ALSO BY SEBASTIAN DE ASSIS

ZENior CitiZEN: Mastering the Art of Aging

The Alchemy of Time

rEvolution in Education

Teachers of the World, Unite!

SPIRALING

MADNESS

Sebastian de Assis

Blooming World Books

For information about special discounts for book purchases, please contact the publisher at the address below.

First Edition

ISBN 978-0-9700722-8-3 (hardcover)
ISBN 978-0-9700722-5-2 (pbk.)
ISBN 978-0-9700722-6-9 (Ebook)

Library of Congress Control Number: 2018900677

Published in the United States of America

Blooming World Books
P.O. Box 443, Corvallis, Oregon 97339
www.bloomingworldbooks.com

*For the generations of the twenty-first century whose inherited
responsibility to the future of humanity is unprecedented*

AUTHOR'S NOTE

In order to avoid the cumbersome dual gender use of the singular third person pronouns, I have opted to refer to all third person instances using the masculine pronouns he/his/him. In my previous efforts to remain gender unbiased in my writings, I have struggled with the burdensome approach of alternating between he and she throughout the text. Determined to stay true to my steadfast commitment to gender equality, as well as my respect and esteem for my fellow female human beings, I insisted on the awkward alternation between he/she and him/her, which has proven to be encumbering to my writing process. Hence, I decided to simplify it with the self-assurance that my values and appreciation for the opposite sex remain unblemished.

As I surmise that many writers feel the same way about the usage of gender pronouns, I suggest that all male writers make use of the masculine pronouns, and all female counterparts employ the feminine pronouns. This would eliminate once and for all the uncomfortable indecision in the face of linguistic political correctness protocol.

Until grammarians institute gender-neutral pronouns, my suggestion above envisions to eliminate the clumsy transitions between pronouns based on gender. In the end, it is our common humanity that unifies us all, regardless of how it shows on the pages.

Contents

The Author

*"Too much sanity may be madness—and maddest of all: to see
life as it is and not as it should be"*

Miguel de Cervantes (1547–1616)

Introduction

I am a madman. I've always known that I am mad. I became aware of it when I was 10-years-old.

I still remember the day I learned I was mad. I was walking on a busy downtown street with my father, both of us munching on succulent hotdogs with "the whole works" while we chatted. With condiments dripping through the side of the hotdog buns and smearing my face with onions and mustard, I halted my steps to wipe off my messy face with my bare forearm. Suddenly, the sight of human misery, which I'd seen many times in the past but never really noticed until that day, captured my attention as if I were seeing it for the first time. A few yards away from me a ragged and barefooted elderly lady scavenged a trashcan in front of a snazzy eatery in search of her daily nourishment. Looking at her as she devoured the pieces and bits of throwaway food she managed to find, all of a sudden my hotdog became tasteless. As I stared at her in awe, I realized that something had happened to me at that moment: it was the first pangs of the birth of the awareness of my madness.

"What's the matter?" My father asked me with his eyes shifting between me and the direction of my fixation. I didn't reply. Obviously there was something that mattered; and yet, it seemed to be as oblivious to him as it was to the many people who walked by utterly indifferent to what seemed to me an unacceptable human condition. Staring at her agape, my child heart was overwhelmed with empathy while my innocent mind was flummoxed with a perplexing sight I could not comprehend. Something was not right in the grownup world. And if that was the social model that awaited me in adulthood, then I was definitely an eccentric child doomed to grow up to be a madman.

From that day on, I realized that my puerile experience of reality had changed forever. I began noticing the loud cacophony of city noises, the crowded sidewalks, and the noxious fumes of motorized vehicles that scratched my throat, burned my eyes, and congested my lungs with poisonous carbon monoxide. I became aware of the tall buildings that hid the mid-afternoon Sun while casting ill-omened shadows in the boulevards. Everything around me looked and felt threateningly strange. I felt as though the innocence of my childhood had been plucked out of my heart without a moment's notice. But nothing was more shocking to my child's eyes than the sight of abject poverty that was seemingly perceived as an integral part of normal society: the long stretch of tents crowding the underpasses in the intersections of busy and noisy highways; the tattered people sleeping on makeshift card-board beds on the sidewalks; the panhandling dejected folks whose faces cried out for help and compassion; all of it struck me as insane as it was unacceptable. In my innocent 10-year-old state of being, I could not fathom why adults didn't do anything about that social travesty. How could they tolerate such a state of affairs? How could it possibly be normal? Did they know what they were doing?—or not doing for that matter. The more I wondered the more disenchanted, bewildered, and concerned I became with the prospect of becoming an adult. Because of the way I felt, I feared becoming a social pariah by reason of insanity. Nevertheless, I came to terms with the possibility that, most likely, I was an abnormal child who would grow up struggling to fit in a normal world.

By the time I reached puberty, the symptoms of my madness were significantly exacerbated. Besides the hormonal changes that were wreaking havoc in my body, in my mind I was perplexed with the emerging awareness of what I perceived to be an illogical reality, albeit professed to be the normal standards. I began questioning whether it would be possible to sustain the continuous sprawling growth of urban centers and the populations inhabiting them. For Pete's sake, even a young madman knows that there's only so much space and resources to go around—and at the current rate of consumption, they will run out in a foreseeable future. Despite this obvious fact, unremitting economic expansion is the unavoidable necessity of the way of life I was being molded to fit in. Although the idea of unfettered growth made no sense to me, I had no choice but to accept it. As a psychological palliative to my disturbed awareness, I found refuge in my own madness.

By my late teens I realized that my mental health state was deteriorating faster than the ozone layer. There was one day in particular, a Sunday when I was reading the newspaper, that I came across a story that convinced me that I was a madman in the normal civilized world. It was the day I learned about the model for peace in the years of my youth. It was called *détente*. I thought it was the most bizarre approach to peace that any sensible intelligent human being could formulate. It was a principle based on fear of mutual self-destruction. Two nations bearing the imposing title of superpower, aimed numerous nuclear weapons at each other and their respective allies, which generated unbearable stressful terror to daily living. Any minute increase in the tension between the deadly rival parties maximized the already high anxiety level—a classic illustration of major mental health crisis. However, as oddly as I deemed *détente* to be, it was the fear of mutual annihilation that preserved the tenuous peace in the world. And if such an irrational approach were not asinine enough, they continued escalating an arms race that could wipe life out of the planet many times over. They claimed, however, that it was the only leverage with which to prevent any reckless impulse to initiate what would be a global catastrophe. Ironically, this outlandish peacekeeping tactic was dubbed MAD (mutually assured destruction).

It was when I became a young adult that the real struggle with my madness began unabated. Now I was feeling the unforgiving pressure "to become someone," which soon I realized it was but an insidious demand to turn me into a fitting cog to keep the rattling dysfunctional socioeconomic machine running. Meanwhile, the dominant cultural standards that parents, teachers, and pundits abided by put an enormous pressure on me to decide what to do; not of my life, but with my life. The Shakespearean dilemma "to be or not to be" was never the question. To do, to have, to earn, to own, to pretend; those were the verbal measuring sticks that must determine the depth of a young person's ambitions and actions. Whatever natural inclinations I had, if they were to conflict with the values predetermined by socioeconomic customs, they had to be discarded as impractical, irresponsible, and even reprehensible. The ultimate objective was to choose a sensible pathway leading to a promising and profitable career; to fulfill an enviable economic function that would bring success, which is translated as financial gains and accolades. Thus, in the face of such dire demands, they tried to coerce me by dint of economic persuasion and fear of lacking necessities, to abrogate my innermost artistic and intellectual inclinations—my ontological vocation, as the revolutionary Brazilian educator, Paulo Freire (1921–1997), puts it[1]—for they had no tangible value in the superficial world of production and consumption I was about to immerse.

By the time I completed the third semester in college, I was utterly disenchanted with the traditional educational system. In fact, I developed contempt for it, which made me understand the words of one of my legitimate teachers in absentia, Friedrich Nietzsche (1844–1900)—a madman in his own right—who said:

> "I have moved from the house of the scholars and I even banged the door behind me. My soul sat hungry at their table too long. I am not like them, trained to pursue knowledge as if it were nutcracking."[2]

Suddenly, my yearnings for knowledge along with my personal aspirations were crushed under an oppressive cookie-cutter educational system whose primary goal was to prepare me to fulfill an economic function in a frenzied society. I could neither comprehend nor adjust to such a frivolous didactic system, and eventually it had a toll on me. It was both incomprehensible and unacceptable to me that two of the most fundamental activities of my life (my studies and my work) were not acknowledged as integral parts of my personhood; the genuine expression of my being in the world. When I noticed that I only seemed to exist when I was not toiling away in the misery of doing something that ran against the grain of my ontological vocation, I realized that maybe I could find reason by exploring my own madness in contrast with what was widespread perceived as the normal cultural model.

Hence, I began an exploratory journey to find out whether I or the world was afflicted with madness. After embarking on a life-journey adventure that took me to three continents and numerous countries through many years, I've been quite content with where I stand now, for I've already learned what took Socrates seven decades to realize: "All I know is that I don't know anything;" well, almost anything. There is one thing I do know: considering how my perception of the world differs drastically from the accepted cultural standards, I must be a madman. Thus, in acknowledgement of my mental, psychological, emotional, and spiritual condition (the causes and consequences of madness extend far beyond the limitations of the biomedical concept), I continue exploring the nature of madness as I see it.

But what is madness?

The answer depends on not only to whom you pose the question, but also on the interpretation of what the condition is supposed to be. Even the dictionary definition leaves plenty of room for ambiguity. It begins by defining it as "the quality or state of being mad," which is a vague statement until the nature of "being mad" is clarified. In attempting to elucidate the meaning of madness, the subsequent entries do not shed light on what exactly madness is either: "rage, insanity, extreme folly, ecstasy, enthusiasm;" all of which can mean different things in different circumstances that do not necessarily relate to madness in psychological terms. After all, feeling ecstatic, enthusiastic, or even enraged is not by any stretch signs of pathological madness. Therefore, in a final attempt to conjure up a feasible definition of madness, the final entry refers to "any of several ailments of animals marked by frenzied behavior."[3] Well, this biomedical approach definition does not convince me either.

So, what is madness, then?

My personal quandary led me to a self-evident conclusion: Madness is in the mind of the observer—and this book is about this observer's perspective.

Although the traditional concept of madness has been present throughout the course of human history, it only became a bona fide disease in the twentieth century. With the advent of complex psychoanalytic theories and the psychotropic wonder drugs with which to treat a growing list of mental maladies, the topic of madness became a specialized matter of medical science. However, by the 1960s, an anti-psychiatry movement began unfolding and its influence is still present today. One of the most notable spearheads of this movement was Scottish psychiatrist R.D. Laing (1927–1989), whose books *The Divided Self and the*

Politics of Experience began expanding the ripple effects of this movement. Dr. Laing argued that schizophrenia was a "special strategy" invented by people to cope with stresses in life (later he rephrased his controversial statement and referred to schizophrenia not as a condition but a "voyage into inner space."[4]) Others, like renowned New York psychoanalyst Thomas Szasz (1920–2012), went a step further and denied the very existence of mental illness. He thought it to be but a label we place on individuals who are different or bothersome to society.[5]

While scientists of the caliber of Thomas Szasz consider mental illness as "a label placed on individuals who are bothersome to society," the arguments I present in this book are based on radically opposite direction: it is a mad society that is bothersome to the individual. And as Dr. Szasz claims that psychiatry is a tool of oppression, I argue that modern industrial society is the one fulfilling this unenviable role. In essence, it is not the individual who is inherently disturbed, but the socioeconomic and political structures of the madhouse we live in that contribute to individual madness. But I am not a scientist. The only expertise I lend to this work is my experience as a madman; someone who perceives what's considered normality as the ultimate insanity. However, my intent is not to place blame on society as the only culprit of the tragedy of human madness. After all, individuals are the creators of the insane social infrastructure that begot the current situation in the first place. There are, I purport, innate human factors in the continuous escalation of the large-scale psychosis afflicting humanity at the early decades of the twenty-first century.

Throughout the evolutionary process of the human species, particularly since the Paleolithic era, or Old Stone Age, when the development and utilization of tools heralded the beginning of technological advancement some 2.5 million years ago, humanity has been thriving and triumphing over the natural world. However, the problem as I see it through the lenses of my madness, is that in the process of conquering the environment in order to overcome the challenges of survival, humanity neglected to rise above the highest obstacle and most daring adversary of its evolution: the internal psychological struggle between two opposing forces within the human nature, which I call the *Homo dementis* and the *Homo clementis*, both of which are in constant conflict with each other. *Homo dementis* is the inherently selfish human condition ruled by raw survival instincts that supersede what's in the best interest of the tribe (community, society, nation, and the planet). On the other hand, *Homo clementis* is the intrinsic emotional nature of humankind that is anchored in merciful and loving communion with the tribe (community, society, nation, and the planet). And according to this madman's theory, the antagonistic interaction between these opposing forces within the species is what's driving humanity mad.

Nevertheless, what I see as a clear vision of a world in desperate need of urgent change is but a blurred image of progress in the eyes of others. Concepts, principles, morals, and values that I deem to be absurdly insane are accepted with open mind and even dutiful sense of righteousness. While I hold serious reservations regarding technological advancements without concomitant human development, my normal fellow-citizens pooh-pooh my position as if I subscribed to some sort of anti-technology Luddism—and nothing could be further from the truth. In addition, my critical view of an economic system that exacerbates our inherent selfishness in highly competitive environments is perceived as a glaring sign of maladjustment to normal standards. To many, I'm seen as a malcontent misfit who cannot adjust to the extraordinary achievements of modern technological industrial societies. Conversely, I marvel at their inability to see—or maybe it's a matter of denial—that we are marching at lightning speed toward the thin edge of the abyss of the ultimate madness: self-destruction.

Finally, I trust that a new understanding of the nature of madness can and will restore humanity's sanity. In the meantime, by virtue of the empirical evidence of my self-diagnosed madness, I beseech that my arguments be exonerated from judgment and forgiven of any unwitting offense by reason of insanity.

After all, these are the words of a madman.

NOTES

[1] The revolutionary Brazilian educator, Paulo Freire, deems "ontological vocation," as he calls it, to be a subject who acts upon and transforms his world, and in so doing moves toward ever new possibilities of fuller and richer life, individually and collectively. For more information see Paulo Freire, *Ped-*

agogy of the Oppressed (New York: Continuum Publishing Company, 1993), 14.

[2] Friedrich Nietzsche, *Thus Spoke Zarathustra,* The Portable Nietzsche, edited and translated by Walter Kaufmann (New York: Viking Penguin, Inc., 1976), 236-237.

[3] *Merriam-Webster's Collegiate Dictionary*, Eleventh Edition (Springfield, MA: Merriam-Webster, Inc., 2007), 746.

[4] Ann Quingley, Book Editor, *Mental Health* (Farmington Hills, MI: Greenhaven Press, 2007), 161.

[5] Ibid.

The History of Madness

ike everything and everyone in the world, madness has a history of its own—and it is a very long and complicated one. But before you can use historical information as a key with which to open the door of understanding the present problems in a reasonably effective manner, you have to be aware of certain fundamental processes and concepts. In other words, you must become historically-minded, which is "a way of thinking," a form of reasoning when dealing with historical materials and present day problems.[1]

I surmise that from the time the *Hominids* rose on their two feet (standing upright and walking on two feet is a basic requirement for inclusion in the human lineage)[2] and took the first steps of a 4 million-year journey, human beings have been battling some degree of psychosis. But by the time the species evolved to *Homo sapiens* 10,000 years ago, my conjecture turns into a much more likely possibility that madness has been walking with us from the beginning of time. In fact, I postulate that within each of the many classifications attributed to the human evolutionary process (*Homo habilis*, *Homo erectus*, *Homo neanderthalensis*, etc.), there has been a couple of ubiquitous categories within the human species that I call *Homo dementis* (characterized by inherent madness) and *Homo clementis* (characterized by inherent compassion); the good and evil within each human being. These two evolutionary components of humanity coexist in direct conflict with each other in a constant struggle for supremacy over human conduct—and *Homo dementis* has been winning the struggle handily.

However, in the course of this long evolutionary journey leading to what humans have become today, it was not until 5,500 B.C.E that a gradual development of organized civilizations began. Few years down

the line came forth the mighty empires of the Egyptians, the Babyloni-
ans, the Assyrians, the Chaldeans, and the Persians, together with some
smaller sates of such peoples as the Hittites, the Phoenicians, and the
Hebrews; all of whom attained a higher level of learning. In the area of
the Indus Valley, the Indian Civilization was born, then China around
4,000 years ago; and finally, on the island of Crete and mainland
Greece, the Hellenic civilization came into being and reached its apex at
around 500 B.C.E[3] But it is in the era known as *Common Era* (the last
2,000 years that characterize the C.E. period) that the development of
Homo dementis escalated to an unprecedented level that culminated in
the twentieth century.

❀

From a strictly scholastic and scientific account of the history of madness, the observations would refer to complex theoretical explanations
of the causes and effects of mental illness from the biomedical model
perspective. According to this view, mental illness is basically the same
as physical illness. Having convinced themselves that mental problems
are diseases of the body, modern psychiatrists treat psychological illness
by physical means. As for treatment, the preferred method is to treat
mental illness with medication, which controls the symptoms of the
disorder but does not cure it.[4] But to approach mental illness from a
biomedical model is bound to lead to misdiagnosis of both the disease
as well as the afflicted person. Madness, the unrefined euphemism for
mental illness, is a complex manifestation of psychological reactions to
a multitude of factors ranging from socioeconomic circumstances to
existential crisis, which the latter is often triggered by the former. Thus,
the concept of mental illness as a biochemical imbalance disease independent of other aspects of the human existence is but an exceptional
argument for the multi-billion dollar pharmaceutical industry. After all,
the practice of psychotropic drugging is big business.

Although psychiatric professionals may ridicule those who question the biomedical model, many an expert in the field attempts to
prove them wrong. As mentioned earlier, Thomas Szasz, a respected
Professor of Psychiatry at Syracuse University in New York regards
mental illness as pure myth. He believes that defining psychiatry as a
medical specialty concerned with the diagnosis and treatment of mental
illness, places psychiatry in the company of alchemy and astrology, all

of which he considers pseudo-science. To him, there is no such a thing as mental illness.[5]

It is important to understand these two different views of mental illness within the context of the history of madness because each reveals a different representation. One, the biomedical model, seems to have been concocted by psychiatrists for reasons of professional advancement and financial gain—and it doesn't hurt that society endorses it as easy solutions for troubled people. The other, not formally denominated but that I call "sociological madness," is rooted in multifaceted cultural, socioeconomic, and environmental circumstances that create imbalances; not in the biochemistry of the brain, but in the living conditions of the individual—and it hurts that this poses an inconvenience for industrialized societies. In essence, it's a matter of investigating madness as a physical ailment or a societal disease that affects the individual. Since I subscribe to the sociological madness approach, I consider the history of madness tantamount to the history of socioeconomic development and all its ramifications; that is, industrialization, division and automation of labor, urbanization, and the other characteristics of modern life. It's a multifaceted perspective that takes into consideration the many manifestations of madness, both in the individual and society.

"That's hogwash," scholars and pundits decry. But from a madman's perspective, in the so-called evolutionary process of the species, the *Homo dementis* (the madman that abides at the core of the *Homo sapiens)* has mutated as well, and definitely not for the better. In fact, of the three main developmental revolutions in human civilization (agricultural, scientific, and industrial), the Industrial Revolution, in spite of its apparent benefits to modern societies, has engendered gradual alienation of people; from their work, their fellowmen and women, nature, and, worse of all, from themselves. And alienation is a terrible and solitary form of madness.

✿

There have been several agricultural revolutions throughout history. The first happened around 10,000 B.C.E., the prehistoric transition from hunting and gathering to settled agriculture. Each ensuing agricultural revolution expanded the advancements of the last one. Together, they unleashed a transformational chain reaction that forever changed social organization. Even before the long gone days of nomadic hunting tribes moving from place to place in search of their next meal, humans were not bound to the land as a necessity of their survival (the Native Americans way of life exemplifies the case). But the development of agricultural production demanded their commitment to tending their crops. Not only they had to stay put, but the acquisition of land, herding, and hording of goods set off a competitive spirit that led to humans warring with each other for the possession of territory. Those who controlled large amounts of resources and had the means to protect them became the dominant elite, for food is an indispensable staple for survival. Consequently, social stratification and class differences in human societies began taking roots as more people ensured their security by solidifying their advantageous economic position. The landless lower classes, however, worked for and purchased food from them with their labor. And by the time the British Agricultural Revolution came about between the 17th and 19th century, unprecedented transformations ensued that aggravated the state of the *Homo dementis* within the modern man and woman.

Despite the extraordinary contributions of the Scientific Revolution that took place in Europe towards the end of the Renaissance period (from the 14th to the 17th centuries), the realization of the possibilities of the human intellect would prove to be dangerously consequential in the following centuries. Although the achievements of this period's notable scientists such as Nicolai Copernicus (1473–1543), who debunked the Earth-centered Universe theory; and Isaac Newton (1643–1727), who established the law of gravity in his work *Principia*, the Age of Enlightenment that came out of this movement was strictly focused on human intellectual capabilities. Thus, the words of another renowned man of this era, Rene Descartes (1596–1650), summarized the new concept of the human existence: *Cogito ergo sum* (I think therefore I am) became the motto of the evolving modern man. However, reducing the complexity of the human being's identity to sheer intellectual capacity is a grievous step toward alienation from another fundamental aspect of human nature as I see it: the *Homo clementis*; that part of us that gives way for the experience of the emotional being; the sensitivity that is fundamental to human development.[6] And as observed earlier, alienation is a serious form of madness.

The emphasis on intellectual prowess in combination with unfettered greed led to a maddening way of life. Since the 1780s, humanity has experienced an unprecedented transformation in every aspect of social organization brought about by the Industrial Revolution. It was at this time that the world witnessed the first breakthrough from a rural handicraft economy to one dominated by urban machine-driven manufacturing. Unable to compete against products churned out by machinery, independent skillful artisans were squeezed out of business and forced to move to urban areas to pursue their livelihood. Now, all they had was their labor to sell to a new dominant class that owned and controlled the machines that produced goods (the means of production). This period marks the beginning of a new impersonal class that came to be known as corporations, which has been sanctioned by the United States highest court as a bona fide citizenry class with equal rights to those of individual citizens.[7]

With expanding populations and ever-growing demand for manufactured goods, the increased scale of production became but inevitable. Consequently, a new complex factory system in which even young children—hired because of their supposed agility to clean under and around the moving machine parts—toiled for as long as twelve hours at a stretch.[8] It was a matter of time for workers to rebel against the machinery-driven economy that changed their lives while binding them to a kind of industrial slavery. Besides being compelled to adapt to a new harsh physical working conditions, the psychological readjustment was even harder, for human beings are not meant to spend excessively long hours alienated from their work activities in a repetitive pattern of production. Thus, they took to drinking and other forms of escapism in order to avoid going (conventionally) mad.

But all forms of individual madness unchained by alienation, discontent, and poverty eventually lead to a large scale collective madness. Once the realization that one's life is bound by undesired servitude surfaces, what ensues is social chaos and revolution—and many social and political unrest unfolded after the mechanization of production. A popular working-class song written in Britain in the 1840s expressed this feeling:

"There is a king and a ruthless king. Not a king of the poet's dreams, but a tyrant fell white slaves know well. And that ruthless king is steam."[9]

❀

By the time the Industrial Revolution reached its apotheosis stage in the 20th century, the madhouse broke loose and a maddening way of living became the norm. And because the socioeconomic transformations accelerated so rapidly, concomitant individual adjustment was inevitable. Indeed, unimaginable advancements took place in the mere fifty years following the turn of the 19th to the 20th centuries: from bicycles to airplanes; from wagons powered by horses to spacecrafts fueled by nuclear energy. Science and technology evolved to unprecedented levels, as it did the production output and the populations consuming those products. From the end of the Roman Empire to the time of Christopher Columbus (1451–1506) overseas explorations, it took thirteen centuries for the world population to reach 200,000,000. Today, it takes only three years.[10] The madness of indiscriminate growth unleashed deadly predatory practices of environmental destruction. Progress was equated to more of everything: more people, more consumption, more greed—and more damage. It created such a vicious cycle of self-destruction that became impossible to go unnoticed; not even by a criminal pathological madman holding a doctoral degree from Harvard University, one of the most prestigious institutions of higher learning in the world. Ted Kaczynski (1942–   ) asserted in the first line of his infamous manifesto that "The Industrial Revolution and its consequences have been a disaster for the human race."[11] Despite his reprehensible and senseless criminal activities, this statement holds truth to observable evidence.

Unfortunately, the disaster is much more devastating than the noticeable footprints that industrial capitalism leaves on the sand of the history of madness. It was the human being who became the main casualty of his own evolutionary failure. In spite of all the astonishing advancements in science and technology, the emotional and spiritual development of the species has remained stagnant at the primitive level of the human evolutionary path. Two brutal world wars and barbaric atrocities against humanity that still go on unabated validate the claim that the 20th century is arguably the most violent century in human history—so far. While intellectual capability evolved at remarkable pace, other equally important modes of human intelligence remain unchanged; and in some cases even degenerated. While the cities became illuminated by electric light engineered by scientific knowledge, the human spirit has been left out in the dark.

As I observe the world today where there is growth without development, freedom without responsibility, democracy without justice, and rhetoric without meaning, I realize that I must be the one who is insane. After all, what is revered as dignified principles and admirable accomplishments I perceive them to be nothing more than sheer lunacy. Evidently, I must be the madman in a normal world where progress is synonymous to expansion of what I recognize as symptoms of indisputable madness.

And for those who may question the stability of my state of mind, I offer my assessment of the madness of history.

NOTES

[1] Carl G. Gustavson, *A Preface to History* (New York: McGraw-Hill Book Company, Inc., 1983), 5.

[2] *Dawn of Humans*, Produced by the Cartographic Division of the National Geographic Society, Washington, D.C. February 1997.

[3] Edward McNall Burns et al, *World Civilization*, Volume 1, Seventh Edition (New York: W.W. Norton & Company, Inc., 1986), 1.

[4] Fritjof Capra, *The Turning Point* (New York: Bantam Books Edition, Simon & Schuster, 1983), 143-144.

[5] Roy Porter, *Madness: A Brief History* (New York: Oxford University Press, Inc., 2002), 1-2.

[6] Hazrat Inayat Khan, *Mastery Through Accomplishment* (New Lebanon, NY: Omega Publications, Inc., 1993), 122.

[7] The United States Supreme Court favorable ruling on the 2010 Citizens United vs. FEC (Federal Election Commission) granted corporations the same legal rights as those of individual citizens. The Citizens United ruling is the most sweeping expansion of corporate personhood to date.

[8] Edward McNall Burns et al., *World Civilization*, Seventh Edition, Volume 2 (New York: W.W. Norton & Company, 1986), 986.

[9] Ibid., 987.

[10] As quoted by Ronald Wright in the documentary *Surviving Progress*, a film by Mathieu Roy and Harold Crooks (Québec, Canada: Alliance Films, 2012).

[11] Theodore Kaczynski, *Industrial Society and its Future*, 1995. http://editions-hache.com/essais/pdf/kaczynski2.pdf

The Madness of History

T he madness of history can be best characterized by a concept developed by the genius of a madman, Friedrich Nietzsche (1844–1900), whose idea of Eternal Recurrence was first introduced in his book, *Gay Science*. He tells the story of a demon that sneaks into the "loneliness loneliness" of one's mind to proclaim that life will repeat itself in an endless tedious process:

> "This life as you now live it and have lived it, you will have to live it once more and innumerable times more; and there will be nothing new in it; but every pain and every joy and every thought and sigh and everything immeasurably small or great in your life must return to you—and in the same succession and sequence...Would you not throw yourself down and gnash your teeth and curse the demon who spoke thus?"[1]

The above quote summarizes the madness of history: a repetitive pattern in which the *Homo dementis* (the internal madman) comes out to manifest itself through exploitation, oppression, morbid selfishness, violence, and all the other ignoble characteristics of this perennial stagnant stage of human underdevelopment. No matter how far back you look in the history of humanity's evolution—and I would argue that there is an element of devolution in the coming of age of the species—there is a vile thread of continuity of inherent animalistic madness. Perhaps, Nietzsche's countryman and fellow distinguished philosopher, Georg Wilhelm Friedrich Hegel (1770–1831), was correct when he uttered his now famous axiom: "The greatest lesson of history is that humankind never learns the lessons of history."

And so the madness has been repeating itself throughout the course of history. Like the Buddhist concept of *Samsara*, the term used to describe the ordinary world dominated by the endless cycle of birth and death (reincarnation), the madness in the world keeps recurring in a vicious cycle of self-destruction that is about to reach its zenith. Barbarian wars, senseless acts of terrorism, horrific crimes against humanity, subjugation of peoples, exploitation and slavery of vulnerable populations, among many other atrocities, have been recorded in the annals of history in accordance with Nietzsche's concept of Eternal Recurrence. The greatest danger, however, is the possibility of things getting worse with the passing of time. As historical philosopher Ronald Wright (1948–   ) pointed out, "Each time history repeats itself, the cost goes up."[2]

Although some historians tend to focus on the study of history based on important socio-political events such as wars and revolutions, most tend to define history as the story of people and the study of our past in the broadest sense. The truth is that our lives today are shaped by decisions and actions made decades, centuries, or even thousands of years ago—and what will happen in the future hinges on decisions and actions being carried out today. Thus, by understanding the past, we may be able to gain a more balanced view of the present,[3] as well as to project the consequences of our current actions into the future.

But as far as the madness of history is concerned, it is not necessary to examine the details of historical events that took place centuries or even thousands of years ago to grasp the cruel cycle of collective self-inflicted pain and suffering. All that is needed is to pick out a few historical patterns and occurrences in order to make sense of the madness we experience today. And among the numerous examples to choose from, perhaps none illustrates the case more emphatically than chattel slavery; the once legal and morally accepted ownership of human beings. Even though the institution of slavery has been abolished in most countries, it has mutated into different guises of socially condoned practices in the post-Industrial Revolution era. "This is a preposterous argument!" I've heard many pundits and academics object whenever I referred to human labor exploitation for profit as a transmuted form of slavery that has the blessings of society. My rebuke has been based on a simple question: How do you think the terms "financial freedom" and "slave wage" came about?

✿

Arguably the most influential philosopher of the Enlightenment Movement of the 18th century, Jean Jacques Rousseau (1712–1778) begins his Social Contract with a statement that is as meaningful as it is undeniable: "Man was born free, and everywhere he is in chains."4 The reasoning supporting Rousseau's controversial tenet is the idea that man is inherently good in his natural state ("the noble savage"), but it is society and progress that corrupt man's natural good. For Rousseau, society is the original sin; but for me, slavery is the original crime in the madness of history—and the aim of world history ought to be human freedom.

Throughout the course of history, slavery has been the predominant factor in the economic lives and development of most civilizations. From the ancient world of Mesopotamia, Egypt, Greece, Rome, and all the way to modern day states, slavery has been the main propelling force that catapulted the economic prosperity of many nations and few individuals. Validated by religious and philosophical misconceptions ranging from the Bible to the writings of renowned Greek philosophers (namely, the Aristotelian concept that some men were born to be masters while others were destined for subjection)5, the endorsement of human ownership has been widely accepted as a normal and ethical practice. In fact, in chapter 3 verse 16 of the book of Genesis, the allusion to the natural right to slavery seems evident with statements such as "...he shall be your master;" and the book of Exodus, chapter 21, verses 4-6, strongly reiterates the pro-slavery claim: "...and the man shall be his slave for life."6 Similar references to the right of slavery abound in the Islamic holy book, the Koran, as verse 16:73 corroborates: "God makes this comparison. On the one hand there is a helpless slave, the property of his master. On the other, a man whom We have bestowed Our bounty, so that he gives of it both in private and in public. Are the two alike? God forbid!"7

With the madness of ownership of human beings validated by both religious and philosophical principles, the "discovery" of the New World opened the flood gates for massive import of subjugated Africans who endured terribly inhumane conditions. They were to become the rightful property of landowners of a stolen new world conquered by dominance and chicanery. The native inhabitants of the pristine lands (the noble savages that Rousseau alluded to) were summarily eliminated with the remaining numbers confined to "reservations;" a euphemism to concentration camps.

Of course, if human bondage is accepted and perceived as an inalienable right, the right to private property of parcels of the Earth is an indisputable entitlement of the fittest, even if possessed by sheer force. To the Native Americans, however, the concept of owning the land was so farfetched that they could not comprehend the madness of owning that which owns us. This common stance is reflected in the words of Chief Seattle's (c. 1786–1866) reply to a government offer to purchase the remaining Salish lands: "The Earth does not belong to man, man belongs to the Earth."[8]

As the winds of madness swept across the west of the newly conquered continent, the religious and philosophical self-validations to take over native people's land strengthened the pseudo-rationale while assuaging the guilt. Manifest Destiny became a God-given right "to possess the whole of the continent that Providence has given us," wrote journalist John Louis O'Sullivan (1813–1895) in 1845 about the westward expansion of the United States, which leaped from his article into the public imagination. "It is a right such as that of a tree to the space of air and earth suitable for the full expansion of its principle and destiny of growth."[9] Although they were able to manifest the destiny of taking over the natives' land, they were incapable of enslaving the noble savages.

After numerous wars, some of which engaged the use of biological weapons (distributing smallpox-infested blankets to natives), the peoples of the three Americas succumbed to the manifest destiny of the foreign invaders. Deprived of their land, culture, and dignity, they were either whisked to reservations in a sort of ad hoc imprisonment or wiped out altogether. It is the unacknowledged holocaust committed on the west shores of the Atlantic Ocean; a crime that the people with God-given rights refuse to admit. After all, Providence has always been on their side of history.

In the meantime, millions of African slaves toiled in the fields to enrich their wicked masters. It was the norm of an insane—and hypocritical—way of being. Ironically, some of the same men who drafted an eloquent document proclaiming that "all men are created equal, that they are endowed by their Creator with certain inalienable Rights, that among these are Life, Liberty and the Pursuit of Happiness," deprived their human private properties of an entitlement that the Creator supposedly bestowed upon all of us. In spite of the hypocrisy underlining this issue, it established the political, social, and economic conditions of the so-called New World. Even today, from the shanty towns of Rio de Janeiro to the projects in the inner-cities of the United States, the legacy of this madness endures.

But then came the liberator; the abolitionary; the savior; the Industrial Revolution. In a new system of mass production, the constant need for consumers made chattel slavery obsolete, for slaves did not earn income, therefore could not purchase anything. Thus, as industrial development expanded throughout the northern regions of the United States, the advocacy for abolition of slavery grew concomitantly. In timely convenient fashion, all of a sudden the sentiment of slavery as an immoral practice spread throughout the north. However, since the southern states' economies depended on slave labor for their continuous prosperity, the American Civil War (1861–1865) became inevitable, as it did the transmutation of slavery into a morally acceptable form of economic oppression. Now, the new impersonal master carrying a whip in his invisible hand became able to enslave everyone.

In the approximately 100-year period between the American Civil War and the Civil Rights Movement of the 1960s, the madness of history did not subside, but merely changed the circumstances in which it played itself out. The reintegration of the traditional African slaves into "the open free society" proved to be a sham, as they still undergo a significant degree of cultural prejudice and social disadvantage. After enduring decades of oppression and discrimination, they must find solace in the fact that at least now the new slave master has leveled the playing field. It is no longer an issue of race, but of economic status that determines the rules of the game for everyone, regardless of the ethnic background. Black, red, yellow, or white; it doesn't matter what the color of the skin is. Economic status is the new letter of abolition from slavery. It is all about financial manumission.

※

The madness of history is the madness of human exploitation. We are the only animals that are both the predators and preys to the members of our own species—and this nefarious approach has only become more complex with the development of exploitation stratagems. The *Homo dementis*, whose malignant DNA is embedded in our historical psyche, never pauses to rest. He's always devising new ways of improving his craft. And the more he engineers new means of manipulation of people, nature, and technology, the closer to the edge of the abyss he moves. And since 1945 with the introduction to the destructive power of atomic energy, we have sped up the pace toward the rim of the precipice to the point we can now look down and see the bottom with great anxiety and fear. At this juncture, considering the situation of the world and the disarray of the human species, if it is true that "each time history repeats itself, the cost goes up," we might be heading to a final payment of our dues.

In an overly populated world in which individuals and nations engage in fierce competition with one another; where increasing hatred and mistrust abound amidst the awareness of Earth's dwindling resources, the collective despair is evident in the day-to-day living. In the news, at work, on the streets; every day we see signs that the madness of history is still unfolding at a terrifying rate.

Perhaps, if we could understand the psychological makeup of the *Homo dementis*, we might be able to take a peek through the chinks of the ethereal skull that hides the essence of the human collective madness.

NOTES

[1] Shelley O'Hara, *Nietzsche within your grasp* (Hoboken, NJ: Wiley Publishing, Inc., 2004), 19.

[2] Ronald Wright, *A Short History of Progress* (Cambridge, MA: Da Cappo Press, 2004), 107.

[3] "Henry Ford, the American car manufacturer, once said 'History is bunk, but most people would disagree. Our lives today are shaped by decisions and actions made decades, centuries, or even thousands of years ago. By understanding the past, we may be able to gain a more balanced view of the present.'" Anita Ganeri et al., Encyclopedia of World History (United Kingdom: Paragon Books, Ltd., 2009), 8.

[4] Jean Jacques Rousseau, *The Social Contract* (New York: Washington Square Press Publications, 1967), 7.

[5] Aristotle discusses this issue in his books *Politics* and *Nicomachean Ethics*. Aristotle, *On Man In The Universe* (New York: Walter J. Black, Inc., 1943).

[6] Roger Sawyer, *Slavery in the Twentieth Century* (London: Routledge & Kegan Paul, Inc., 1986), 235.

[7] Dawood, N.J., comp. and ed., *The Koran* (London: Penguin Books, 1990), 192.

[8] For the complete speech of Chief Seattle, refer to the text of Native American Chiefs compiled and edited by Kent Nerburn, *The Wisdom of the Native Americans* (New York: MJF Books, 1999), 193-199.

[9] Editors of Time-Life Books, *The Wild West* (New York: Warner Books, Inc., 1993), 28.

The Psychology of Madness

For thousands of years people have been searching for answers to these perennial elusive questions: Who am I? What's unique about me that makes me different from other people while at the same time I am the same as they? What does it mean to be me? Or, if you're an unconventional madman, why do the accepted cultural norms feel so abnormal? These questions, among many others like them, are natural reflections of the individual's search for self-discovery. It is the ultimate pursuit of identity—and the foundation upon which the study of psychology stands.

The scientific interest in the study of psychology emerged in the 19th century as an informal branch of philosophy. Since psychology (the study of the psyche) extends beyond the medical domain, because it is unverifiable by conventional scientific methods, it can only be explored through a philosophical approach. Nevertheless, psychology often has been defined as a science of human behavior and mental processes. But since few of us are scientists by trade, though we are all practicing psychologists constantly asking questions about our identities, the debate on whether psychology is a science or a branch of philosophy should be settled by now. Indeed, psychology is but philosophy of human behavior; even within the context of Freud's complex psychological theories. Personally, when I'm practicing psychology in relation to myself, I call it the "philosophy of self-inquiry."

Just as there is a distinct difference between science and philosophy, madness and mental illness are also unique in nature. Despite the claim by professionals in the field of psychiatry that they're both the same, from a socio-psychological perspective each has its own characteristics. For instance, a case of dementia brought about by say, Alzheimer's disease, can be feasibly recognized as an organic mental disorder that causes impairment of intellectual functions. However, Alzheimer's disease remains a mystery to the scientific community. There are theories linking it to possible environmental causes of the illness, such as loneliness. Renowned French psychiatrist Jean Maisondieu (1939–   ) does not hesitate suggesting that Alzheimer's may be a "cry, a refusal, a sort of social and intellectual suicide." He suggests that they do it so as not to see themselves growing old. In fact, many psychotherapists embrace the hypothesis that Alzheimer's disease is a progressive way to avoid confronting the approach of old age and death.[1]

Madness is a different beast. While mental illnesses such as dementia and schizophrenia are investigated from a biomedical standpoint, madness requires a much broader approach to evaluating its myriad characteristics; both in the individual and collective psyche as well. Historically, it has held wild assumptions ranging from punishment from the gods to demonic possession. But madness is a matter of delusion, which by definition is a "false belief that is firmly held, despite objective and obvious contradictory proof of evidence and despite the fact that other members of the culture do not share the belief."[2] In essence, it is dissociation from the norm. This is the type of madness I believe I've succumbed to; and this is the madness I'm interested in exploring: the one "that other members of the culture do not share the belief."

❀

The psychology of madness is explored through the complex and diverse field of psychoanalysis. Interested in diagnosing my peculiar case of the condition, I took an interest in the subject matter. In addition to learning about interesting theories from towering figures in this area of study such as Ivan Pavlov (1849–1936), William James (1842–1910), Carl Gustav Jung (1875–1961), Wilhelm Reich (1897–1957), and Sigmund Freud (1856–1939), I realized that I should apply their knowledge to my self-diagnostic investigation. Since Freud is considered the father of psychoanalysis, it is only natural to begin with him.

Freud wrote his seminal work, *Civilization and its Discontents*, in the summer of 1929; the year of the Great Depression and four years before the democratic election of Adolf Hitler (1889–1945) and the coming of the Third Reich. The work compares "civilized" and "savage" human lives in order to reflect upon the meaning of civilization and to identify the neurotic aspects of society itself. Likely influenced by the horrors of the First World War, Freud's pessimistic view reflects his insistence of the violent and cruel nature of humanity, and proposing that humans are driven by a desire for destruction. This information corroborated my concept of *Homo dementis* (madman) that has been present throughout the evolutionary process of the human species. This observation aside, Freud's book is a study on the fundamental tensions between civilization and the individual.[3]

Caught in the middle of the tension between conformity to a neurotic way of living and the isolation of madness, I came to terms with the possibility that I'd acquired what I termed *Pathological Perceptual Impairment*; that is, the inability to understand and accept the means through which the culture (society) strives to deify the sacrosanct motto of *The Pursuit of Happiness*. Like an imaginary place that you go to—instead of an experience of being—the road to the pursuit of happiness is paved with stressful living conditions, alienation, disconnect from nature, and a sense of perpetual despair. The angst is aggravated by the awareness of unsustainable population explosion that goes along with unremitting economic expansion; both of which create an insatiable appetite for natural resources in order to sustain the unsustainable dual growth. Unable to comprehend the normality of what I perceive to be suicidal madness, I learned to acknowledge and accept my unrelenting impairment.

Based on Freud's *Pleasure Principle* in which the strive for happiness is the driving force inspiring people to endure the continual hardships of life, the pursuit of happiness is in direct conflict (tension) with the awareness that people are constantly threatened with suffering from three directions: from the body, which is doomed to decay; from the world, which may rage against the familiar comfortable with merciless forces of destruction; and finally from relations with others, which Freud contends that is perhaps more painful than any other[4]—and Jean Paul Sartre (1905–1980) validated with his widely quoted saying: *Le enfer c'est les autres* (hell is other people).[5] But despite the long-quest for finding meaning in the chaos of human life, a satisfactory answer is yet to be discovered.

Despite our failure to answer questions regarding the state of human madness, even someone with mediocre powers of observation will be able to see that the answer to the current human situation lies in the observation itself: the meaning of the purpose of life when life's existence is threatened can only be its recovery. Anything else is an act of madness. Therefore, if you find yourself trapped in an unsustainable situation, your primary objective always should be to find the way out, as Wilhelm Reich observed:

> "It is possible to get out of a trap. However, in order to break out of a prison, one first must confess to being in a prison. The trap is man's emotional structure, his character structure. There is little use in devising systems of thought about the nature of the trap if the only thing to do in order to get out of the trap is to know the trap and to find the exit."[6]

The tragedy of our collective trap is that what's destroying life simultaneously sustains the demands of modern industrial societies, as individuals and nations pursue a delusional sense of happiness through economic prosperity. From a collective standpoint, happiness hinges on scientific and technological advancement fueled by unfettered economic expansion, which serves a contradictory dual function of development as self-destruction. And to add aggravation to it, this maddening process takes place in an extremely competitive environment that exacerbates indifference while widening the gap among people, social classes, races, nations, or whatever the dividing line happens to be determined. This duality of simultaneous development and self-destruction is a manifestation of the perennial *Homo dementis* within the *Homo sapiens*. In the meantime, *Homo clementis* (the dormant compassionate element of human nature) is completely stifled, disregarded, and ostracized from participating in the development of *Homo sapiens*, whom by now have cemented its devolutionary status as *Homo ignorantis* (the ignorant human).

※

Since the pursuit of happiness is intrinsically connected to economic prosperity, happiness itself becomes a commodity for consumption, like everything else produced by the economic system. The psychology of this madness is quintessential to what Wilhelm Reich refers to as "the little man," or the common man, who is unable to enjoy happiness in full freedom, for he does not know how to cultivate it with loving care, as a gardener cultivates his flowers and a farmer his wheat.[7] It is much easier to consume it as a "product of joy" than to cultivate it as recurrent experience of being. Thus, "the little man's" pursuit of happiness becomes his economic prosperity goals. The more money he makes, the more happiness he can buy—or so he believes, until he realizes how naïve, ephemeral, and elusive his happiness really is. And in order to continue on his pursuit of happiness, he must participate in the inglorious rat race. But the trouble with the rat race is that even if you win, you're still a rat.[8] In my turn, I'd much rather be a stray cat in the pursuit of my self-fulfilling madness.

As the rat race exemplifies, the pursuit of happiness is but the pursuit of a lifestyle in which money and prestige define success and achievement. What's often not mentioned is the exorbitant cost one must pay for it: the sacrifice of quality of life and health of being. The constant pressure to succeed; the daily stress to get ahead in the race against other rats and the one the individual engages with himself. It seems as though the prize is always out of reach, for when you get there you realize there's another there to reach in a typical Nietzschean concept of Eternal Recurrence. Like a hamster franticly running inside a caged wheel, the human rats can't get anywhere. Locked in materialistic ambition, there is not enough wealth and social recognition to fill in the emptiness of the poverty of being. Ironically, this is the desirable and accepted normal standard of living.

So, where does madness stand amidst this absurd sense of normality? Is everyone who resists and rebels against such an oppressive existence truly insane? After all, madness is perceived as a deviation from behavioral patterns that run parallel to the dominant cultural principles.

Perhaps, madness is but a component of the psychology that attempts to define it.

NOTES

[1] Marie de Hennezel, *The Art of Growing Old, Aging with Grace* (New York: Viking, Penguin Group, 2010), 57-59.

[2] Harold I. Kaplan, M.D., Benjamin J. Sadock, M.D., *Comprehensive Glossary of Psychiatry and Psychology* (Baltimore, Maryland: William & Wilkins, 1991), 49.

[3] Sigmund Freud, *Civilization and Its Discontents* (New York: W.W. Norton & Company, 1961.

[4] Ibid., 25-26.

[5] From Jean Paul Sartre's play, *No Exit* (*Huis Clos*). *No Exit and Three Other Plays* (New York: Vintage International Edition, Alfred A. Knopf, Inc., 1976).

[6] As quoted in Kathleen Riordan Speeth, *The Gurdjieff Work* (New York: Pocket Books, 1976), 56.

[7] Wilhelm Reich, *Listen, Little Man* (New York: The Noonday Press, 1974), 40.

[8] A quote attributed to comedian Lily Tomlin. Peter McWilliams, Editor, *The LIFE 101 Quote Book* (Los Angeles, Prelude Press, 1996), 300.

The Madness of Psychology

T he modern concept of psychology relates to the study of human behavior and mental processes. Based on this approach, it is evident that a baseline of what constitutes normal behavior and healthy mental processes must be established by the scientific community leading the study. In this context, psychology is an experimental and comparative analysis of dysfunctional behavior and unhealthy mental processes. Conversely, it must also be determined what is functional behavior and healthy mental processes. And here is where the misunderstanding begins.

Since psychology evolved from a philosophical branch to pseudo-scientific methods, the history of its development from 1879 to the late 20th century has been dominated by a series of nine different approaches: Voluntarism, Structuralism, Functionalism, Psychodynamic (pioneered by Sigmund Freud), Gestalt psychology, Behaviorism, Humanistic psychology, Cognitive psychology, and Social psychology. By the end of the 20th century, psychology fragmented into many fields and also combined with other disciplines including neurophysiology, evolutionary biology, computing, linguistic, and anthropology.[1] However, from a strictly cultural standpoint, the misconception about madness happens when it's investigated from biomedical approaches that classify it as a form of mental illness. But is it?

Madness seems to extend far beyond the medical grasp and extrapolates to artistic and intellectual manifestations. Many brilliant philosophers (Nietzsche and Rousseau), talented writers (Hemingway and Tolstoy), imaginative painters (Van Gogh and Goya), among numerous other creative individuals have shown characteristics of what is commonly considered signs of madness. Although many of them have been "diagnosed" as mentally ill, there is no scientific evidence that their struggles with depression or mood swings were not caused by the sensitivity of their unique human nature, rather than an ill-fated biochemical imbalance that befell upon them by an unfortunate luck of their DNA draw. A classic modern example of artistic talent misdiagnosed as mental illness is the case of international bestseller author, Paulo Coelho (1947–   ), who was temporarily confined to an insane asylum where he endured electroconvulsive therapy. This outdated ghastly treatment—if you could classify physical and psychological torture as treatment—is based on the idea that mental disorder results from electrical disturbances in the brain. After ten to twenty sessions of electric shocks applied every other day, the patient's brain is "reorganized" allowing him to return to normal;[2] that is, adjustment to the dominant perception of what it means to be normal.

All of this may sound literally crazy, especially because it's written by a self-proclaimed madman. However, as I mentioned earlier, many renowned experts of the caliber of Dr. R.D. Laing and Thomas Szasz have subscribed to this seemingly outlandish reasoning. The fact is that mental illness has no conventional medical roots to back up its validity with scientific evidence (like trying to prove the existence of God by virtue of the outspread belief in it). Unlike a broken arm that can be identified through an X-ray, or a tumor that can be spotted in a MRI or CAT scan, mental illness is as elusive as it is subjective in its diagnosis. Despite the plethora of claims that mental illness is rooted in dysfunctional biochemistry in the brain, deficiencies or surpluses of particular neurotransmitters, or the product of unfavorable genetic heritage, the etiology (cause or origin) of most mental illnesses remain obscure and definitive answers about the condition continue to be as elusive as ever. Even the *Diagnostic and Statistical Manual* (DSM), the Bible of the American Psychiatric Association, is enmeshed in controversy, even at the highest reaches of the profession itself.[3] But irrespective of how mental illness is classified, there is something borderline insane about the pseudo-medical science of psychiatry. And considering its close relationship with pharmaceutical corporations, suspicion arises effortlessly.

✣

"Psychiatry is probably the single most destructive force that has affected society within the last sixty years," Dr. Thomas Szsasz proclaimed categorically. This statement is printed on the back cover of the excellent documentary film titled *The Marketing of Madness,* produced by Citizens Commission on Human Rights. This is the story of the high-income partnership between psychiatry and drug companies that has created an $80 billion psychotropic drug profit center. The documentary exposes the shenanigans of this partnership while questioning the validity of psychiatrists' diagnosis and the safety of the drugs they prescribe.[4] As it is, the spurious medical science of psychiatry classifies any unpredictable human behavior as a mental health issue to which powerful—and profitable—psychotropic medications supposedly can help manage the concocted disease. A typical example of this fraudulent strategy is a "disease" named generalized anxiety disorder (GAD). The public relations firm for the British pharmaceutical giant GlaxoSmithKline initiated a massive marketing campaign to promote, Paxil, the miracle drug with which to manage this newly invented disease. Soon, local newscasts around the country reported that as many as 10 million Americans suffered from the unrecognized disease. What Cohn & Wolfe, the drugmaker's P.R. firm, was doing had less to do with marketing a drug product, but to promote a corporate-sponsored "disease awareness" campaign focusing on a mild psychiatric condition with a large pool of potential sufferers,[5] as well as avid consumers who'd generate significant profits.

Recent litigation trends reflect a dramatic increase in successful lawsuits against the pharmaceutical industry to compensate victims of debilitating and even deadly effects of psychotropic drugs. According to the Citizens Commission on Human Rights, the legal drug dealers—or corporate pushers to be exact—are having their share of costly losses in the courts of law:

> "Billions of dollars have been paid in settlements and fines because of the false and misleading marketing of psychotropic drugs...Since December 2006, state and federal authorities have exacted more than $5.1 billion in criminal and civil fines, penalties and settlements from manufacturers of antidepressants and other psychiatric drugs."[6]

But that is not strong enough deterrent to the powerful pharmaceutical industry. After all, the upward trend in business is very promising. In 1987, Americans spent $2.8 billion on psychotropic drugs. By 2001, that figure soared to $18 billion. A mere three years later it jumped to $34 billion, and in 2008, drug makers made $40 billion from psychiatric drug sales internationally.[7] As of 2015, the industry was raking in $70 billion a year.[8] At this pace of profitability, the likelihood that new mental illnesses will not continue to expand is close to nil. No wonder the American Psychiatric Association's Diagnostic and Statistical Manual of Mental Disorders (commonly known as DSM); the indispensable volume of the business of therapy, routinely adds new mental disorders to each updated edition. Author Steven Pressfield (1943–   ) gives a good personal experience account on how this trend develops in the business world:

"I once worked as a writer for a big New York ad agency. Our boss used to tell us: Invent a disease. Come up with the disease, he said, and we can sell the cure. Attention Deficit Disorder, Seasonal Affect Disorder, Social Anxiety Disorder. These aren't diseases, they're marketing ploys. Doctors didn't discover them, copywriters did. Marketing departments did. Drug companies did."[9]

Evidently, the madness of psychology orbits around the demand for profit, not the welfare of the sufferers it creates through the concoction of new diseases. If there is an imbalance that is more troubling than the biochemical function of the brain, it's certainly the selfish greed of an ethically disturbed industry of sickness. Seemingly, it is not the brain that is not functioning properly; it is the emotional heart that has become desensitized by the travesties of a socioeconomic system that disregards the most essential human needs. Perhaps this is why I consider myself to be a madman, though I am not a mentally ill person. In this sense, I don't think that I am crazy at all; in fact, I think those who embrace the culture of normality are. I just happen to experience reality from a different perspective of the normal social standards.

In my dogged effort to understand my peculiar type of madness, I continue to pursue an explanation for my particular case, which led me to a definition that set off a new awareness about my condition:

"Mental disorder is difficult to define. Generally speaking, mental disorders are conditions that involve either loss of contact with reality or distress impairment...the symptoms that define them are open to subjective interpretation."[10]

Since I've definitely lost contact with perceived normal reality and have become distressed impaired—and defining symptoms are open to subjective interpretation—I had no qualms diagnosing myself with a psychological-emotional illness caused by socioeconomic and cultural imbalance; a disharmony with the mainstream behavioral patterns. This inability to comprehend and adapt to accepted codes of normality has convinced me of my status as a bona fide madman.

And as the pursuit of profit seems to be at the center of what's perceived to be the normal standards, the next step of my investigation ought to focus on the complexity of the economic system that nurtures the industry of madness.

NOTES

[1] Anne Rooney, *The Story of Psychology* (United Kingdom: Arcturus Holdings Limited, 2015), 9.

[2] Fernando Morais, *Paulo Coelho, A Warrior's Life* (New York: Harper-Collins, Publishers, 2009), 132.

[3] Andrew Scull, *Madness in Civilization* (New Jersey: Princeton University Press, 2015), 14.

[4] *The Marketing of Madness: Are We All Insane?* Documentary produced by the Citizens Commission on Human Rights. ISBN 978-1-4031-8759-8

[5] Ann Quigley, Book Editor, *Mental Health* (Farmington Hills, MA: Greenhaven Press, 2007), 55-56.

[6] This statement appears in the cover letter enclosed in the DVD package of the documentary produced by the Citizens Commission on Human Rights, *The Marketing of Madness: Are We All Insane?* This excellent journalistic work provides the facts about psychotropic drugs, their side effects and dangers, as well as the marketing that fuels the profits.

[7] Ibid.

[8] Robert Berezin, M.D., *Psychiatric Drugs Are False Prophets With Big Profits*, posted on July 5, 2015. https://www.psychologytoday.com/blog/the-theater-the-brain/201507/psychiatric-drugs-are-false-prophets-big-profits

[9] Steven Pressfield, *The War of Art* (New York: Warner Books, Inc., 2002), 26.

[10] Neel Burton, M.D., *The Meaning of Madness: Thinking of "mental illness" as more than just illness*, Psychology Today, September 24, 2012. https://www.psychologytoday.com/blog/hide-and-seek/201209/the-meaning-madness

The Economics of Madness

O ften times I wonder whether economists misunderstood the meaning of the words that Protagoras (481 B.C.E.–411 B.C.E.) uttered twenty-five centuries ago: "man is the measure of all things." It seems that, at least in economic terms, the individual man became the sole measure of all things, especially in regards to economic advantages over the other contributing members of society. Perhaps, had Protagoras redacted both the subject pronoun and the verb (men— and women—are the measure of all things), the confusion over the meaning of his words would have been dissipated. But as it is, the dominant economic system of *laissez-faire* capitalism takes the meaning of his message to a literal context. It's all about the one (man) who outdoes the others in the open competitive field of business, as each embarks on the pursuit of his happiness often times in detriment to the happiness of others.

The economics of madness was first introduced to the world by Scottish economist Adam Smith (1723–1790) in his *magnum opus The Wealth of* Nations. In this work about economic productivity aspiring to expand the wealth of nations, Smith fervently extolled the notion that individuals who engage in the pursuit of their own selfish interests benefit society as a whole.[1] Published in 1776 (a symbolic coincidence with the year of the birth of the nation that would become the flagship of his doctrine), *The Wealth of Nations* became the landmark treatise on *laissez-faire* market economy (the term *laissez-faire* comes from the French expression "*laissez-faire la nature,*" which translates as "let nature take its course.") His theories, some of which might have made sense at the dawn of the Industrial Revolution, grabbed the world with the invisible hand of competitive free market forces and never let go of the controlling reins. Henceforth, the stallion of capitalism has been galloping as though a horseman of the Apocalypse directed its destiny into the twenty-first century.

Smith started out on the right track. Vehemently opposed to mercantilism (the economic theory that trade generates wealth and is stimulated by accumulation of profitable balances, which a government should encourage by means of protectionism), he argued that the prosperity of all citizens could be best attained by encouraging individual citizens to pursue their own interest without competition from state-owned enterprises. Influenced as he was by the ideals of the Enlightenment, he believed that both mother nature and human nature could guide an economic system of natural liberty in which free market forces would propitiate equitable distribution of wealth. Although he thought of himself as the champion of the poor against the economic injustices inherent in state-supported mercantile privileges, his *laissez-faire* doctrine later became the favored theory of private industrial entrepreneurs who exploited the poor even more than mercantilist governments ever did.[2] Ironically, "let nature take its course" economic approach did not apply to human beings in factory specialized labor that annihilated workers' souls by treating them as a part of the machine they operated.[3]

With the Industrial Revolution picking up steam—literally—in the nineteenth century, the widespread exploitation of workers paved the way for new ideas to counteract the negative effects of Adam Smith's influence on the emerging market economies. Since the production of wealth, not the welfare of workers, was Smith's primary objective, the political economy of industrialized nations was focused on increasing the riches and power of countries, which were dominated by the elite class that controlled the means of production. As the working and living conditions of the populace degenerated, many opposition voices spoke up against the exploitative situation that expanded as rapidly as the industrial system itself. Thus, philosophers and economists like the Englishman John Stuart Mill (1806–1873), insisted that the distribution of wealth can be regulated by society for the benefit of the majority of its members, and that the state might properly take preliminary steps toward the redistribution of wealth by taxing inheritances and by appropriating the unearned increment of land.[4] However, among all the humanitarian thinkers of the nineteenth century, none exerted more impactful worldwide influence than the German philosopher Karl Marx (1818–1883).

Indeed, Marx's ideas revolutionized the world in a way never experienced before in human history. His insights brought about modern sociology, transformed the study of history, and profoundly affected philosophy, literature and the arts.[5] But more importantly, he instated a new consciousness in which the ultimate goal of history became the liberation of humanity from the shackles of economic oppression engendered by industrial capitalism. He purported that in the *laissez-faire* approach to economics, the worker becomes a commodity; the production of which is subject to the ordinary fluctuating laws of supply and demand that affect the value of labor and therefore wages. Hence, those who employ the workers (the capitalists) build up their wealth through the labor of their workers, and they become wealthy by keeping for themselves a certain amount of the value their workers produce. In this sense, capital is nothing but accumulated labor. And as the worker's labor increases the employer's capital, the latter acquires more machines and other sophisticated and cost-effective ways to produce more goods and services. Unable to compete against large enterprises, large numbers of self-employed workers go out of business, therefore forcing them to sell their labor on an increasingly competitive job market. This intensifies competition among workers trying to land a job, and therefore lowering wages.[6] Pressured by the circumstances of the economic system, workers are compelled to accept whatever employment they may find in order to survive.

❀

By the early twentieth century, the world situation was chaotic at best. With chattel slavery finally abolished in the Western World (Brazil was the last country to sign an emancipation act on May 13, 1888), albeit replaced by a new modern form of industrial slavery in which workers were "bound" to the machines as appendages of the production system, a new era in socioeconomic and political organization was about to begin. Unlike the pre-industrial age when artisans were free to set their own hours and have certain control over their own labor, workers became "enslaved" by the factory system that utterly alienated their working experience. In addition to the industrial technological advancements, the fast expansion of urban centers aggravated both the psychological condition of the increasingly alienated individual whose mental health became significantly compromised. The British writer, Aldous Huxley (1894–1963), summarizes the consequences of urban living this way:

> "City life is anonymous and, as it were, abstract. People are related to one another, not as total personalities, but as embodiments of economic functions...Subjected to this kind of life, individuals tend to feel lonely and insignificant. Their existence ceases to have any point or meaning."[7]

This miserable existential context within an exploitative working and political climate is a recipe for revolution. Thus, the ideas of Karl Marx flourished like a rose of hope in a barren desert of despair.

After ruling Russia with an iron fist since 1894, Czar Nicholas II (1868–1918) was forced to abdicate his throne on March 15, 1917[8] as strikes and widespread revolt broke out in Petrograd (St. Petersburg). Some seven months later, the Bolshevik Revolution overthrew the government while the world was engulfed in one of the most brutal wars in human history. It was at this time that the revolutionary ideas of Karl Marx became institutionalized for the first time under the dictatorial regime of a new imperialistic nation: the Soviet Union. Like Napoleon Bonaparte (1769–1821) who rose to power under the banner of the French Revolution's values of *liberté, egalité, fraternité* (liberty, equality, fraternity) and crowned himself the Emperor of France, the Soviet Union, too, betrayed Marx's humanistic principles and turned them into tools of corruption and oppression. Although it claimed to adopt Marxist values of social and economic justice that contrasted with the exploitative practices of industrial capitalism, the leadership of the Soviet Union became an authoritarian monopolistic state that exercised as much exploitation as capitalistic nations. Erich Fromm (1900–1980), the notable German-American social psychologist and humanistic philosopher, expressed this sentiment in his writings:

> "The Soviet Union with its ruthless economic exploitations of workers for the sake of quicker accumulation of capital and the ruthless political authority necessary for the continuation of exploitation, resembles in many ways the earlier phase of capitalism."[9]

In his foresight and wisdom, Karl Marx himself recognized decades earlier that his ideas were being corrupted by special interests. According to Friederich Engels (1820–1895), Marx's lifelong friend and collaborator, Marx grew so irritated at misinterpretations of his doctrine that towards the end of his life, Marx himself declared: "All I know is that I am not a Marxist."[10]

The most unfortunate consequence of this historical failure is that Karl Marx's humanistic ideals were tainted by the misuse of his philosophy by the failed Soviet Union experiment. Like the values of Jesus of Nazareth (c. 6 B.C.E–c. 29 C.E.) who preached love and brotherhood but whose churches—particularly the Catholic Church—turned them into tools of chicanery, exploitation and thievery, what political groups fight as "Marxism" has superficial resemblance to Marx's economics teachings. Similarly, the various "Marxist" parties and states of today have nothing in common to Marx's scientific socialism.[11] Nations like the so-called "Democratic" People's Republic of Korea (DPRK) whose leadership passes on from father to son as in any old monarchical system, disparages the values of one of the greatest humanistic thinkers of all times.

The other unfortunate consequence for humanity—and the Earth and the future of both—is that capitalism has been victorious in this ideological economic battle. Even decades before the fall of the Soviet Union in 1991, capitalism has been the dominant economic force in the world. Today, traditional communist nations like China have given in to capitalism overwhelming force (China's billionaires have their own list in Forbes magazine's wealthy directory.)[12] However, it has changed significantly—and arguably not for the better—into an economic system of mass consumption in which the fundamental principle is to produce more and more, while instigating the desire for consumption through widespread marketing. Alas, in this transformational process of the economic system, the *Homo sapiens* has also been transformed into the *Homo consumens*, as Fromm calls this vilified version of the human being:

"What is the effect of this type of organization on man? It transforms him into *Homo consumens*, the total consumer whose only aim is to have more and to use more. This society produces many useless things; and to the same degree many useless people. Man as a cog in the production machine becomes a thing and ceases to be human...when he is not producing, he is consuming."[13]

As the *Homo sapiens* becomes the *Homo consumens*, the impersonal economic system also is anthropomorphized into a quasi-person with bona fide characteristics of an individual. For instance, whenever a particular event, action, speech, among other relevant expressions of opinion of potential consequences—and even banal comments expressed in 140 characters—the stock market reacts as though it were an actual independent being. Every day in the news media there are references to "today the markets reacted" to whatever happened in the world or an influential personality said. Perhaps, the Supreme Court of the United States of America was correct when it validated the concept that corporations are, indeed, individual citizens with equal rights to regular human citizens. After all, corporations are the "life-force" of the market that reacts to outside stimulus as any average citizen does. Hence, as humans become dehumanized by the inexorable demands of the economic system, the market takes their place as the heart of society as it pumps the blood of profitability throughout the social body, therefore nurturing it with the much needed economic growth.

Within this context, corporations, especially the large financial institutions, have become a distinct new dominant class managed by individuals who function as lackeys of a much higher order—and are compensated handsomely for their servitude. The problem for the erstwhile society of human citizens, however, is that this new dominant class has absolutely no invested interest in the welfare of the population it dominates. In fact, neither the individual citizens nor the health of the economy is an issue of primary concern, as the collapse of the housing market of 2008 that led to the Great Recession is a classic example supporting this argument.[14]

Hence, despite the Aristotelian concept of man as a social being, the indifference and divisiveness within society engender what I call Collective Solipsism; that is, aggregated selfishness in the making of one society divided by voracious competition among citizens in the pursuit of their own selfish interests. And to make matters worse, this economic system of madness exacerbates the worst aspects of human behavior. With each individual for himself, motivated by unfettered greed, and dishonestly convincing himself that his selfish endeavors will trickle down to benefit society at large, is a bogus economic theory that reveals itself in the growing widening gap between the haves and have-nots. And as long as fierce competition prevails over cooperative efforts, the fallacious notion that the selfish pursuit of profit is what nurtures the common good is not only a lie, but a mendacious psychotic economic policy.

Perhaps, humanistic engineers of social planning in the twenty-first century will address the fundamental issue that Rousseau emphasized in his *Social Contract* in the Age of the Enlightenment: "Every man has by nature a right to all that is necessary to him."[15]

In the meantime, the millions of underprivileged citizens must learn to survive in the madness of economics.

NOTES

[1] Adam Smith, *The Wealth of Nations* (New York: Bantam Dell, 2003).
[2] Edward McNall Burns et al., *World Civilizations Seventh Edition in Two Volumes, Volume 2* (New York: W.W. Norton & Company, Inc., 1986), 875.
[3] Charles Van Doren, *A History of Knowledge* (New York: Ballantine Books, 1991), 216.
[4] Edward McNall Burns et al., *World Civilizations*, 994.
[5] Peter Singer, *MARX* (Great Britain: Oxford University Press, 1980), 1.
[6] Ibid., 24.
[7] Aldous Huxley, *Brave New World Revisited* (New York: Harper & Row Publishers, Inc., 2000), 23.
[8] It is an ironic coincidence that the despot who took on the title of Czar, which is in reference to the great Roman ruler Julius Caesar, abdicated on the same day (March 15) that Caesar was assassinated in the Roman Senate in 44 B.C.E. to what is known as the Ides of March.
[9] Erich Fromm, *The Sane Society* (New York: Henry Holt and Company, Inc., 1990), 102.
[10] Peter Singer, *MARX,* 38.
[11] Wilhelm Reich, *People in Trouble* (New York: Farrar, Straus and Giroux, 1976), 50.
[12] For a list of China's 20 richest people in 2016 see http://www.forbes.com/pictures/hdij45jl/1-wang-jianlin-33-bil/?ss=china-billionaires#3a644b5164ca
[13] Erich Fromm, *The Revolution of Hope: Toward a Humanized Technology* (New York: Harper & Row Publishers, Inc., 1968), 39-40.
[14] For a great example of this economic travesty, see the 2015 film *The Big Short* directed by Adam McKay. Based on a true story book titled *The Big*

Short: Inside the Doomsday Machine by Michael Lewis, it shows how irresponsible financial speculations created the housing bubble that led to the financial crisis of 2008.

[15] Jean Jacques Rousseau, *The Social Contract* (New York: Washington Square Press, 1967), 24.

The Madness of Economics

Cooperation has long lost the competition against, well, competition. Unfortunately, two of the fundamental principles of cooperation, empathy and compassion, are not only underrated in the dominant economic system, but also undesirable emotional characteristics that are perceived to hinder the expansion of commerce. What is good for business has alarming consequences for humanity and the environment.

Just as empathy (the ability to understand and share the feelings of another) and compassion (sympathetic concern for the sufferings or misfortunes of others) distinguish the essence of cooperation, greed (intense and selfish desire for something, especially wealth and power) and selfishness (excessive concern with self and disregard of others) are the defining attributes of competition. Each duality lies on the opposite side of the comparative spectrum, and therefore they cannot coexist without contradicting their underlying distinctiveness. Thus, because the free market economic system is based on the assumption that competition is its driving force, empathy and compassion must be discarded.

What ensues, then, is the systematic development of economic strategies that maximize the potential for greed and selfishness to thrive in detriment to fostering the value of empathy and compassion. Through a methodical nationalistic propaganda (the craft of marketing) that subliminally associates the broad concept of human freedom with the narrow notion of free market, industrial capitalism becomes an essential pseudo-element of society's cultural identity. Once the economic system is validated as a quintessential cultural value, policies and laws are established to ensure the continuation of an inhumane and dysfunctional socioeconomic system that is in cahoots with the political administration of society—with untoward consequences for the nation, regardless of how much wealth a few individual citizens accumulate. And even though the madness of economics is all around us, the blinds of indifference and denial obscure the vision of a warped reality. Perhaps, if we remove the blinds for a moment, we'll be able to see the peripheral conditions of insanity.

In order to dispel misinterpretations of this madman's analysis of the dominant economic system, let me begin by stating that what's under the investigative microscope is not capitalism itself, but its harmful consequences. It should be clear by now that one cannot eliminate the function of capital in economic activities (as mentioned earlier, communist nations engage in the practice just the same), since capital is nothing other than the means of production working for the community. Thus, it is not capital that is harmful, but rather capital in private hands, especially if this private ownership is able to control the social structure of economic organization. Private capitalism has led to antisocial conditions, for he who possesses the means of production acquires economic power over others.[1] Once this power is harnessed, it acquires a proprietary function that is nearly impossible to be relinquished. In this case, the unspoken mantra of this privileged group is as simple as it is effective: money to get power, and power to protect money.

❀

The madness of economics is buttressed on egregious income inequality and extremely unfair distribution of wealth among the producers of the wealth of nations: all workers. From a madman's standpoint, one of the most incomprehensible features of capitalistic economic practices regards the issue of wages. It makes absolutely no sense to me why there is an established minimum wage, which is commonly referred to as slave wage, but no ceiling to maximum wage, which I refer to as slave-master income. Although it's a well-known fact that there are millions of hard-working people in the wealthiest nation on Earth who, in spite of laboring full-time, are unable to eke out a living without receiving public assistance. Conversely, a handful of top executives in multinational corporations and powerful financial institutions can "earn" (I use this verb with tongue-in-cheek), obscene salaries and compensations for their "contribution" (I use this noun with overt sarcasm) to society.

The end-result of this travesty is a truly maddening economic statistic that boggles the mind, confounds the spirit, and bewilders even a modicum sense of fairness.

According to a study by Oxfam, an international confederation of 18 non-governmental organizations (NGO) working with partners over 90 countries to end injustices that cause poverty, the wealthiest 62 people now own as much as half of the world's population, or 3.5 billion people. In the meantime, the wealth of 62 people has risen 44 percent since 2010, while the wealth of the poorest 3.5 billion has fallen 41 percent during the same timeframe.[2] This is not by any means a mere reflection of economic injustice--this is undeniable madness!

Amnesty International, another non-governmental organization focused on human rights, provides some additional statistical details of the consequences of this madness of economics: At least 963 million people go to bed hungry every night; 1 billion people live in slums; 2.5 billion people have no access to adequate sanitation services; and 20,000 children a day die as a result.[3] As the organization asserts, no solution without human rights at its core will have any long-term sustainable impact on the lives of those in poverty.

Another controversial issue that relates to the inequitable distribution of wealth is taxation. Although I'm not an economist, nor do I claim to have expertise in this pseudo-science,[4] I find the rationalization supporting a reduction of taxes to stimulate the economy ludicrous at best. Conservative arguments purport that cutting taxes to big business, large corporations, and wealthy individuals is seemingly the most important initiative in the creation of jobs (mostly slave-wage jobs). However, my common sense leads my inference in the opposite direction. Since traditional capitalism has long been mutated into consumerism, it is the spending of money that actually stimulates the economy and creates jobs—and the market's Consumer Price Index (CPI) keeps track of it. Thus, if the workers who earn the least have more disposal income (an oxymoron considering that they barely earn enough to pay for essential living expenses), they will consume more goods and services, therefore stimulating the consumerist nature of the economic system; and consequently, create more jobs. On the other hand, taxing high income businesses, corporations, and wealthy individuals at a robust rate, it would stimulate the economy and the job market concurrently by adding revenue to the national treasure, which in turn would reinvest in the economy through public services—and all of it without even scratching the surface of the well-to-do net worth. It seems like a win-win situation that would do away with the inauspicious zero-sum approach that hurt so many on behalf of a few.

As for the skeptical die-hard free market winner-takes-it-all advocates, I say that you cannot pooh-pooh this madman's argument without taking a close look at the Scandinavian countries. Sweden, Denmark, Norway, and Finland have been applying the high-taxes model without compromising their prosperity and democratic values; to the contrary, both have been enhanced. Despite the hefty taxes assessed on their citizens, these countries have consistently sustained through the years a standard of living that is much higher than the charges meted out on their people. Besides their solid economic development, each of these nations flaunt a well educated population, universal health care for its citizens, and a public safety net that erases concerns about untoward circumstances in the present or in old age. Notwithstanding, the crime rate in these nations are extremely low, particularly in comparison with the ever-growing violence and incarceration in the United States.

However, one of the most disturbing aspects of the madness of the dominant economic system is its reliance on debt—of individuals, businesses, and nations—as a valuable commodity of trade. At first it seems contradictory that debt, which alludes to deficit, can be a source of profit. But in reality, the entire economic system, especially the financial sector, relies on debt to increase gains. It is so pervasive in the United States economy that you could say that debt is as American as apple pie.

Seemingly, this trend developed as capitalism transitioned to consumerism. The traditional capitalist approach to generating wealth through reinvestments and savings has been reversed and replaced by the coerced need for consumption—Personal Consumer Expenditure (PCE) tracks this important aspect of the economy. And since the modern version of capitalism depends on consumption for the system to survive, it purposefully fosters the belief that the pursuit of happiness lies in the amount of money necessary to be happy; a misleading notion that Lucretius (99 B.C.E.–55 B.C.E.) already knew and Leo Tolstoy (1828–1910) echoed some 2,000 years later: "Seek among men, from beggar to millionaire, one who is contented with his lot, and you will not find one such in a thousand."[5] And contemporary chroniclers of wealth have reached the very same conclusion:

> "No matter what their income, a depressing number of Americans believe that if only they had twice as much, they would inherit the state of happiness promised them in the Declaration of Independence. The man who receives $15,000 a year is sure that he could relieve his sorrow if he had only $30,000 a year; the man with $1 million a year knows that all would be well if he had $2 million a year...Nobody ever has enough."[6]

In fact, spending is not only the measuring stick of happiness, but a fundamental aspect of economic growth. Since every segment of society depends on consumption of goods and services—including the federal, state, counties, cities, and municipalities that must collect all sorts of revenues to balance their budgets—the encouragement to accumulate debt is a must.

❁

Beginning at the individual level, accumulation of debt has become imperative to economic stability and expansion. Bewitched by the seduction of using credit to fulfill an illusion of prosperity and short-term pleasures, naïve consumers unwittingly give in to debt-bondage. Used on a daily basis, "plastic money" is like an addictive financial drug people carry in their wallets easily accessible whenever there is a need for a consumerist fix. It's no surprise that the idea of a new currency system that would substitute cash for a permanent credit-card mechanism has circulated in recent years, which likely would increase both consumption and debt. Even as it is, workers in the lower echelons of the financial pyramid are already burdened by debt as a means to close the gap between income and expenses—survival that is. According to Bankcard Holders of America (BHA), more than 70% of Americans carry some sort of credit-card debt. In 1994, the collective national credit-card debt was tallied at more than $279 billion.[7] In 2016, it was calculated at $747 billion.[8] At this rate, debt-bondage will become a wage-labor slavery economic model in which workers are perpetually bound to debt. Hence, the likelihood of a lifelong enslavement is as high as the interest rates applicable to credit-card debt. And considering that more than half of American workers claim to feel disengaged from their jobs,[9] the quality of life is significantly diminished in spite of the excessive consumption of superfluous goods.

Meanwhile, the financial institutions and the privileged individuals profiting from the meretricious economic system are flying high. Opposite to the high interest rates assessed to credit-card debt, the interest rates on savings account have been negligible for a long time. At the time of the 2008 economic meltdown created by irresponsible financial speculations, the Federal Government doled out over $700 billion of tax payers money to Wall Street and slashed the interest rates to near zero to rescue the nation's big banks; the main culprits of the economic collapse. As a result, the financial institutions that caused the problem in the first place made billions of dollars, while the savings accounts of average citizens were nearly stagnant. As banks enjoyed the benefits of paying measly rates on CDs and money market accounts, American households lost hundreds of billions of dollars in interest earnings. At the same time, the Wall Street mob and their investment firms handed out a jaw-dropping $20 billion in cash bonuses to their lackeys.[10] And if this were not enough to drive a man mad-out-of-his mind, the venturing for profits by exploitation of the national debts of impoverished nations most certainly will.

❁

In the madness of economics, governments accumulate debt—some of them massive amounts due to stratospheric interest rates—just as citizens owe money to private banks. And just as individuals' debt is a valuable commodity of trade (think Collaterized Debt Obligation (CDO), which bundles up extremely overrated mortgage debts that are sold as "investment commodities to gullible investors), the debt of nations is sumptuous fodder for the wealth of nations—and for opportunistic vulture capitalists who prey on them. From Argentina to the Republic of Congo across the Atlantic Ocean, developing countries are drowning in debt and unable to keep up with the unrelenting accruing of interest rates. In Argentina, for instance, the middle class collapsed under the heavy weight of $81 billion in foreign debt, which was the largest sovereign debt default in history. The upper class, however, were shored up by the sturdy pillars of their wealth. In the meantime, Jay Newman, an American investor associated with the hedge fund firm Elliott Management, and another eccentric billionaire investor by the name of Kenneth

Dart (an American citizen who forfeited his citizenship and operates in the Caribbean to shield his wealth from the government), used a highly specialized investment scheme known as vulture funds.[11] They buy debt in bedeviled countries at pennies on the dollar and turn them into massive riches for themselves in detriment to some of the world's most desperate populations. In vulture capitalism, traders make their fortunes on the backs of the weak and poor.[12]

Like credit-card companies that sell laid-off factory workers' old accounts to debt collectors, vulture funds operate in similar fashion, but at a much higher stakes. The most aggressive vulture funds apply an array of legal tools at their disposal; from the courts of law to the old fashion way of having a politician-in-your-pocket approach. And it's all worth it. Profits in this unique specialty can range from 300 percent to 2,000 percent per deal, and the cost is borne by the world's poorest countries. While Liberia was falling apart, FH International, an investment firm run by vulture capitalist Eric Hermann, sued in a New York court demanding $13 million for a debt from 1978; a piece of a loan made by Chemical Bank. Since no lawyer appeared in court on behalf of Liberia, which was immersed in a brutal civil war at the time, FH international won the case. "If you pick on a country like Liberia, they're not going to be able to afford big lawyers," one vulture investor said. "If you don't show up in court when you are sued, you lose."[13]

Alas, the impoverished nation of Liberia becomes a source of revenue for the luxuriant life style of a human vulture.

✺

In the face of such predatory capitalist practices, it is no wonder that even the Pope has become a vocal critic of modern market capitalism. Lambasting the "idolatry of money and the dictatorship of an impersonal economy in which man is reduced to one of his needs alone: consumption,"[14] the 266th Pope of the Roman Catholic Church (an institution that has historical ties with imperialist powers) doesn't mince words in his criticism of a no-holds barred economic system that scavenges individuals and nations in detriment to the most basic human needs. But when you think that the madness of economics has reached rock-bottom, a noxious element emerges from the swamp of profit-seeking ogres that can make you literally sick.

Among all the industries in the all-encompassing capitalist system, none is more degrading than the health care and its accessory pharmaceutical business. If speculating on essential human necessities such as food, housing, and education were not reprehensible enough, pursuing profit by exploiting the health care needs of those who contribute to the overall health of a productive society is at minimum a violation of basic ethics, and at worst an egregious crime. In fact, it is a transgression that is openly sanctioned by *laissez-faire* capitalism in the United States. It has extrapolated to a level in which even deadly diseases have become valuable commodities of trade. Cancer, for instance, one of the most dreadful and widespread illness of our time, has become an industry in and by itself.[15] And since acquiring health insurance to cover the astronomical expenses of treating life-threatening diseases—or any medical need for that matter—has become cost-prohibitive for millions of people, the misfortune of being afflicted by a life-threatening disease can lead, if not to death, most certainly to bankruptcy.

In tandem with the ill-administered "health" care industry is what is commonly known as the Big Pharma. Flying high on Wall Street, financial advisors enthusiastically recommend adding stocks in this profitable sector of the economy to their clients' portfolios. Except for pharmaceutical companies that don't have a large number of drugs in development, analysts avow that some drug companies make for some good long-term investments.[16] And why wouldn't they? After all, Americans spend more on medicines than all the people of Japan, Germany, France, Italy, Spain, the United Kingdom, Australia, New Zealand, Canada, Mexico, Brazil, and Argentina—combined![17] Besides, the United States is the only developed country in the world that does not control prescription drug prices, and the lobbyists for the pharmaceutical industry have ensured the passing of laws that have added years to the average length of time their products are protected from competition by patents. Other laws have allowed companies to profit from medical discoveries made by taxpayer-funded scientists, as well as tax credits so lucrative that as a group they pay far lower taxes on average than other major industries.[18] In the meantime, both the health care insurance premiums and the cost of lifesaving drugs skyrocket with profits in a sick free market economic system.

Perhaps the most egregious example of despicable greed and scathing irresponsibility in the ailing industry of "health" care is that of loathsome CEO of Turin Pharmaceuticals, a despicable human vulture by the name of Martin Shkreli (1983–   ). He orchestrated an absurd 5,000 percent price hike of a medication called Daraprim, which is used to treat toxoplasmosis, a parasitic disease that affects AIDS patients, pregnant women, and those with weakened immune system.[19] Not to be obscured by the shadow of shame, CEO of Mylan Pharmaceuticals, Heather Bresch (1969–   ), who earned nearly $19 million in total compensation in 2015 alone, set off a relentless series of price hikes of the lifesaving EpiPen (epinephrine), a drug that stops potentially fatal allergic reactions. Even though epinephrine itself is a very cheap drug, costing less than $1 per milliliter—and there is less than a third of that in a EpiPen—within few years of acquiring the rights of the drug, Mylan Pharmaceuticals jacked up the cost from $100—already an exorbitant profit margin—to $600, a modest increase of 500 percent. The notorious aspect of this particular example is that Mylan Pharmaceuticals is guaranteed to sell plenty of units because epinephrine degrades quickly, so users have to replace their EpiPens every year. And because EpiPen has virtually no competition, health insurers often cover most of its cost; and yet, the company had no qualms to raise the price repeatedly without much resistance.[20]

❀

And so the madness of economics goes unabated. From unregulated financial speculations to the administration of prisons by private enterprises (even crime is a commodity for profit),[21] the insane economic system has no restrictions in its predatory practices. Even judges fall prey to the temptation of corruption, as the case of ex-Judge Mark Ciavarella (1950–) from Luzerne County, Pennsylvania, illustrates. He left the bench in disgrace for sending youth offenders to for-profit detention centers in exchange for millions of dollars in illicit payments from the builder and owner of the lockups.[22] Indeed, everything becomes fodder to nourish the insatiable economic system beast—and people and the environment are the unwitting delicatessen to its voracious appetite.

As the irrepressible need for continuous growth marches on, environmentally conscious citizens strive to curb its forward motion and minimize the damage along the way. In the end, however, all we can do is ride the tsunami hoping we will not wipe out under its massive weight. As long as population and economic expansion continue growing at the same time and pace, the desperate cries of "save the Earth" will be unheralded, unheard, and unheeded. It doesn't matter how much recycling, downsizing, reducing our carbon footprint, or any and all the other efforts to slow down the locomotive of capitalistic expansion. Unless there is a sense of urgency that compels us to change course expeditiously, the train of progress will either derail or crash against the wall of (in)convenient apathy. Alas, it seems like it's already picked up so much speed that the prospect of derailing off its tracks might be the least damaging alternative, either we do it willingly or not.

Sometimes I wonder whether my madness, like the socioeconomic-political system, has reached the point of no return. I try to remain optimistic, but as the news media reminds me every day, the most important aspect of modern life is the economy, stupid. It's all about the Gross National Product (GNP); the Dow Jones Industrial Average (DJIA); the Standard and Poor's 500 (S&P); the Nasdaq Stock Market; the unemployment rate; and all the other economic measurements that do not take into consideration the quality of life, the health of the environment, and the hope for a sustainable future. As it is, we find ourselves in a quintessential Catch-22: if we don't have a strong growing economy, we can't afford the services we depend on (education, social safety nets, health care, and even resources to protect the environment). But at the current rate of growth, the long-term survival of the planet is in serious jeopardy, and so is the human species.

Meanwhile, career politicians continue drafting economic policies and passing laws that will ensure unremitting economic expansion. These self-serving professionals of politics disguised under the mantle of public servants have their own selfish interests to pursue. And because their political careers are financed by private capital (they wouldn't be able to run for office otherwise), an important question remains to be answered: Can we trust them? The answer, it seems obvious to me, is as straightforward as it is undeniable: Definitely not!

Perhaps my sane fellow citizens have an explanation, and maybe even a reason to trust, though I don't think it'd be convinced. As long as the politics of madness is in place, I shall remain skeptical and distrustful of those purporting to serve the common good while pursuing their own selfish interests.

NOTES

[1] Rudolf Steiner, *The Renewal of the Social Organism* (Spring Valley, New York: Anthroposophic Press, 1985), 11, 25.

[2] *The Week*, January 29, 2016, 16.

[3] These statistics are listed on a card for a recruiting new members campaign to join Amnesty International. For more information and learn how to contribute to their laudable worldwide struggle for human rights, visit http://www.amnesty.org.

[4] For a cogent descriptive interpretation against economy as a legitimate science, see the brief video with Canadian geneticist and activist David Suzuki at https://www.youtube.com/watch?v=4NiauhOCfsk.

[5] Alan Thein Durning, *How Much is Enough?* (New York: W.W. Norton & Company, Inc., 1992), 37-38.

[6] Ibid.

[7] Diane Hales, "Smart Ways To Get Yourself What Out Of Debt," *Parade Magazine*, February 13, 1994, 20.

[8] Erin El Essa, *2016 American Household Credit Card Debt Study*, Nerd Wallet, Inc. Comprehensive details of the study is available at https://www.nerdwallet.com/blog/average-credit-card-debt-household/

[9] Reported on News Hour, *Public Broadcast System*, January 5, 2017.

[10] Michael Crowley, "How Wall Street, creator of the financial meltdown, profits at the expense of the middle class," *Reader's Digest*, September, 2010, 39-41.

[11] Aram Roston, "Vulture Capitalism," *Playboy*, December 2010, 60-62, 175-186

[12] There is a quote by Leo Tolstoy that illustrates this sentiment: "I sit on man's back, choking him and making him carry me. And yet, I assure myself and others that I'm sorry for him, and wish to lighten his load by all possible means; except, by getting off his back."

[13] Aram Roston, "Vulture Capitalism," 62.

[14] Rana Foroohar, "Saving Capitalism," *TIME*, May 23, 2016, 29.

[15] For an excellent comprehensive account of this travesty of capitalism, refer to Ralph W. Moss, Ph.D. book *The Cancer Industry* (Sheffield, U.K: Equinox Press, 1996).

[16] "Don't write off Big Pharma," Money & Markets, *Corvallis Gazette-Times,* March 29, 2011, A7.

[17] Melody Petersen, *Our Daily Meds* (New York: Sarah Crichton Books, an imprint of Farrar, Straus and Giroux, 2008), back cover.

[18] Ibid., 10.

[19] Matt Krantz, "11 Drugmakers Wield Pricing Power," *USA Today*, August 26, 2016, B1.

[20] "Issue of the week: Uproar over EpiPen price hikes," *The Week*, September 9, 2016, 34.

[21] Michael Moore, the award winning filmmaker, exposes the multi-million for-profit prison business in his excellent documentary titled *Capitalism: A Love Story*. See selected references at the end of this book for details.

[22] Tim Wendel with staff and wire reports, *Newsline*, USA Today, February 19, 2011, A1.

The Politics of Madness

P olitics, a word of Greek origin (*Politiká*, meaning affairs of the cities), is intended to address issues of concerns of society in a process of governance. In his work, *The Republic*, Plato expresses his thoughts on the ideal state ruled by philosophers (educated committed citizens) to fulfill the ultimate goal of justice. In the Eastern World, *Kung Tzu* (551 B.C.E.–479 B.C.E.), or Confucius as he's known in the Western World, envisioned politics as a tool with which to achieve the highest ideal of what he called *Ta Tung* ("Grand Commonwealth"); a state where men of talent and virtue were chosen to positions of responsibility based on the divine duty of loyalty. But observing politics in the world today, it's impossible not to wonder what happened to the Platonic goal of justice and the Confucian values of responsibility and loyalty in politics. But if these are the normal ideal principles of governance, then we can rest assured that what we have today is akin to politics of madness.

Seemingly, what used to be an honorable representation of people's best interest has become an art and a science of manipulation. In fact, according to dictionary definition, this inference is validated almost verbatim: politics is the art or science of government; the art or science concerned with guiding or influencing governmental policy; the art or science concerned with winning and holding control over a government.[1] It is the latter definition, however, that makes you raise an eyebrow of suspicion, for "winning and holding control over a government" without genuine concern for the interest of the people it's supposed to serve has the potential to lead to corruption. Although the influence of money in politics is a long and pervasive American tradition, the pattern has been significantly exacerbated since the inception of the super PACs² following the 2010 federal court decision in the case of *SpeechNow.org* (an organization that pools resources from individual contributors to make independent expenditures) vs. Federal Election Commission. Thenceforth, capital became more powerful than the right to vote itself, because it can sway millions of voters through marketing, advertisement, and propaganda. And as Jean Jacques Rousseau warned in his *Social Contract*, "Nothing is more dangerous than the influence of private interests on public affairs."³

Hence, the "general will" (Rousseau's famous notion that alludes to the will of the people) is compromised by the interference of special interest groups that supersede the will of the population that politics is supposed to serve. In this case, neither the citizen nor the state is legitimately free by democratic standards, since wealth and power take, by proxy, the reins of the decision making process, therefore corrupting politics. In such a political climate, Congress and elected officials at large, owe their allegiance not to the citizens who cast their votes, but to individuals and entities that finance their political campaigns. This is why, in spite of the democratic rhetoric, we have been led to a bedlam of lies about freedom when in reality we've been enslaved and trapped in a camouflaged web of corporate and governmental machination that continuously enfeebles our "general will." As the great humanistic American attorney and author Gerry Spence (1929–) observes:

> "...the people of a nation are enslaved when, together, they are helpless to institute effective change, when the people serve the government more than the government serves them."⁴

Thankfully, there are always committed citizens who rebel against the politics of madness. They organize, protest, and bring their cause to the national spotlight; like the rebellious youth of the Counterculture Revolution did in the 1960s. Although most of the time thousands of people set out on marches and rallies to bring attention to a worthy cause, sometimes one single person imbued with conviction and courage can ignite the fire of social transformation—and history shows numerous examples of such spirited individuals. In the case of the prostitution of the political system (when corporations pay money to be in bed with elected officials, prostitution is the only appropriate term to describe the relationship), a most unusual citizen stepped to the plate to challenge this travesty. Unlike the vigorous young men and women of the counterculture movement of the 1960s, a nonagenarian lady took upon herself to fight against the pimps of democracy single-handed.

❀

Doris Haddock (1910–2010), or Granny D. as she became popularly known, was one of the oldest political activists in the world. A former housewife and office assistant, she was content enjoying her retirement for more than twenty years. After her husband and another close friend passed away within years of each other, Granny D. started questioning her lifelong beliefs and convictions as she searched for a purpose in her life. Convinced that the corrupted political system in the United States had been hijacked by special interests, she decided to fight against the influence of capital buying out the democratic process behind the back of the people. She was determined to put the kibosh on corporations investing their capital in electoral campaigns through the purchase of morally cheap political candidates. Thus, this genuinely mad woman (per perceptional interpretation of normality) embarked on a walking journey across the United States to protest the betrayal of democracy by money in politics. She laced up her sneakers in Los Angeles and walked 3,200 miles in fourteen months all the way to the nation's capital to bring attention to the issue of campaign finance reforms.5

At first, she was dismissed by the corporate-owned media as a "naïve innocent grand-mother" whose actions were considered soft-news unworthy of coverage (they obviously had no invested interest in covering the story), she received national attention when *The New York Times* ran a story about her activism. Soon afterwards, the media went on a frenzy about this elderly lady whose vitriolic message against the prostitution of democracy exposed many politicians as if they were pimps hiding under their fedora hats of public servants. That's when the business-oriented media realized that Granny D. was not soft-news as it was originally dubbed. In fact, her message was as hard as a brick smashing through the window of political corruption. Like the old adage that says "money talks," Granny D. literally walked her talk to show an apathetic nation that if money is to be equated to the First Amendment right, then those with more money have more speech rights than the majority of the population; and that's an ethical violation of the fundamental principles of democracy. She made her position clear in a speech she delivered on July 23, 1999 at the Reform Party Convention in Dearborn, Michigan:

> "It is said that democracy is not something we have, but something we do. But right now, we cannot do it because we cannot speak. We are shouted down by the bullhorns of big money. It is money with no manners for democracy, and it must be escorted from the room...While wealth has always influenced our politics, what is new is the increasing concentration of wealth and the widening divide between the political interests of the common people and the political interests of the very wealthy who are now able to buy our willing leaders wholesale...What villainy allows this political condition? The twin viral ideas that money is speech and that corporations are people. If money is speech then those with more money have more speech, and this idea is antithetical to democracy. It makes us no longer equal citizen."[6]

Granny D.'s walk across the United States galvanized the national attention to campaign finance reform. She exposed even more the obvious fact that the power of Big Money has corrupted both politics and the accomplice elected officials benefiting from this immoral and undemocratic practice. Thus, at the age of 94 and still fed up with politics as usual, she decided to take the heavily underdog role of running for the U.S. Senate.[7] Although she lost the race as expected, she put out a feisty campaign decrying the corruption of the political system while personifying the quintessential American democratic ideals of a government of, by, and for the people. Former President Jimmy Carter (1924–   ) extolled her efforts by acknowledging her as "a true patriot, and our nation has been blessed by her remarkable life." Even a member of the Republican Party in the Senate and former Presidential candidate, John McCain (1936–   ), commended her swashbuckling activism: "I believe she represents all that is good in America. She has taken up this struggle to clean up American politics."[8]

❁

Western politics has been founded on the principle of democracy. Since Aristotle (384 B.C.E.–322 B.C.E.), one of the most influential philosophers in the Western World, asserted that man is a political animal, much attention has been devoted to this important element of political science. Since humans must live in associations and devote attention to the family and to the public affairs of a commonwealth, he stressed his views regarding political organization in his renowned work, *Politics*. In his discussion about governments, he divides them into three forms: monarchy, aristocracy, and constitutional government, as well as three perversions of them, which are tyranny, oligarchy, and democracy.[9] However, considering that democracy is such a reverential idealistic concept, having the word associated with perversion sounds like a condemnable heresy. But in the politics of madness, democracy is just another casualty of the perversion of human nature.

At the apex of the Cold War between the communist and capitalist empires—the two failed beasts of oppression—the Western "free (market) world" boastfully proclaimed that communism was a utopian model of political and socioeconomic organization that could never succeed. Meanwhile, the propaganda exhorting the values of the marriage between capitalism and democracy assured that this holy matrimony begot the child of freedom—the euphemism for free enterprise. Nevertheless, observing the circumstances of capitalism and democracy in the world today, it is evident that what has come out of this union is a seriously dysfunctional child in the throes of suicidal thoughts. One needs not to probe too deeply to realize that capitalism has failed as miserably as its nemesis. As for democracy, capitalism idealistic spouse, it has proven to be a myth that deludes the masses with a false sense of participation. As Granny D. demonstrated, capital has become the determining factor in a so-called democratic process. This is evinced by the number of political candidates who have abandoned their campaigns because of their inability to raise funds from wealthy donors, lobbyists, and corporate sponsorship. In fact, the reputation of democracy has gotten so bad that it has been equated to a large brothel where the whores do not wear skin-tight hot red pants, but business suits with dignified pinstripes. It's been said that the largest brothel in America is the Congress of the United States.[10]

Like the communist utopia of an egalitarian society, the illusion of equal participatory rights attributed to democracy is just as deceptive, especially at a time when capital can decisively influence the result of elections. Since the divided U.S. Supreme Court in Citizens United vs. Federal Election Commission in 2010, the power of money to influence government decisions by freeing them to spend their millions to sway elections for president and Congress, democracy has lost much of its credibility as a fair participatory process. As Granny D. asserted in her speech quoted above, "If money is speech then those with more money have more speech, and this idea is antithetical to democracy. It makes us no longer equal citizens." Furthermore, the argument that communism is unachievable because people are unique and unequal by nature, which is not the point since it's the equal treatment of citizens that is the crux of the matter, democracy is doomed by the very same argument, for the one-person one-vote system overshadows this inherent human distinction. After all, how can the vote of an uneducated boorish person have the same democratic value of a well-informed intellectual citizen?

In addition to the blatant disparity in judgment between a learned citizen and another without a modicum of intellectual qualifications, the latter can be easily manipulated by political propagandist in mass movements of discontent.[11] It's particularly more aggravating when the masses of intellectually uncouth citizens are bewildered, frustrated, and disenchanted with the oppressing conditions of their lives. Joseph Goebbels (1897–1945), the Minister of Propaganda of the Third Reich, understood it well and he instructed the Führer how to manipulate the throngs of blindly patriotic fools. Under Goebbels' guidance, Adolf Hitler (1889–1945) was able to control and lead millions of distressed people to commit unspeakable atrocities for the fatherland. In spite of his nationalistic fervor, Hitler had the utmost contempt for the masses whose will he submitted to his own, as the passage below indicates:

> "The masses are utterly contemptible. They are incapable of abstract thinking and uninterested in any fact outside the circle of their immediate experience. Their behavior is determined, not by knowledge and reason, but by feelings and unconscious drives. It is in these drives and feeling that 'the roots of their positive as well as their negative attitudes are implanted.' To be successful, a propagandist must learn how to manipulate these instincts and emotions...Whoever wishes to win over the masses must know the key that will open the door of their hearts...In post-Freudian jargon, of their unconscious."[12]

Although many a naïve citizen shall think that only the likes of Hitler would make use of such manipulative tactics, in reality it is more widespread than ever before, especially at a time when the advancements in technological communication have gone "viral." And to make matters worse, the millions of chronically anxious people in desperate need of reassurance are even more susceptible to being manipulated by professional political demagogues than in any other critical time in history. Unlike the mid-twentieth century when assembling a crowd involved the physical presence of people, in today's world pervasive television broadcasts, the internet, and a slew of electronic media make it possible to gather a crowd of millions in individual living rooms; and persuading them to act as directed becomes a matter of manipulating their basic instincts, small-minded beliefs, and shallow patriotic emotions. Hence, under these circumstances, genuine democracy in which popular suffrage bestows a representative government of the people, by the people, for the people, becomes but a commodity coveted by the wealthy and powerful to fulfill their own selfish interests.

❀

Perhaps, the compass that may guide us out of the politics of madness in the twenty-first century can be found some two thousand years ago in the Eastern World; in the Confucius ideal of the "Grand Commonwealth" (*Ta Tung*), that state in which people of talent and virtue take on the responsibility of stewardship of the welfare of the nation. The ideal rulers who are considered of their subjects' best interest and provide both moral leadership and adequate social welfare, while imbued with an unswerving sense of duty and loyalty to the people they serve. However, one could certainly argue that Confucius' teachings are as utopian as Adam Smith's or Karl Marx's. But there is an important element in the philosophy of Confucius that distinguishes it from his Western counterparts of many later centuries: the moral principle of *Jen*, which signifies humanity; human-heartedness; true-manhood; the importance of the relationship between man and his fellow men; love; benevolence; kindness. *Jen* is the essence of Confucius' ethical teachings.[13] A leader guided by *Jen* is not concerned about lack of wealth; he is concerned about fair distribution of wealth. He is not concerned about poverty, but about insecurity. When there is fair distribution, there will be no poverty; when there is harmony, there will be no complaint of shortage; when there is contentment, there will be no rebellion.[14]

As idealistic as Confucianism may seem, unless there is a revival of *Jen* in political and socioeconomic organization in the twenty-first century, democracy will be irreversibly corrupted by the madness of politics.

NOTES

[1] *Merriam-Webster's Collegiate Dictionary*, Eleventh Edition (Springfield, MA: Merriam-Webster, Inc., 2007), 960.

[2] Super PAC is a type of independent political action committee that may raise unlimited amounts of money from corporations, unions, and individuals for political purposes. Super PACs are not permitted to contribute to or coordinate directly with political parties or candidates.

[3] Jean Jacques Rousseau, *Social Contract and Discourse on the Origin of Inequality* (New York: Washington Square Press, 1967), 70.

[4] Gerry Spence, *Give Me Liberty!* (New York: St. Martin's Press, 1998), 8.

[5] Doris Haddock with Dennis Burke, *Granny D.: You're Never Too Old to Raise a Little Hell* (New York: Villard Books, a division of Random House, Inc., 2003).

[6] Ibid., 267.

[7] Marlo Poras, *Run Granny Run*, a documentary DVD (New York: Arts Alliance America, LLC, 2007).

[8] Doris Haddock with Dennis Burke, *Granny D.: You're Never Too Old to Raise a Little Hell*, Praise for *Granny D.*

[9] Louise Ropes Loomis, Editor, *On Man in the Universe* (New York: Walter J. Black, Inc., 1943), 322.

[10] Gerry Spence, *Give Me Liberty!*, 209.

[11] For an excellent discourse on the nature of mass movements, refer to Eric Hoffer, *The True Believer* (New York: Perennial Classics, an imprint of Harper-Collins Publishers, Inc., 2002).

[12] Aldous Huxley, *Brave New World Revisited* (Perennial Classics, an imprint of Harper-Collins Publishers, Inc., 2000), 40-41.

[13] Ch'u Chai with Winberg Chai, *The Story of Chinese Philosophy* (New York: Washington Square Press, Inc., 1961), 241.

[14] Ibid., 12.

The Madness of Politics

A t the dawn of the twenty-first century, the madness of politics rose like a dim-lighted Sun in the botched political horizon of America. Had it happened in a Third World country, the people of the United States would have derided the affair with caustic amusement. However, the paradoxical event took place in the affluent state of Florida during the heatedly contested presidential election of the year 2000. In unprecedented circumstances, a recount of the votes was necessary to determine the winner of the election—and and that's when the controversy began.

Since the governor of the State of Florida was the brother of one of the presidential candidates, the suspicion of favoritism and unfair play was but inevitable, which already had occurred even before the controversy came about. This is how it happened: In the months leading up to the November 2000 election, the Governor of the State of Florida, Jeb Bush (1953–   ), ordered local elections supervisors to purge 57,700 people from the voter rolls, most of whom (around 90 percent) were voters of his brother's opposite political party.[1] Under the pretext that they were criminals not allowed to vote (most were innocent of crimes, though the majority were guilty of being black), the strategy proved to be critical to the outcome of the election: Florida's Secretary of State declared George W. Bush (1946–   ) winner of Florida, and thereby president, by a plurality of 537 votes over candidate Al Gore (1948–   ).[2] And thus the twenty-first century unleashed the madness of politics.

Almost two decades into what's likely to be the most critical century in the history of human civilization, the socio-political situation worldwide is at a crescendo topsy-turvy state. Afflicted with grave environmental crises, economic stagnation, explosive population expansion, geopolitical chaos, among countless challenges both at regional and global levels, it is befuddling not to acknowledge that madness has taken over the "brilliant" human mind. There is a possibility, albeit very slim, that is not madness but ignorance that assails the proud reasoning bipeds.

Since the debacle of the dubious—and likely fraudulent—2000 election result in the flagship nation of democracy and leader of the free (market) world, the sociopolitical situation in the United States has deteriorated piecemeal, as it has around the world it leads. And in the wake of yet another extremely controversial election in which a megalomaniac billionaire businessman with no experience in politics narrowly wins the archaic electoral vote system, in spite of a corrosive campaign laden with inflammatory rhetoric of hatred, discrimination, misogyny, and documented video evidence admitting to sexual assaults, the reputation of democracy has been smeared in shame. It is as though the sword of Damocles hung over the head of hope.[3]

In the face of sliding public opinion polls, the abrasive egocentric political candidate boisterously claimed that the election was rigged against him; that was being stolen from him through a large-scale voter fraud, biased media coverage, and a conspiracy of international banks and globalist elites conniving against him—contradictorily, he is a foremost member of the elite he purports to reject. Bellowing to his boorish angry supporters that their America was being stolen by dark foreign forces, the rhetoric of Donald Trump (1946–   ) is unprecedented in American political history.[4] Ironically, his portentous oratory denouncing the illegitimacy of the U.S. elections came to haunt him. Against all odds and to the astonishment of the nation and the world, he was elected and became the 45th President of the United States, casting doubts about legitimacy of the election he proclaimed to be rigged. However, to make matters worse, the undeniable evidence of the "dark foreign forces" he claimed to be working against him, were allegedly decisive factors to his winning the election. After the U.S. intelligence community disclosed—and with utmost confidence—that Russia's President Vladimir Putin (1952–   ) was behind the hacking that influenced the outcome of the election in Trump's favor, the cat was out of the bag. And yet, the newly appointed leader of the free (market) world denied the evidence of the agencies committed to protecting national security and interest. Sad.

When people in the capital cities of the allies of the United States take to the streets to protest the incoming president, while celebrations take place in the capital city of America's archrival Cold War era enemy, you know that something has gone awry. And when the newly elected president who claimed that "international banks and globalist elites" were in cahoots to conspire against him, and yet he selects members of these financial and corporate elite groups to join him in office, you also know that chicanery played a major role in bamboozling the unsophisticated 26 percent of eligible voters who swayed the presidential pendulum in Trump's direction.[5] For someone who promised to "drain the swamp," he brought a number of alligators to his inner circle.

Unlike the biochemical-triggered mental illnesses, the madness of politics is highly contagious, especially when it's spread through the leading powerful nation in the world. Although the dissemination of right-wing nationalism ideology—similar to what gave rise to the Third Reich in the early 1930s—has been escalating over the years, the controversial election of a political outsider with radical nationalistic views has dangerously injected the sentiment with a high dosage of vigor. Far-right populist political candidates in France, Germany, Italy, the Netherlands, among other nations in the old continent have gained significant headway while inspiring their counterparts across the Atlantic Ocean. At the time of this writing, European nationalist leaders gathered in Koblenz, Germany, declaring their platform as realistic alternatives to the continent's governments. Invigorated by Trump's victory in the United States, the European nationalistic parties hope for similar success in tapping anti-establishment and protectionist attitudes in upcoming elections. Although bolstered by Trump's election, radical European right-wingers such as France's Marine le Pen (1968–   ) claims that Trump was elected on the back of the ideas the European nationalists have been propagating for quite some time (the middle-east refugee crisis has aggrandized their cause and inflamed public opinion). Speaking to his political counterparts at Koblenz, Geert Wilders (1963–   ), Dutch anti-Islam leader and presidential hopeful, said "I believe we are witnessing historic times...the genie will not go back into the bottle again, whether you like it or not."[6]

In my turn, I think what we are witnessing is the madness of politics in action; a time bomb that can go off at the slightest disturbance.

❀

Unfortunately, the revival of the radical nationalistic movement is not confined to European nations. In Brazil, one of the biggest "democracies" in the world with more than 100 million voters, a new surge of right-wing politics has been on the rise (an anomaly considering that the country endured one of the most brutal military dictatorships for over 20 years). To celebrate the victory of Donald Trump in the United States, an upcoming radical right-wing devout Christian politician by the name of Jair Bolsonaro (1955–   ), a congressman with presidential aspirations who has been touted as the "Brazil's Trump," tweeted in impeccable Trumpian style: "Congratulations to the American people. In 2018 Brazil will follow in your footsteps."[7] Reasserting his political position during the Machiavellian impeachment proceedings of the outgoing worker's party president Dilma Rousseff (1947–   ) , Bolsonaro cast his vote dedicating it to the Colonel who was in charge of tortures of political prisoners during the military dictatorship years (Rousseff was captured, tortured, and jailed from 1970 to 1972). Like Trump, Bolsonaro's supporters are mostly Christian, middle-class white people disgruntled with the status quo.

With the backing of a growing Evangelical Christian movement in the fast-dwindling largest Catholic nation in the world, the "perennial country of the future," as Brazilians wittily refer to their motherland, has been steadily slipping into its own brand of "democratic dictatorship:" a corrupted capitalist hypocritical Christian nation. Even the progressive-leaning city of Rio de Janeiro has succumbed to the wave of right-wing victories in local elections across Brazil. Marcelo Crivella (1957–   ), an evangelical bishop and nephew of the billionaire founder of the influential Universal Church of the Kingdom of God, beat his left-wing opponent by nearly 20 percent in the city's mayoral election.[8]

Corruption and demagoguery, intrinsic elements of the madness of politics, are trademarks of political regimes in Third World countries—be it democratically elected or usurped by military dictatorships. When the Brazilian economy was booming and the country was being touted as an emerging economic power (a member of the BRIC nations: Brazil, Russia, India, and China), the populist government wanted to show the world that Brazil had arrived at the world stage at last. Thus, they contended to sponsor the two major international sports events in the world (the World Cup and the Olympics) in a few years hence. What they didn't foresee, however, was that their financial health would become anemic therefore sickening the nation's economic prosperity, which was aggravated by a massive corruption scandal involving dozens of politicians and billions of dollars. Consequently, what was envisioned to be a showcase for the economic prosperity of a democratically elected government of the free (market) world, turned into a financial disaster for the nation and its people, though it proved to be highly profitable ventures for capitalist investors and their corrupt political lackeys.

Besides the betrayal of public trust through degenerate shenanigans to graft the national treasury, one of the most despicable factors of political corruption is hypocrisy. In the case of the largest Latin American country, one congressman typifies the madness of politics. Eduardo Cunha (1958–   ), the former house speaker who led the charge of Dilma Rousseff's impeachment, is in jail accused of taking millions in bribes. But what makes him an interesting character is the fact that he was elected as a conservative evangelical Christian—the same kind of voters who helped place Donald Trump in power. A pseudo-moralist who preached traditional Christian values, he betrayed his pretentious beliefs, his ingenuous constituents, and his battered nation. He exemplifies the prevalent con artistry of politics that mingles religious faith with political agendas in order to dupe gullible devout citizens. And even though corruption of such a large scale has been presumably limited to Third World countries, what happens in the shadowy deals between lobbyists and U.S. elected officials is suspicious at best.

Unfortunately, corruption is ubiquitous in the madness of politics. Even in small poverty-stricken countries like El Salvador, the temptation of greed goes undeterred among politicians. Former Salvadoran President Tony Saca (1965–   ) was arrested for alleged embezzlement and money laundering. A former radio sports announcer, Saca was president from 2004 to 2009, and during his time in office his personal fortune swelled by some $10 million; an amount inconsistent with his modest earnings that he could not justify. His successor, President Mauricio Funes (1959–   ), was also involved in corruption scandals and had to flee to Nicaragua under the pretext of requesting political asylum.[9] These spurious "public servants" and their kin betray, steal, and sometimes even commit murder with impunity, as it was the case of a Salvadoran army colonel who was sentenced for his part in the 1989 massacre of six Jesuit priests, their housekeeper and her daughter but was released from a 30-year sentence through an amnesty law after serving only 15 months in prison.[10]

❋

For those who may wonder what the corruption in Latin America—or anywhere else in the world—has anything to do with politics in the United States, the answer is as simple as it is important: everything, because corruption in politics is so widespread that transcends national barriers. There is not a single continent in the free (market) world that can be spared from this ethical transgression. Be it in Africa where Gambian's former President Yahya Jammeh (1965–   ) ruled for more than two decades and plundered the small impoverished nation's coffers; or Asia where corruption scandal surrounded embattled South Korea's former President Park Geun-hye (1952–   ) who was accused of funneling $36 million to support a merger of two Samsung corporation affiliates; or in the European Union where the EU Commissioner Cecilia Malstrom (1968–   ) came on record stating that "the extension of corruption in Europe is breathtaking and it costs the EU $120 billion euros a year;"[11] and, of course, the United States is no exception to the far-reaching tentacles of corruption.

For the sake of illustrating the point in case—without delving into the complex web of corruption in the political scene in the United States—the multinational American corporation Halliburton provides the appropriate exemplification, as well as its former CEO and former Vice-President of the United States, Dick Cheney (1941–   ), whose shenanigans opened a crack in the door of corruption in American politics for the rest of the world to see.

After dragging the nation into a war in Iraq based on lies and fabricated misinformation—or "alternative facts," as it's known in the Trump political era jargon—the Bush-Cheney administration ensured that the giant Halliburton obtained lucrative contracts with the Federal Government. KBR, Inc. (Kellogg, Brown & Root), a subsidiary of Halliburton until 2007, was given $39.5 billion in Iraq-related contracts over a decade. In fact, many of the deals did not require any bidding from competing firms, such as a $568 million contract to provide housing, meals, water and bathroom services to soldiers. This particular contract led to a Justice Department lawsuit over alleged kickbacks, as reported by Bloomberg.[12] In addition, while KBR was being investigated for bribery in Nigeria, it was partnering with a company that bribed officials in Kazakhstan. But bribery scandals were nothing new to Halliburton and KBR. After a years-long federal investigation, KBR pleaded guilty in 2009 to multiple criminal counts of violating U.S. foreign corruption laws by bribing Nigerian officials (KBR agreed to pay $402 million as part of a settlement). Three years later, Albert "Jack" Stanley (1943–), KBR's former CEO, was sentenced to 30 months in federal prison for his role in the scandal.[13]

Here is where the resemblance of what happens in lowly Third World Latin American countries, colonial powers of Europe, and the imperial United States of America meet in the common ground of political corruption. But in order to avoid extensive comparative analysis of corruptive activities, which is not the purpose of this writing, a comparison between Halliburton and the Brazilian construction giant company, Odebrecht shall suffice. Both companies applied similar bribery techniques to lock in highly profitable contracts with their national governments as well as foreign states. Besides its broad involvement in one of Brazil's most notorious corruption scandals that implicated many members of the country's political and business class, Odebrecht admitted to paying $788 million in bribes from 2001 to 2016 to secure lucrative construction contracts in 12 countries. In a plea bargain deal, the company agreed to pay some $3.5 billion in fines and to release documents showing its payouts.[14] Halliburton, on the other hand, used secretive banks and offshore tax havens to funnel $182 million in bribes to Nigerian officials in exchange for $6 billion in engineering and construction work for an international consortium of companies that included its then subsidiary KBR, Inc. As a result, in 2010 Nigeria indicted former U.S. Vice President Dick Cheney, who was CEO of Halliburton before he was elected, only to later exonerate him when Halliburton agreed on a $35 million settlement.[15]

The reason I emphasize these underhand dealings between corporations and governments is because they compromise democracy and violate the public trust. With this in mind, it would behoove us to heed Rousseau's warning that "nothing is more dangerous than the influence of private interests in public affairs," for when selfish economic interests outweigh the welfare of society, the consequences can be disastrous. A classic example of this charade is the "investment" of $26 billion to host the 2016 Rio de Janeiro Olympics. While big businesses profited handsomely with building contracts, the city declared a financial state of emergency even before the games began.[16] The aftermath of the games is a city deeply immersed in serious financial crisis and unable to pay for its basic services. In a city marred with pervasive abject poverty where the infrastructure (hospitals, sewage, education, etc.) is in dire straits, $26 billion could have gone a long way to improve the quality of life of its citizens. Instead, it aggrandized the bank accounts of big business' executives and their corrupted accomplices in a "democratically" elected government. But that is the fundamental mandate in the madness of politics where selfish financial interests must always prevail over the common good.

Either is the construction giant Odebrecht in Brazil or the mega Halliburton Corporation in the United States, the influence of capital in politics has extrapolated to an unprecedented level of corruption. There was a time when the threat to democracy came from revolutionary movements arising from the discontent of the masses, as Spanish philosopher José Ortega y Gasset (1883–1955) claimed in his seminal book *The Revolt of the Masses*[17] where he argues that countries should be ruled by the intellectual elite to avoid the decaying influence of mob control on the arts and government. However, contrary to Gasset's observation about the threat from the populace in the first half of the twentieth century, today, at the early stages of the twenty-first century, what we witness is a threat from the financial elites that control and manipulate the fickle minds and feeble voices of the masses. These elites, mobile and increasingly global in outlook, refuse to accept limits or ties to nation and place. As they isolate themselves in their networks and enclaves, they abandon the middle class, divide the nation—the Trump effect in American politics—and betray the idea of democracy.[18] They've become both the scourge and the enemies of democratic societies.

At a time when populism pervades politics and spreads like a contagious virulent disease around the world, the dangers of private interests in public affairs is greater than ever before. As populist politicians blow the clarion of nationalism and incite division among different people, the world trembles to the sound of prejudice, hatred, and gratuitous hostilities. As walls rise—at nations' borders and figuratively among people—we forget the ones we have demolished that brought rejuvenated hope for humanity. A wall in and by itself is a symbol of division. Either in its physical form (the Berlin Wall) or its symbolic sociological representation (apartheid), the disconnecting element of any kind of wall is as detrimental to unity as it is a threat to social harmony among peoples and nations. But what have we learned from the Berlin Wall? What have we learned from apartheid? Alas, Hegel was right when he said that "the greatest lesson in history is that humankind never learns the lessons of history"—or worse yet, Ronald Wright's claim that "each time history repeats itself, the price goes up."

And as we march along the pathway of history toward an unknown future, we must remain vigilant of the perils along the way. We live in dangerous times, which call for radical measures. Unfortunately, those who are most apt at building walls have already taken action to the radicalization of politics, which they've turned into a religion in itself: the religion of madness.

NOTES

[1] Greg Palast, *The Best Democracy Money Can Buy* (New York: Penguin Putnam, Inc., 2003), 1, 2.

[2] Ibid., 12.

[3] The sword of Damocles dates back to an ancient moral parable popularized by the Roman philosopher Cicero in his 45 B.C.E. book "Tusculan Disputations." The story centers on tyrannical king Dionysius II who grew tired of those who envy his power without knowing the dire dangers he constantly faced from his many enemies. To prove his point, the king lavished a flatterer named Damocles with the abundance of his court so he could taste for himself the good fortune—and dangers—of the monarch's life. Thus, he seated Damocles on a golden couch where above his head a razor-sharp sword tenuously hung only by a single strand of horsehair. After several nervous glances at the blade dangling above his head, Damocles asked to be excused asserting the king he no longer envied the ruler's good fortune. This parable gave way to the expression "sword of Damocles" to convey a sense of constant fear and danger.

[4] "Trump claims the election is 'rigged'," *The Week*, October 28, 2016, 6.

[5] According to the *New York Times*, Donald Trump received 59,705,000 votes out of 231,556,000 eligible voters. 111,907,000 (48% of eligible voters) did not vote for Donald Trump or Hillary Clinton. To view a chart visit https://mises.org/blog/26-percent-eligible-voters-voted-trump

[6] Geir Moulson, Associated Press, "European nationalists buoyed by Trump," *Corvallis Gazette-Times*, January 22, 2017, A2.

[7] Beth McLoughlin, "Brazil's Trump?" www.usnews.com, January 19, 2017. http://www.usnews.com/news/best-countries/articles/2017-01-19/brazils-controversial-congressman-jair-bolsonaro-eyes-the-presidency

[8] "The world at a glance," *The Week*, November 11, 2016, 8.

[9] Ibid.

[10] "Today in History," *Corvallis Gazette-Times*, January 24, 2017, A2.

[11] "Corruption across EU 'breathtaking'- EU Commission, *BBC*, 3 February 2014. http://www.bbc.com/news/world-europe-26014387

[12] Angelo Young, "And The Winner For the Most Iraq War Contracts Is...KBR, With $39.5 Billion In A Decade," 3/19/13. http://www.ibtimes.com/winner-most-iraq-war-contracts-kbr-395-billion-decade-1135905

[13] "U.S. Oil Industry Giant Paid Millions To A Company At The Center Of A Huge Corruption Scandal," *The Huffington Post*, 3/30/2016. http://www.huffingtonpost.com/entry/kbr-unaoil-corruption_us_56fafbf1e4b0a06d5803f5b8

[14] "The world at a glance," *The Week*, January 27, 2017, 8.

[15] Will Fitzgibbon, "Files point to $182 mn Halliburton bribery scandal in Nigeria," The Indian Express, February 9, 2015. http://indianexpress.com/article/world/world-others/files-point-to-182mn-halliburton-bribery-scandal-in-nigeria/

[16] Jonathan Watts, "Rio de Janeiro governor declares state of financial emergency ahead of the Olympics," 17 June 2016, The Guardian, https://www.theguardian.com/world/2016/jun/17/rio-de-janeiro-financial-emergency-olympic-games-2016

[17] José Ortega y Gasset, *The Revolt of the Masses* (New York: W.W. Norton & Company, Inc., 1957).

[18] Christopher Lasch, *The Revolt of the Elites and the Betrayal of Democracy* (New York: W.W. Norton & Company, Inc., 1995), back cover.

The Religion of Madness

M any a thinker has attempted to define religion, though definitions may vary as widely as those who have tried to identify
the phenomenon of creed: "Religion is the daughter of Hope
and Fear, explaining to ignorance the nature of the Unknowable." Am-
brose Bierce (1842–1914). "Religion is what the individual does with his
own solitariness." Alfred North Whitehead (1861–1947). "Religion is a
unified system of beliefs and practices relative to 'sacred things.'" Emile
Durkheim (1858–1917). These are just a few among numerous other
interpretations of the ritual of faith. But of all the characterizations of
religion, perhaps none has generated more outrage in the Western
Christian world than Karl Marx's: "Religion is the opiate of the people,"
which has been removed from its entire context that reads: "Religion is
the sigh of the oppressed creature, the heart of a heartless world, just as
it is the spirit of a spiritless situation. It is the opiate of the people."[1]
Marx's description reflects a humanistic rebellion against the intellectu-
alization of religion that has been disconnected from what religion—
most notably Christianity—is supposed to be in action: love thy neighbor as you love thyself. Unfortunately, as Erich Fromm pointed out, "the
principle underlying capitalistic society and the principle of love are
incompatible."[2] Thus, another religion had to be born to accommodate
the incongruity.

Just as there are various individual interpretations of the meaning
of religion, dictionary definition also offers an array of meanings, ranging from "commitment or devotion to religious faith or observance" to
"a cause, principle, or system of beliefs held to with ardor and faith."[3]
The latter definition is what buttresses a modern undeclared religion,
which is but a cause, principle, and a system of economic beliefs held

with ardor, and yes, faith. Sprouting from the gospel of Adam Smith's sacred book *The Wealth of Nations*, the socioeconomic religion of capitalism has forged a unifying bond with Christianity from the early days of the Industrial Revolution. And based on the history of Christianity in pre-industrial era, the partnership between an economic system driven by the selfish pursuit of profit and a religion with a history of power-hungry cleric corrupted by materialistic objectives was but inevitable.

❀

It started out with a humble child born in a manger to a carpenter and his devoted wife. Jesus of Nazareth (c. 4 B.C.E.—c. 36 C.E.) was primarily an enlightened teacher who offered a new outlook on the purpose of life and harmonious relationships with his fellow human beings. The problem, however, was that Jesus' teachings were revolutionary. He challenged the established religious authorities and the hypocrisy of their self-righteousness, while claiming that the Kingdom of God is rooted in service to others. Thus, his teachings stirred the hearts of people and created social instability, something the Jewish religious authorities dreaded. Since his views differed drastically from the ancient traditions of his time and culture, he was perceived as threat and therefore persecuted. But he continued conveying the wisdom of his mind through the nobility of his soul by both the spoken word as well as by the example of his living. His teachings can be summarized in one word: love; not in the superficial and egoistic meaning of the term, but an all-encompassing emotional experience of oneness with everything that exists, especially his fellow-human brothers and sisters.

Like the great Greek philosopher Socrates (c. 470 B.C.E.–399 B.C.E.) who was immortalized through the words of his pupil Plato (427 B.C.E.–347 B.C.E.), Jesus never wrote a single word about his teachings, nor did he found an organized religion. Rather than a founder, he was a foundational figure to a major religion that would revolutionize the world. The function and title of the founder of the Christian Church was delegated to a Pharisee of Asia Minor named Paul, also known by his native name Saul of Tarsus (c. 5 C.E. – c.67 C.E.).

After making several trips throughout Palestine in search of those who witnessed the teachings of Jesus, Paul underwent a supernatural experience in which he came to believe that Jesus was actually the Messiah of Israel and that God had called him to preach the message of Jesus to all people. Indubitably, in today's world a mental illness would be attributed to such a bizarre behavior: delusional disorder, paranoia, schizophrenia, or any other of the hundreds of denominations listed in the Diagnostic and Statistical Manual of Mental Disorders, the bible of the American Psychiatric Association. But whether Paul was insane or not, he founded a magnanimous religion that rested on three main principles of his understanding of Jesus of Nazareth's experience: Jesus is the son of God and the Messiah foretold by the prophets of Israel; by his death, Jesus atoned for the sins of all and opened the gates of heaven for humanity; and the Mosaic law, by the fact of Jesus' death and resurrection, had been abrogated and replaced by the Law of Jesus.[4] By establishing the dogma of the new Christian Church, Paul set out to transform the world—and not necessarily for the better.

From the ones who proclaim to be the chosen people of God (the Jews) a unique new religion emerged and the world has never been the same. From the mythical Old Testament of the Jews a new testament written in recondite language established the foundation of a new creed. In addition to allowing for several different interpretations—some of which have validated concepts that Jesus himself abhorred, e.g. oppression, intolerance, and slavery—the numerous translations in the course of centuries certainly distorted the original archaic writings of the apostles. Consequently, what many pious believers perceive to be a sacred book turned into a powerful tool of conquest and tyranny.

As other prophets came along, principally the Prophet Mohammad (571 C.E.–632 C.E.), new empires rose to compete with the Christian Church for influence and territorial control. Thus, in 1095 C.E. the monarch of the Christian Empire, Pope Urban II (c. 1035 C.E.–1099 C.E.), waged the first war in the Holy Land in what came to be known as the Crusades; a series of brutal battles for conquest and domination that lasted until the end of the thirteenth century. Sometimes mercenaries paid by the pope fought for the Church in a motley army of crusaders who exhibited their Christian charity by slaughtering Jewish and Muslims, including women and children.[5] But after experiencing the enticing taste of plundering riches and subjugation of people, the Crusades, which were but a masquerading form of piracy, opened the door for future opportunities for massive takeovers and cruel exploitation of the innocent inhabitants of the New World.

☠

It would take dozens of thousands of words to cover even a smattering of the crimes the Christian Church committed against native peoples around the world. From its collusion with imperialistic European monarchies (the pope even had the audacity to divide the world and bestow each half to two European superpowers)[6] to the cultural cleansing and genocides meted out in the Americas, Africa, Asia, and Oceania, the Christian Church has been carrying a heavy cross of guilt in the Way to Cavalry of history.

As Christianity commenced with the birth of a humble loving man, the annihilation of indigenous peoples began with Christopher Columbus (1451–1506) expeditions under the sponsorship of the Catholic Spanish monarchs. At a time when "the truth" was "the fact" that the Earth was flat and the Sun subserviently rotated around it, Columbus subscribed to the heretic belief that the world was actually round, and that he could reach the coveted destination of India by sailing through a western route. After commissioning the crowns of England and Portugal and being turned down by both, he secured the financing he needed from Spain to prove his theory was correct. Although he was unwittingly right, he was wrong to assume he'd reached India when he made landfall on the American continent on October 12, 1492. That was the day that marked the beginning of the end of the Native Americans, whom Columbus erroneously called *Indios*.

Ironically, the loving friendly people Columbus encountered were much more like Jesus of Nazareth than the representatives of the impious Church founded in his name, as documented in his writings to the King and Queen of Spain:

> "So tractable, so peaceable, are these people that I swear to your Majesties there is not in the world a better nation. They love their neighbors as themselves, and their discourse is ever sweet and gentle, and accompanied with a smile; and though it is true that they are naked, yet their manners are decorous and praiseworthy."[7]

Despite the natives welcoming demeanor, which elicited deserving of praise comments from the foreign intruders, by the early 1500s when it was clear that the possibility for great wealth and slavery abound, the discourse changed radically. Because European Christianity made it impossible for the Europeans to view the Indians in a way that allowed a fair or equitable negotiation for the takeover of their lands, they were immediately labeled as savages of primitive culture whose only valuable asset as people was as a source of slave labor. In their turn, they were unable to understand the absurd concept of private property and the selling of their homeland to these odd-looking bearded white people invaders. Thus, when the *Requerimiento* (an infamous Spanish document demanding submission) was presented to the native peoples of America, the only thing they understood was that they were doomed to vanish:

> "We ask and require you...to acknowledge the Church and the ruler as superior of the whole world and the high priest called the Pope... (if they didn't submit, the Spanish warned them)...We shall take you and your wives and your children and shall make slaves of them...and we shall take away your goods and shall do you all the harm and damage we can."[8] And so they did.

By the time the Indians realized that they could not comprehend the European way of life and thinking, their only final recourse was in the battlefield where they courageously countered gun powder with arrows, spears, and spirit. In spite of their bravery, their homeland, ancient culture, and the numerous nations that lived in the Americas for millennia, they were all obliterated by the chosen people of a wrathful God. With the self-proclaimed assurance that the Lord is on their side, and with the Bible in their hands, the duplicitous pious devotees of the Christ, like his erstwhile apostle Judas Iscariot (c. 30 B.C.E.–c. 33 C.E.), have been betraying the fundamental principles that made Jesus of Nazareth known as the Prophet of Love. As for their rhetorical holy commandments, thou shall not kill, covet, or steal, they have been conveniently neglected to give way to their ravenous greed and unfettered yearning to subjugate whom they considered to be "inferior peoples," as Chief Red Cloud (1822–1909), the great leader of the Oglala Lakota nation attested:

> "They made us many promises, more than I can remember, but they never kept but one: they promised to take our land, and they took it."[9]

Along with all the worthless paperwork treaties, the Bible was one of the most influential tools for taking over their land and deracinating their cultural traditions. The Hawaiian Islands offer a good showcase for their strategic shenanigans.

☸

By the time Dwight Baldwin (1798–1886) and his wife Charlotte Fowler (1805–1873) arrived in Hawaii in 1831, the Native Hawaiians were already undergoing a vigorous process of deracination of their language and cultural traditions. As medical missionaries to the Sandwich Islands (as the archipelago was called before renamed the Hawaiian Islands), they came as representatives of the American Board of Commissioners for Foreign Missions (ABCFM), one of the first American Christian missionary organizations. The following year, they were joined by Reverend William Alexander (1805–1884) and his wife Mary McKinney (1810–1888). And by the will of God and the fortunate of serving the Lord among the Hawaiian natives, their offspring eventually would establish one of the largest public corporations in the State of Hawaii: Alexander & Baldwin, Inc. But first, some preaching had to be done to set up the opportunistic entrepreneurial venture.

Amidst the efforts to eradicate the Hawaiian language and culture (cultural genocide), the missionaries, in cahoots with a growing number of businessmen concocting underhand tactics to divvy up the land among themselves, spread the Gospel of the Lord while chucking out native traditions piecemeal. After all, native Hawaiians were considered savages and inveterate sinners, therefore the missionaries had the disingenuous moral duty to civilize and save them from eternal doom. This position was clearly stated by one of the members of the American Board of Commissions for Foreign Missions (ABCFM) as he interpreted events through the narrow perspective of his myopic vision:

> "Forty years of experience with white men had only confirmed the Hawaiians in vice and deepened their depravity. From now on, however, the Gospel would be the civilizing instrument, and Hawaiian civilization would be Christian civilization."[10]

And with Christian civilization, as it's always been from time preceding the Crusades, substantial profits consistently ensue. Hence, after the Great Māhele (to divide or portion) of 1848, which destroyed the traditional system of land ownership in Hawaii (before the Great Māhele foreigners were not permitted to purchase or lease land), the Hawaiian Islands became a real estate archipelago that was taken over by capital investments—it is considered one of the most significant events in the history of Hawaii; only the overthrow of the Hawaiian Kingdom is deemed more important. Therefore, it was a matter of time for the descendants of missionaries Dwight Baldwin and William Alexander to purchase hundreds of acres of land on the island of Maui to cultivate sugarcane. By the early 1900s, after acquiring many more acreage and two main railroads on the island, the company was incorporated as Alexander & Baldwin, Inc.; a corporate byproduct of Christian missionary service. Indeed, it's undeniable how truthful the old African saying below is:

"When the white people came we had the land and they had the Bible. Now we have the Bible and they have the land."[11]

🌀

One of the most misunderstood statements about religion in general and God in particular comes from Friedrich Nietzsche's infamous book, *Thus Spoke Zarathustra*: "God is dead; God died of his pity for man."[12] The outrage and controversy about what conservative Christians consider a blasphemy is, indeed, unwarranted. Those unfamiliar with the work of Nietzsche would be surprised to learn that he had the utmost respect for Jesus of Nazareth whom he referred to as "the noblest human being."[13] It was to Christianity as an organized religion that he directed his most vitriolic condemnation, calling it "the one great curse, the one great innermost corruption...the one immortal blemish of mankind."[14] As for "God is dead," what he meant was humanity killed God and replaced Him with our own ideological and scientific materialism, which we came to worship as the new revered God. Unbeknownst to many, Nietzsche was a philosophical prophet whose mission was to address the modern world's spiritual crisis.

From the very early years of the twentieth century, the promise of an unfolding brave new world was in the air. As economic and technological advancements progressed at unprecedented rates, Nietzsche's concept of a dead God being replaced by the idolatry of scientific materialism was becoming evident. Consequently, as a new man-made god manifested out of human ingenuity, the founding of a new religion became necessary to worship the new deity. Since economic development is the driving force propelling the extraordinary accomplishments of modern society, the economic system itself became the *de facto* religion of the new era; a state religion in which priesthood is deeply rooted in politics. By linking the principles of democracy with free market (*laissez faire*) economics, capitalism became the new religion, which devout Christians embraced wholeheartedly without having to give up their sanctimonious faith. In fact, based on the history of Christianity in the exploitation of vulnerable populations, the new economic religion was a perfect match. From the loving empathetic Jesus the King to an impersonal indifferent king of exploitation, a far-reaching transformation to religion took place, as Gerry Spence relates in the passage below:

> "The goal of the New King is to subjugate the Earth and its population to the most insidious tyranny ever experienced by man; a tyranny that is guarded with religious zeal by its very victims, who mouth the dogma of the New King's system with such slogans as 'with liberty and justice for all,' and 'government of the people, by the people, and for the people.' It is tyranny with a state religion. The religion of Free Enterprise. It is a tyranny supported by the people as their sacred right, one that enslaves the people while it convinces the people they are free."[15]

As capitalism became a bona fide religion around the Western World, the indoctrination of its consecrated values was cleverly embedded in the collective psyche as the most righteous institution of freedom; the freedom to pursue selfish interests with utmost greed—and in detriment to the welfare of all. With a new political-economic religion established, a new god to be worshipped had to be invented;[16] and the god is capital (perhaps this is the reason the national motto of the paragon nation of capitalism says "In God We Trust). But as history has evinced, when new religions arise, others are created to challenge its dogma with another pernicious doctrine; the counter-reactionary forces of convictions of faith; the enemies of truth, as Nietzsche professed:

> Convictions are more dangerous enemies of truth than lies."[17]

Hence, an opposing political-economic religion was begotten in the Eastern World.

※

An inevitable response to the exploitation of workers in the fledgling years of the Industrial Revolution, Karl Marx's humane socioeconomic philosophy was first implemented in Russia approximately a year before the end of World War I (1914–1918). Unfortunately, like the many interpretations of Christianity have led to different understandings of what Christianity is supposed to be, the profound ideas of Marx have been interpreted in fundamentally opposite directions. The first version, the one that was applied in what later would become the Soviet Union, was the interpretation of Vladimir Ilyich Ulyanov (1870–1924), better known by the alias Lenin, which became known as Leninism (socialist political and economic theories for the organization of society based on Marx's writings). The second version, a more virulent and violent interpretation and implementation of Marx's principles and Leninism, came seven years later with the passing of Lenin. Joseph Stalin (1878–1953), the stronghold dictator who ruled the Soviet Union from the mid 1920s until his death in 1953, instituted a corrupted version of Marxism that blemished the reputation of Karl Marx's humanistic approach to socioeconomic organization. Unrelated to the fundamental principles Marx promulgated, Stalinism was characterized by state terror, centralized state collectivization, and unquestioning subordination to state authority. It was the ultimate dictatorship. Like the Roman Catholic Church of years yonder, the Union of Soviet Socialist Republic turned into a despotic, oppressive, and power-hungry society. In essence, Stalin was to Marx what Saul of Tarsus was to Christ: a distorter of principles.

Thus, the new religion of communism was doomed to fail, even as new versions came about. Marxism became just another tool of oppression based on a meretricious political-economic religious practice. In fact, Stalin betrayed Marx even more poignantly than Judas betrayed the Christ. Indignant with such travesty, a growing number of brilliant socialist thinkers denounced the new besmirched paradigm of socialism, Wilhelm Reich being one of them:

"It is the dynamic vicious circle which turned every single socialist leader during the first half of the twentieth century into a bureaucrat of statist power over men...The socialist appears as the 'progressive leader' toward 'freedom'. He is in reality a builder of slavery."[18]

Like capitalism, communism turned into a failed political-economic religion that fiercely opposed traditional capitalist beliefs and practices. Their differences, however, is not as stark as it seems at first. While capitalism's god is capital and the exploitation of workers is carried out by individuals and corporations that own the means of production, in the religion of communism the state is the worshipped god that controls the means of production and is in charge of the exploitation of workers. Indeed, they are more alike than they are different, for both enslave their citizens in distinct fashion: capitalism under the false appearance of freedom (free market), and communism under the pretext of equality in which people submit to state authority. They both beguile and betray. And because their political-religious objectives are so antagonistic to each other, an ensuing cold war between them was but inevitable; a war that remained cold only because of the fear of going MAD (mutually assured destruction). Thus, these unique new expressions of unorthodox religions help corroborating what history has shown: religion—of any kind—has a propensity to foster the suppression of human freedom and unhindered corruption of the human being.

Today, both the religions of capitalism and communism have changed, significantly. The former has transformed into consumerism in which the wealth of nations is determined by the amount of consumption of its citizens, which must increase incessantly lest the entire system collapses. Communism, on the other hand, though still exists in its original deceptive political form in some regions of the world (e.g. North Korea), has changed by emulating its religious-political nemesis. China is the classic example where billionaires coexist with peasants and the ruling Chinese Communist Party. And Russia, the country where the system originated in 1917 before becoming the mighty USSR empire, which came crumpling down on the weight of its own grandiosity in 1989, there is not a vestige of its communist past—except for the authoritarian oligarchic regime.

Regardless of the mode of expression it manifests itself, the practice of dogmatic religion—spiritual, political, or otherwise—is indicative of mental and emotional disturbances; not only in the individual practitioner, but at the collective organized group as well. It is, indeed, a form of madness that can only be diagnosed by analytical observation and critical judgment. And because they all profess certitude of inviolable righteousness aimed at mass appeal, religious organizations can be dangerous institutions. Often times their zealotry reaches such a high level of intensity that becomes sheer madness—the madness of religion.

NOTES

[1] John Bowker, Editor, *The Oxford Dictionary of World Religions* (New York: Oxford University Press, 1997), xv.

[2] Erich Fromm, *The Art of Loving* (New York: Harper & Row, Publishers, Inc., 1989), 118.

[3] https://www.merriam-webster.com/dictionary/religion

[4] John Renard, *The Handy Religion Answer Book* (Canton, MI: Visible Ink Press, 2002), 127.

[5] Charles Van Doren, *A History of Knowledge* (New York: Ballantine Books, 1991), 109.

[6] Pope Alexander VI created a line of demarcation in 1494 dividing the world in half between Portugal and Spain, the two European superpower nations at the time. Spain would gain control and appropriate all lands discovered west of the line (370 leagues or 1,770 km west of the Cape Verde Islands), while Portugal would claim territorial control of lands east of the line. This agreement is known as the Treaty of Tordesillas. .

[7] Dee Brown, *Bury My Heart at Wounded Knee* (New York: Holt, Rinehart & Winston, 1970), 1.

[8] Judith Nies, *Native American History* (New York: Ballantine Books, a division of Random House, Inc., 1996), 73.

[9] Dee Brown, *Bury My Heart at Wounded Knee*, 449.

[10] Gavan Daws, *Shoal of Time* (Honolulu, HI: University of Hawaii Press, 1974), 62.

[11] Barry Denenberg, *Nelson Mandela: No Easy Walk to Freedom* (New York: Scholastic, Inc., 1991), 59.

[12] Walter Kaufmann, editor and translator, *The Portable Nietzsche* (New York: Viking Penguin, Inc., 1982), 202.

[13] Friedrich Nietzsche, *Human All Too Human* (Lincoln, NE: University of Nebraska Press, 1986), 229.

[14] Walter Kaufmann, *The Portable Nietzsche*, 656.

[15] Gerry Spence, *From Freedom to Slavery: The Rebirth of Tyranny in America* (New York: St. Martin's Press, Inc., 1993), 86.

[16] In one of Voltaire's aphorisms he says: "*Si Dieu n'existait pas, il foudrait l'inventer*" ("If God did not exist, it would be necessary to invent him.")

[17] Friedrich Nietzsche, *Human All Too Human*, 234.

[18] Wilhelm Reich, *The Murder of Christ* (New York: Farrar, Straus and Giroux, 1971), 66.

The Madness of Religion

igmund Freud characterizes religion as an illusion; a false belief system instigated by the fear of uncertainty in the face of the dangers of life. As the child grows up into maturity, the desperate need for guidance and protection, which was previously provided by parental guardianship, turns into a void of insecurity. Terrified by the consistent looming perils of living and the dreadful anticipation of inevitable death (Freud's theory of the death instinct), the search for the benevolent rule of a divine Providence arises to fill in the vacuum created by independent adulthood.[1] Thus, God becomes the numinous surrogate father who allays the fear of the dangers of life with promises of security and the bliss of blessed eternity.

But before the pearly gates of heaven are opened to the pious believers, they must endure the trials and travails of living a life of continuous challenges and uncertainties; and they must, of course, abide by the mystifying rules of the Bible and submit to the authority of the Church. It all begins with the first basic tenet of the Christian dogma: the self-deprecating belief that people are born sinners; a concept that Jean Jacques Rousseau vehemently rebutted. To him, "it was society that was wrong, society and 'progress' that have corrupted the natural good in men."[2] But to the Church, we are all byproducts of the original sin; the immoral act of physical love that blemishes the purity of the soul tempted by carnal temptation. Therefore, this first nefarious principle that turned love—physical or otherwise—into a desecrated religious offense, became the key that opened the gates of hell on Earth for the masses of nincompoop to come in. It was the end of paradise and the genesis of the madness of religion.

The Book of Genesis, the first chapter of the undecipherable scriptures, recounts an unimaginative mythological story of how it all began—and heralds the ensuing madness that religion would wreak in the world. This introductory chapter of the Holy Book is by all rational, philosophical, and scientific standards a book of mythology. In fact, if compared with Nordic, Celtic, or Afro-Brazilian mythologies, Christian mythology is uninspiring at best. It starts out telling the story of the first woman, Eve, who was born from the rib of Adam, the unoriginal male womb of life:

> "Hence, Jehovah God had a deep sleep fall upon the man and, while he was sleeping, he took one of his ribs and then closed up the flesh over its place. And Jehovah God proceeded to build the rib that he had taken from the man into a woman and to bring her to the man."[3]

As a lackluster folk story, the telling of a woman coming into being from a man's rib is a terribly pedestrian tale. But as a religious statement to the creation of humankind, it is an absurd credence bereft of both imagination and even a modicum of common sense. Nevertheless, devout Christians embrace this asinine narrative as the backbone of their adamant religious belief referred to as creationism.[4] And in spite of the overwhelming scientific evidence that the Earth is about 4.5 billion years old, biblical literalists vigorously reject the evidence. Instead, they assume the Bible's view of the Book of Genesis in the historical account of creation. It is, indeed, the extrapolation of idiocy into the realm of madness.

Never mind the outrageous chauvinistic assumption that man, through a most bizarre cesarean section, became the crucial element in the parturition of the first woman; the one who has the womb and who is called mother. By reversing the natural order of natural birth, the feminine element of human nature was delegated to an inferior category, as the first hierarchical class division commenced. But if that were not prejudicial enough, the first woman, was blamed for causing Adam's downfall by succumbing to the serpent's temptation to eat the forbidden fruit from the tree of knowledge of good and evil. She shares the fruit with him, they take pleasure in the joy of knowledge, and they are expelled from the Garden of Eden by a wrathful God, who apparently does not want His children to learn the difference between good and evil—or love and perfidy.

As the hackneyed fairy-tale continues, the ill-fated couple procreated and established the perennial tragedy of the human existence. They have three children: Cain, Abel and Seth. Cain represents the progenitor of evil who kills his brother Abel setting off a dysfunctional pattern in human relations that has never been undone. Thus, the mythological story of the Book of Genesis as a religious truth turned out to be a portentous prophecy of the future of humankind: the fratricide Cain committed was the first act toward genocide when large numbers of brothers are killed.

Since the original murder, which originated from the original sin that an unoriginal creed determined to be the truth, men have been murdering their most noble brethren without compunction.

From the early days of its inception, the Christian Church has attempted to monopolize the right to determine what reality is. It has held the gavel of truth in one hand and the sword of punishment on the other. Although the truth often has evaded its perception, the sword meting out chastisement never has failed to deliver.

Blinded by its own dogmatic ignorance and haughty self-assuredness, the Church determined that the geocentric theory (the astronomical theory that puts the Earth at the center of the Universe) was an irrefutable fact. When the Scientific Revolution that began with Nicolai Copernicus (1473–1543) established the heliocentric theory (the astronomical model in which the Earth and planets revolve around the Sun), the Church repelled it with utmost vehemence. After all, the geocentric theory was a consecrated belief interpreted from the Bible that had been in place for more than a thousand years. The heliocentric theory, however, posed a threat to the wisdom and authority of the Church that robbed man of his proud position at the center of God's creation. Consequently, it became a heresy to which the Inquisition (the internal judicial system of the mighty Roman Catholic Church) punished by death through the ghastly method of burning the heretic at the stake. Thus, the madness of religion had managed to turn a basic knowledge into a cardinal sin.

For nearly seven hundred years countless number of people were burned alive for defying the authority and monopoly of knowledge of the Church. Among the famous historical figures who barely escaped the horrific persecution, Galileo Galilei (1564–1642) had to betray himself and forgo his championing the heliocentric theory lest he'd be put to death. Another less known character, a Dominican friar, philosopher, and cosmological theorist who came to be known as a "martyr of science" was not so fortunate. Giordano Bruno (1548–1600) was convinced by his studies and observations, that the Universe and all its parts had qualities identical with life. He understood that many distant stars were like our Sun with planetary systems around them. But perhaps his most radical view, which the constricted Church could not fathom, was the idea that the Universe was infinite, and therefore could not have any celestial body at its center. However, it was his philosophy and theology that most likely sealed his heresy conviction, as Wilhelm Reich relates:

> "Bruno believed in a universal soul that animated the world; this soul to him was identical with God...Bruno had discovered the road that leads to knowing God, and therefore he had to die. And die he did, indeed, a death of nine long years, from 1591 to 1600, when on February 16th in the early morning he was led with prayers, by the heirs of Jesus Christ, to the stake and given over to the flames, all in the name of love of the Creator."[5]

It comes as no surprise that the strict and bigoted dogma of the Christian Church, which reached the apex at the time of the Inquisition, would pave the way to the conservative movement of evangelical fundamentalism we witness today. And since both Christianity and Islam embrace the fundamentalist culture in which the interpretation of their sacred books is perceived as literally true, the rest of us who view all the madness of religion with great skepticism gasp in disbelief of what the believers are capable of doing.

❀

Religious fundamentalism is on the rise—everywhere. Be it Islam or Christianity, the two religion superpowers in the world of creed (they play similar roles in religion as the Soviet Union and the United States did in politics), the widespread wave of radical faith has been corrupting the function and purpose of religion in social life. It's becoming increasingly more political, belligerent, and intolerant of the diversity of humanity. It's been corroding the fabric of our human bond, as we fall apart in the separation of discord.

Christian fundamentalism began in the late nineteenth and early twentieth century as a reactionary movement against liberal interpretations that deviated from biblical inerrancies such as the virgin birth of Jesus, the resurrection of the Christ, among several other traditional convictions. Today, however, it has extrapolated from the realm of blind faith and turned into a powerful political force to be reckoned with. Notwithstanding, it has become an immensely profitable multi-billion dollar industry where evangelical pastors rake in high earnings from gullible—and mostly low income—believers.

Many devout Christians will say that the Church is God's bride. But from a secular humanistic perspective, it seems more logical to state that the Church is the bride of the pastor. And considering that the Church has become a major source of income, the dialectical inference of what has become of both priesthood and its bride is unbecoming of what religion is supposed to be: an expansive and diversified money-making machine called Christianity, Inc. In the gambling style of the free market economy, the business of Christianity has turned into a slot-machine with nonprofit status (501) (c) (3) organizations. Nonprofit, however, is a misnomer, for the managers of the Church who profit handsomely from the marketing of their willing bride.

Indeed, the number of multi-million dollar megachurch evangelical organizations around the world is mind boggling. These large religious corporations are tax exempt for billions of dollars a year ($7.2 billion in 2005 alone—and it's been growing steadily).[6] In the first decade of the twenty-first century, the number of megachurches has more than doubled. Lakewood Church, the largest in the United States led by charismatic televangelist Joel Osteen (1963–), whose net-worth is conservatively estimated at $40 million, has an annual budget of $70 million and draws a weekly televised audience of nearly 7 million viewers—and over 20 million monthly in more than a hundred countries. Incidentally, the largest megachurch in the world, Yoido Full Gospel Church in South Korea, has a membership of 850,000 people and an annual budget of $200 million.[7] With such high margins of profit, the temptation to jump on the bandwagon of Christianity, Inc., is stronger than physical lust—and many opportunists "men of faith" have been jockeying for the pole position.

According to the Hartford Institute for Religion Research, there are roughly 350,000 religious congregations in the United States. Of those, about 314,000 are Protestant and other Christian churches, and 24,000 are Catholic and Orthodox churches. Non-Christian religious congregations are estimated at about 12,000.[8] Like all other businesses, thousands of churches open and close each year, and so do the number of pastors-entrepreneurs come and go; but the ones who manage to stay in business have the potential to make bank.

"We make plenty of money...but we just live normal lives,"[9] says Joel Osteen, the leader of the largest megachurch in America whose luxurious lifestyle is a far cry from the normal lives the majority of his followers. But he makes no apologies for his wealth because he believes it is God's blessings in his life.[10] Although he is the heavyweight in the evangelical ring where the faithful is always ready to rumble, there are a plethora of slick televangelists cashing in the desperate credulity of simple-minded uneducated folks searching for an answer to their anxieties and sorrows. The list of these religious crooks is so extensive that naming them would take more time and space than they are worth. However, in order to illustrate this dishonest cadre of hypocritical peddlers of pseudo-Christian morality, a selected few must take the spotlight of shame.

From Francis Schaeffer (1912–1984), an American Evangelical Christian who is to the conservative religious right what Karl Marx is to communism, to the likes of Mike Murdock (1946–   ), Peter Popoff (1946–   ), and Benny Hinn (1952–   ), three of the slickest, filthiest, and worst among the worst of all televangelists, some popular pastors managed to pave their way through mainstream culture with their silver tongue debauchery. One of the most prominent—and wealthiest—is Pat Robertson (1930–   ), the octogenarian host of the popular 700 Club televangelist program, which airs on his own Christian Broadcasting Network. The man who questioned if there is "in all the history of human folly a greater fool than a clergyman in politics"[11] was also a presidential candidate in the 1988 election campaign. With a net worth estimated at somewhere between $200 million and $1 billion, and a penchant for luxurious lifestyle that contradicts the simplicity Jesus advocated, he routinely analyzes and praises the stock market in his television show as if it were a fundamental component of the Holy Scriptures. In fact, he allocates regular segments of his broadcast ("Money Monday" and "Bring It On") to financial and investments topics. No wonder one of his former business associates who flew often with Robertson on his private jet never saw him open a Bible or seek private time for prayer, but "he always had the *Wall Street Journal* open and *Investor's Daily*."[12]

A Christian capitalist investor and media mogul who is touted to be an extraordinary financial expert, Pat Robertson is first and foremost a wily businessman. In his nineteenth book titled *Right on the Money: Financial Advice for Tough Times*, Robertson covers everything from how to get out of debt to investing in commodities. The book's dust jacket flap text states that "...this man of God is also a multifaceted business leader and expert in finance. In fact, he ranks within the top 1 percent of the nation's fund managers."[13]

Robertson's reputation as a savvy financial advisor blends in with his Southern Baptist Christian background in a manner that is highly conducive to lucrative business opportunities. Thus, through a heart-wrenching fundraising drive on his television station to help alleviate the woes of refugees feeling the genocide in Rwanda, several million dollars for the tax-free charitable trust "Operation Blessing" fattened his "religious" enterprise's coffers. However, what reporter Bill Sizemore of the *Virginian-Pilot* discovered was an ignominious anti-Christ activity:

"Operation Blessing purchased planes to shuttle medical supplies in and out of the refugee camp in Goma, Congo (then Zaire)...except for one medical flight, the planes were used to haul heavy equipment for something called the African Development Corporation, a diamond-mining operation distant from Goma. African Development is owned by Pat Robertson."[14]

Here is a question that begs to be answered: how can wealthy Christian ministers like Pat Robertson, who are supposedly committed to serving the Lord, reconcile their actions with some of the few unambiguous messages from the Bible? Unlike the recondite language that prevails in the scriptures, the Biblical passage below is clear and leaves no room for ambiguity:

"You must love your neighbor as yourself...Jesus said to him: 'If you want to be perfect, go sell your belongings and give to the poor and you will have treasure in heaven, and come be my follower.' When the young man heard this saying, he went away grieved, for he was holding many possessions. But Jesus said to his disciples: 'Truly I say to you that it will be a difficult thing for a rich man to get into the kingdom of the heavens. Again I say to you, it is easier for a camel to get through a needle's eye than for a rich man to get into the kingdom of God.'"[15]

Alas, greed for money is not the only path to the downfall of hypocritical sinister ministers. There is also the temptation of the flesh; the irrepressible carnal desires that burn the erotic passion of human sexuality. First there was Jimmy Swaggart (1935–), a televangelist who led a multi-million dollar evangelical empire and fell from grace. Despite being a sanctimonious moralist who preached the word of the Lord with abandon, he apparently neglected to abide by it himself—most certainly the tenth commandment: thou shalt not commit adultery. In 1988 he was involved in extra-marital sex scandal with a prostitute, which resulted in his defrocking. Three years later, he succumbed to temptation again with another prostitute.[16]

But to the relief of the religious conservative flock, at least Swaggart's case was a heterosexual act. Ted Haggard (1956–), however, the evangelical pastor and founder of the New Life Church, committed similar sin but with multiple aggravations: he alleged engaged in a three-year long affair with a male prostitute and also admitted purchasing crystal methamphetamine. Later in an interview with a media outlet, he said that "probably, if I were 21 in this society, I would identify myself as a bisexual."[17] Not to be outdone, the Catholic Church was embarrassed and disgraced by numerous abominable cases of child molestation by its pedophile priests.

And when it seemed that the madness of religion had reached the apex of a chronic pathological disorder with its excessive greed, hypocrisy, and sexual transgressions, it erupted with a maddening hatred that has stunned even the most violent among the human species.

Religion has long been a powerful tool with which to keep a strong hold on the human species—through fear, guilt, and yes, hatred. Seemingly, it all begins with the opposing duality of good and evil, which religion combats with the rusty sword of dogma. The problem, however is that in the midst of the ideological struggle, the hatred of evil (whatever is perceived to be the antagonist of God's will, which is also liable to open-ended interpretations) manifests in physical form through all sorts of aggression against those misperceived or concocted to be the enemies. Furthermore, any other dogma differing from the one a particular religion espouses as "the truth," shall be chastised as a representative of the evil it battles against. And religions manifest themselves in multi-faceted expressions of their alienated states—a state of madness.

One of the most notorious and pervasive organizations of hatred is the notorious Ku Klux Klan. Nothing short of a domestic terrorist organization misguided by the alienated state of hatred, the Klan, as it is popular known, is the oldest and most infamous American hate group with a strong Christian identity. When the Klan was formed in 1865, it was a single, unitary organization. Today, there are dozens of competing Klan groups. Although black Americans have typically been the Klan's primary target, it has also attacked Jews, immigrants, homosexuals, and Catholics.[18]

Sometimes, religious hate groups develop within the political state to uphold a particular doctrine. In recent decades, none of these manifestations of political state-religion is more notorious than Nazism, which went as far as establishing its own god-like leader, the Führer. Subscribing to megalomaniac theories of racial superiority, political hierarchy, and extreme Social Darwinism, the Nazis of the Third Reich dragged the world into the hell pit of what is arguably the most devastating war in human history. In addition to harbingering the extremely dangerous nuclear age, millions of people were killed in battle and murdered in concentration camps of hatred. Ironically, the survivors and descendants of this appalling genocide have become impetuous oppressors of their neighbors, whose homeland they've occupied after the Nazi-incited war. In spite of all the horrific outcomes of the Nazi unorthodox religion, this nefarious political dogma still thrives today among the alienated youth and ignorant old as the neo-Nazi movement.

However, the manifestation of maddening hatred is supposedly more justifiable and effective through traditional religious practices.

Like the time of the ghastly Inquisition when cruel crimes were committed in the name of "the truth," an equally barbaric manifestation of religious madness has been spreading like a wildfire straight out of the hell of hatred. In an extremely skewed misinterpretation of the religious book of Quran, Islamic fundamentalism has set off a new wave of hatred and horrifying murders not seen, at least in traditional religious terms, since the time of the Inquisition. From flying suicide missions that turn commercial airplanes into missiles—like the kamikazes of World War II Japan but with dozens of innocent people aboard—to gruesome beheadings of the perceived enemies and traitors of the faith/cause, this new madness of religion is reviving the dark ages of civilization. Sharing many worshipping similarities with Christianity and Judaism, Islam, too, claim to possess the monopoly of truth, which the sacred scriptures of the Quran represents: the infallible word of God, a manuscript of a tablet preserved in heaven, revealed to the Prophet Mohammed (571 C.E–632 C.E.) by the Angel Gabriel.[19] Even though the Prophet Mohammed disclaimed power to perform miracles, he firmly believed that he was the messenger of God sent forth to confirm previous scriptures, namely that of Christianity and Judaism. And with the demand for absolute submission to the will of Allah, a war of gods and dogmas has exploded into a grisly new way of violence and hatred. Thus, *Jihad* has become an "honorable" religious cause to murder and die for—and the encouragement to death is rewarded with the preposterous promise of 72 virgins in the afterlife.

Soon, the fruits of the unholy matrimony of religion and politics begot wars of belief systems that have been pushing the international community to the edge of the abyss of self-destruction. Not only Islam, Christianity, and Judaism (the three dominant religions in the world) have been at dogmatic war with one another, they also have indissoluble bonds with governments and states. In fact, Israel is a predominantly Judaic nation whose national flag displays the symbol of its religiosity, and so are the symbols of Islam and Christianity embossed on the banner of other nations.[20] And even those unofficial religious nations that do not display the emblem of their faith on their national banners, they, too, cannot divorce the state from the creed they espouse (the United States being the classic example among many others). Therefore, religious wars are often camouflaged in the intricacies of socioeconomic and political divergences; or, as it is the case in the Arab-Israeli wars, their mutual hatred is exposed like a festering wound that doesn't seem to heal with time. And despite their bitter animosity that extrapolates to deadly enmity, historically, they are like congenitally united Siamese twins that cannot tolerate the union. Hence, the madness of religion becomes a socioeconomic and political issue, which the conflict between the fledgling nation of Israel and Palestine epitomizes.

In a world where in many countries the separation of state and religion is delineated by a narrow blurred line, the risk of dogmatic intolerance is high and increasingly perilous. Even in nations like the United States whose Constitution unequivocally proclaims the separation between government and faith, the evidence contradicts the rhetoric. After all, shouldn't the newly elected presidents be sworn in with their right hands on the Constitution of the United States instead of the Bible? Isn't it an undeniable evidence of the unspoken infiltration of religion in governmental affairs? Maybe this is why every four years while watching the ceremonial oath of office, I cannot help but think of the old popular saying: an image is worth a thousand words. It is the confirmation of a fact that is already verifiable through political agendas of career politicians and their flagship parties.

Whether or not we have the courage to acknowledge that the madness of religion rules the world, the many powder kegs of hatred around the world can explode at the lightest flickering of conflict—and the consequences can be utterly ruinous. Either religious, political, economic, or otherwise, the madness of religion seems to evolve and change according to the needs of the time. The meaning of the motto "In God We Trust," also changes; be it a fatherly ruler, ideology, or capital, people always worship with blind trust a god to whom they surrender their rational minds and oppressed hearts with unquestioned obedience.

Today, a new form of religion is king; a religion inspired by human achievements in which man has become his own god. This new religion is science, and its dangerous gospel has been spreading like a deadly virus that is transforming the *Homo sapiens* into *Homo technicus* who must rely on *deus ex machina* (an unexpected power or event saving a seemingly hopeless situation) for its survival.

Hence, what was originally intended to be an extraordinary accomplishment for the evolution of the human species has turned into the science of madness.

NOTES

[1] Sigmund Freud, *The Future of an Illusion* (New York: W.W. Norton & Company, Inc., 1989), 38.

[2] Jean Jacques Rousseau, *The Social Contract and Discourse on the Origin of Inequality* (New York: Washington Square Press, 1967), viii.

[3] Genesis 2:21, 2:22.

[4] Creationism is the belief that the Universe and all living organisms originate from specific acts of divine creation, contrary to the documented scientific approach of natural processes of evolution.

[5] Wilhelm Reich, *The Murder of Christ* (New York: Farrar, Straus and Giroux, 1971), 104-105.

[6] For detailed data on megachurches and their pastors refer to http://www.onlinechristiancolleges.com/megachurches/

[7] Ibid.

[8] For a comprehensive "Fast Facts about American Religion," refer to http://hirr.hartsem.edu/research/fastfacts/fast_facts.html#numcong.

[9] Interview with Oprah Winfrey at http://www.oprah.com/own-oprahs-next-chapter/why-pastor-joel-osteen-makes-no-apologies-for-his-wealth

[10] Ibid.

[11] This popular quote is ubiquitous on the internet quotes sites, and has even turned into trinkets sold on online retail outlets.

[12] Greg Palast, *The Best Democracy Money Can Buy* (New York: Plume Book, Penguin Putnam, Inc., 2003), 241.

[13] Pat Robertson, *Right on the Money: Financial Advice for Tough Times* (New York: Hachette Book Group, Inc., 2009).

[14] Palast, *The Best Democracy Money Can Buy*, 240.

[15] Matthew 19:19, 19:21-24.

[16] For a video of his confession and plead for forgiveness before his wife and congregation see https://www.youtube.com/watch?v=yWkVa-_sd24

[17] Kevin Roose, "The Last Temptation of Ted," *GQ*, January 26, 2011, http://www.gq.com/story/pastor-ted-haggard

[18] Southern Poverty Law Center, "The Year in Hate and Extremism," Intelligence *Report*, Spring 2016/Issue 160, 44.

[19] N.J. Dawood, translator and notes, *The Koran* (Baltimore, MD: Penguin Books, Ltd., 1974), 9.

[20] The symbol of Islam, the crescent moon and star, is featured in the flags of several Muslim countries. The cross is also depicted on the flags of several nations, including Great Britain whose Red Cross on a white back-

ground represents England's patron Saint St. George, known as Saint George's Cross.

The Science of Madness

N ever since the early 1800s has the world been so dramatically affected by the advancements in science and technology—except that today the consequences have proven to be catastrophic. Not even when weavers and textile workers declared war on the machines in northern England in 1811 can be matched with what's happening now. Back then, the Luddite uprising witnessed gangs of men wielding swords, hammers, and axes, as they stormed the automated factories that usurped that work and livelihood. Two hundred years later, extraordinary developments in automation continue to cause political and social upheaval. A recent study found that 85 percent of manufacturing job losses from 2000 to 2010 was caused by automation[1]—not outsourcing or immigration as some populist public officials preach from the pulpit of their political churches. Although U.S. factories now produce twice as much products as they did in 1984, the output is carried out with only one-third of the workers.[2] And the prospect of machines taking over human labor in the near future is ominously real. A study conducted by Oxford University predicts that 47 percent of U.S. jobs will be automated over the next two decades. Some 1.7 million truckers could be rendered redundant by self-driving vehicles, and computers could replace millions more store cashiers, insurance underwriters, and tax preparers.[3] This trend heralds a massive unemployment apocalypse, courtesy of the evolving science of madness.

Since the Scientific Revolution that began with Nicolai Copernicus (1473–1543) science has evolved at an increasingly astounding pace; not only in technical knowledge, but in its impact in the evolution of the human species—or devolution, depending on individual interpretation. When Copernicus overthrew the geocentric view, which was the

Church's consecrated dogma for more than a thousand years, the Earth lost its privileged position as the center of the Universe. Instead, the planet was delegated to a substandard class of countless cosmological bodies roaming an unimaginably vast Universe. Unwittingly, Copernicus scientific knowledge robbed man from his proud megalomaniacal position as the central figure of God's creation.[4] Disappointed and distraught with the verifiable scientific fact that man was not the crown jewel of creation—and not even "the beauty of the world, the paragon of animals," as Shakespeare referred to[5]—he found an alternative solution for his egocentric quandary: he turned his own scientific achievements into the center of his own universe. Science became a religion and technology its god.[6]

Ironically, the science of madness is incongruent with the religion of madness. In fact, they are antagonistically positioned and cannot reconcile at any step of the way. From the very beginning their disagreement arises as their opposite views of life on Earth unravels. Science, with its rational analytical means of acquiring information through scientific methods, measurements, and notations is based on empirical evidence. Traditional religions, however, rely on faith-based assumptions drawn from recondite sacred texts that leave plenty of room for manifold interpretations. Thus, like two courting individuals adamantly locked in their opposite belief systems, the marriage of science and religion could never succeed. In fact, it is doomed even before a marital proposal can be articulated. With one being rational and the other allegorical, their perceptions of knowledge are, indeed, incompatible.

From the deadly divisive struggle between the geocentric and heliocentric theories to the acrimonious disagreement between evolution and creationism, science and religion have been battling for supremacy of knowledge for centuries. The active nature of science, in contrast with the passivity inherent in dogmatic religious beliefs, are so radically opposed that they remain juxtaposed in parallel realities. Hence, amidst the conflicting dualities of evolution and creationism, secular humanism and religious fundamentalism, original sin and inherent love, among other divergent positions between science and religion, the conciliatory solution was to turn science into an independent religion in its own right with technology as the object of worship. By developing highly sophisticated artificial intelligence, as well as producing unnatural

foods, synthetic drugs, titanium-made limbs, mind-numbing entertainment, and a slew of unessential products for profit, technology has
taken the center stage that used to belong to humanity. In fact, technology has become so pervasive in modern life—and based on the large
number of people moving about always with their cell phones in hand—
it has turned into a bona fide appendage of the human body to which
the mind has succumbed to. A few visionaries of the twentieth century
foresaw the unfolding of the madness of science; the great German-
American social psychoanalyst Erich Fromm was one of them:

"A specter is stalking in our midst whom only a few see with clarity. It is
not the old ghost of communism or fascism. It is a new specter: a completely mechanized society, devoted to maximal material output and consumption, directed by computers; and in this social process, man himself
is being transformed into a part of the total machine, well fed and enter-
tained, yet passive, unalive, and with little feeling."[7]

It is important to clarify that even a madman recognizes the extraordinary benefits of science to human civilization. It is not science in and by
itself that is the culprit of modern social travesties; to the contrary, it
has been a boon to the quality of life of the human species. However,
even though the astounding scientific advancements—particularly in the
twentieth century—have brought about the development of life-saving
vaccines, effective medications to treat dreadful diseases, salubrious
and convenient sanitation, mass food production, efficient transportation systems, broad-range communications, and a plethora of benefits
that contribute to quality living, science also has had devastating consequences to and in spite of the same quality living it contributed to create. At first, science seems like a gift wrapped up in a tantalizing package, but upon opening it a curse is released and wreaks havoc in human
life. It is very much like the Greek myth of Pandora's Box (Pandora
means "the gift of all"), whose unrestrained curiosity and in violation of
Zeus' instructions, unleashed every kind of trouble by opening the box
entrusted to her—and in the human case, it is the box of science. From
Pandora's Box, troubles that people had never known before flew out
like ravenous boding evil bats spreading the rabies of misfortune. But if
the comparison of Pandora's Box to science may sound disconcerting,

the good news is that the last thing that flew out of the ominous box was hope.[8]

As mentioned above, science is not the problem; but alone, it is not the solution either. What the discovery of fire meant to the Stone Age, science and the technology it derives from is to the Electronic Age. As a resource and tool for expanding the human potential and consciousness, science and all its components are fundamental to the evolution of the species. But if science is not the problem, and yet its consequences have been detrimental to both individual and collective welfare, what is the underlying cause that can lead to the answer of this dilemma? Firstly, there is the human nature whose irrepressible thirst for knowledge cannot be restrained—and science offers an exceptional opportunity to explore the farthest frontiers of possibilities of the human experience. Now, the crux of the matter lies on how and what we do with the knowledge we accumulate through the use of this powerful intellectual tool. The how is answered by the empirical evidence of socioeconomic practices in which everything, including science, works in behalf of the profit motive of individuals and large entities as well. Thus, when science is at the service of profit, the essential characteristic of science's intrinsic purpose—the expansion of knowledge—is severely compromised, therefore assuming the inferior position of being a mere accessory for an ulterior motive: the pursuit of profit.

❁

Beginning with the human intellectual nature, we know by experience that we all have a Darwinian survival necessity to acquire and accumulate knowledge. It is an inherent human trade that is observable in early childhood when the need to learn is imperative to self-development. The bio-social educational process unfolds in stages: the infant learns to walk; the child learns to read; the adolescent learns that life is an evolving challenge; the mature adult learns to cope; and the elder, granted that all the learning of a lifetime was worthwhile, learns to surrender. Intellectually, however, the thirst of knowledge remains unquenchable for a lifetime. And because the unrestrained human passion for learning is exacerbated by the gradual accumulation of knowledge, learning becomes like an addicting drug; a potent psychological drive to accumulate more knowledge, understanding, and ultimately, to gain an expanding awareness of at least some of the infinite mysteries of life that torments us with the anxiety generated by our ignorance. But the problem is that we're stuck in a nauseating merry-go-round of knowing only that the more we learn the more we realize that we do not know, which makes us even thirstier for more knowledge. It becomes a perennial vicious cycle that leads to everlasting intellectual frustration.

As we march on through the educational desert with an insatiable thirst of knowledge, science becomes like the distant oasis that shall placate our intellectual dehydration. However, the thrill and excitement of a constantly evolving science that yields more and more knowledge all the time only reaffirms what Socrates (c. 470 B.C.E.–399 B.C.E.) realized millennia ago: "All I know is that I don't know anything." Nevertheless, we turn to science with the highest expectations of minimizing the amount of disappointment of knowing that learning is a Sisyphean task that will never lead to the Holy Grail of Knowledge. But science is the staff upon which we lean on as we walk through the path of knowledge.

Science, like a magical fire, has illuminated the dark path of human civilization. But it also has left a shadow behind that is proving to be as problematic as the original darkness on the path. Seemingly, for every scientific and technological advancement, there is a costly price tag associated with it. There is also an investment cost to deliver the results that science procures, which is expected to be recouped in various profitable ways. This necessary and inevitable partnership of science and free enterprise engenders a serious problem: it transforms both the nature and the fundamental purpose of the pursuit of knowledge. And once the profit motive is inserted in the scientific equation, the common denominator is always the pursuit of financial gains; and the numerals representing humanity and the environment become mere accessories of a business mathematical process.

When I was a knowledge-starved teenager searching for answers to my countless questions, I remember reading an article in a reputable economics publication that made absolutely no sense to me at the time. Somewhere in the middle of the Indian Ocean, a cargo ship had dumped tons of rice to the bottom of the ocean floor. It was not an accident; to the contrary, it was the only purpose of the navigation. And the reason for the deliberate action—not to mention the expense to transport the rice there--baffled my mind: to maintain the artificially high value of the commodity (rice) on the stock market. Although today I begrudgingly understand how the capitalist system works, the lunacy of disposing of tons of food in a region where millions live on the brink of starvation can only be identified as disturbing sociological madness; a madness caused by the virus of greed.

The relevance of my recollection above to the issue of science is pertinent; after all, agricultural science has evolved at a remarkable pace in the last decades. From the time of the Neolithic Revolution (approximately 10,000 years ago) that transformed human societies from a lifestyle of hunting and gathering to one of agriculture and settlement, science has exerted an enormous influence on food production outcome. Today, public traded agrochemical and agricultural biotechnology corporations (e.g. Monsanto Corporation) reveal the role of science in high volume agricultural production, which incidentally has been contributing to the unrelenting population explosion. And because food is a commodity on the stock market whose value is closely monitored and often manipulated by multinational food production corporations (the rice dumping example illustrates the point), the science involved in this process has been prostituted by the economic interests of the pimps of the business world. In addition, the use of highly toxic pesticides to increase production as well as the genetic alteration of basic food components, can and should be viewed with great skepticism. After all, once the selfish profit motive takes predominance over the interests of people, the environment, and the comprehensive welfare of life as a whole, it must be regarded with utmost misgivings, lest a Malthusian nightmare may awaken us from our delusional reverie of unremitting growth.

Although many a pundit derides the concept of a Malthusian nightmare, the undeniable truth is that agricultural science has made it all too real. The Malthusian nightmare concept derives from the population growth thesis of Thomas Robert Malthus (1766–1834). In his famous and controversial *An Essay on the Principle of Population*, Malthus asserts that populations grow exponentially while food production grows at arithmetical rate. He purports that there is a disparity between the potential rate of growth of population and the potential rate of growth of means of subsistence. Therefore, the risk for a demographic-centered catastrophe is all too real. If what Malthus calls "preventive checks" (the conscientious monitoring of population control) are insufficient, then whatever is necessary will be done instead by the "positive check," which in reality doesn't sound positive at all. According to Malthus, positive checks are external forceful interferences in which population decline and balance through the unholy trinity of war, pestilence, and famine.[9] And considering the current astronomical rate of population growth, which increases the demand and consumption of vital limited resources, the prospect of a Malthusian nightmare is tantamount to the religious concept of Armageddon. Since no significant measures to curb population explosion are currently in place, humanity is being quietly lulled into a chilling night sleep.

Science, be it agricultural, bio-chemical, engineering, or any of its manifold exploratory fields, always seems to generate negative results—like the lengthy frightening list of side effects of the many pharmaceutical drugs on the marketplace of illness. Evidently, for every benefit that science bestows upon humanity, there are several consequences that endanger both our welfare and that of the planet and the myriad life forms inhabiting it. The carcinogenic pesticide-laced food we consume, the polluted air we breathe, the contaminated water we drink, the massive deforestations, the sprawling urban centers, the electronic addictions, all the way to the ever-growing threat of a nuclear holocaust are all byproducts of scientific knowledge misused. It is as though the balance between nature and human ingenuity has been severely compromised by economic greed and sociopolitical irresponsibility. Perhaps, if science was mostly committed to the improvement of life on Earth—and its benefits available to all without restrictions—then it would cease to be an intellectual tool with which to create wealth for a few privileged beneficiaries of a chaotic and corrupted economic system.

Since science is not limited to strictly scientific and technological innovations, maybe the partnership of science and the humanities can yield more enduring positive results than the disastrously overused affiliation of science and free market economics in which the ultimate goal is always to make a profit. In humanistic social sciences, however, the investigation of human life and activities can help us find solutions to our numerous challenges, as well as a pathway leading to genuine and comprehensive human development. It may well be our last chance for survival in the twenty-first century—and we're running out of time.

❀

If there is a science that can pull us back from the brink of the abyss of self-destruction, it ought to be the undervalued social sciences: the scientific study of human society and social relationships, particularly political science, sociology, anthropology, and social psychology. Although economics is traditionally regarded as a social science, Canadian scientist and environmental activist David Suzuki (1936–   ) adamantly rebukes the assumption that economics is a science. He argues that "economics is so fundamentally disconnected from the real world it is destructive."[10] On the other hand, due to the critical environmental crisis of our time that's been threatening the survival of the human species and our planet at large, I suggest that environmental science to be studied as a fundamental social science as well.[11] Since the ultimate goal of science is to understand, explain, and expand the knowledge that should improve the human condition, then, considering the dismal situation of our historical time, the social sciences are arguably the most important science of all.

Although the word science alludes to mental images of technicians in research laboratories, in its broader concept science is the intellectual and practical activity encompassing a variety of systematic studies that take into consideration, theories, experiments, and observations. As such, it is applicable to all sorts of human endeavors, including socioeconomic and political activities. Since the science of madness is deeply rooted in the sociological and political circumstances of our time, both sociology (the study of the development, structure, and functioning of human society) and political science (the branch of knowledge that deals with political activity and behavior) are paramount to unearthing an antithetical approach to, if not a cure, at least alleviate the pressures of modern insanity. However, unlike physics, biology, chemistry, among other types of science that rely on verifiable data that leaves nearly no room for speculations, both sociology and political science must embrace philosophical approaches if they are to deliver scientific alternatives to the functioning of human society and solutions to the myriad problems we face in the twenty-first century.

Like a child raised within a particular socioeconomic environment tends to absorb those values throughout his developmental process, society evolves in similar pattern. Both the individual and the group have a natural propensity to respond and adapt to the cultural environment they are exposed to as they mature. In the case of a child, the one reared by a financially privileged family that espouses conservative views of the world and traditional religious principles, will likely grow up to model significantly different beliefs from a child raised in poverty who is bereft of economic and educational opportunities. These inherent factors will determine the direction the individual will take in life, though a few strong and self-reliant personalities may willingly take the road less traveled by. In likewise fashion, society responds exactly the same way.

Hence, growing up in a society that regards certain rights as inalienable, whether they are authentic or not, determines the dominant culture in which millions of children absorb as the only legitimate values they must abide by. And regardless of how vague and obtuse the moral concepts they're compelled to take up may be, the belief systems manifest themselves enmeshed in an intricate web of brainwashing social, economic, political, and religious values that can be detrimental to the most fundamental inalienable right of all: the freedom to be authentic and fulfill one's ontological vocation to be more fully human.[12] Thus, within the context of this distorted situation, entire populations are misled to embrace a reality of madness as if it were the exemplary standard of normality. It is the quintessential social science of madness.

As millions of children are indoctrinated from early childhood to be patriotic (reciting the Pledge of Allegiance daily at school) and religious (having faith in God, Allah, or Jehovah, while believing in unimaginative mythological fables), by the time they grow into young adulthood they've been primed to take on a new belief system that links all of the above with politics and economics. They've been groomed to become fervent advocates of a different kind of allegiance and religion: free market economics. Soon they're trained to hone their economic function skills in preparation for a highly competitive job market where they will peddle their labor; the disposable commodity of the free market. Concomitantly, they're coerced to buy in the economics cultural value of consumption in which the measuring stick of success is determined by the amount of money, goods, and properties they can accumulate in the course of their finite lifetime. Thus, besides the sacrosanct trinity of love of God, country, and family that was inculcated into them in childhood, as adults they learn to develop the love of money, too.

Once enamored with the socioeconomic culture of love of money, some nefarious characteristics of human nature prodded by the economic system are inexplicably overlooked or ignored altogether. Trapped in an iniquitous behavioral pattern dictated by greed and selfishness and spurred by fierce competition, a culture of madness ensues that blinds the collective perception of the incalculable damage capitalism produces along with its many superfluous goods. And the impairment is as multiple as it is diverse. At the individual level, there is the disturbing alienation from work, self, others, and nature. But it is at the collective level that the problem mushrooms into a frightening environmental deterioration as it's never been witnessed in the history of human civilization. In the meantime, the incessant demand for continuous economic expansion, which comes in tandem with a rapidly growing population, depletes natural resources and overloads the infrastructure necessary to accommodate the unsustainable growth of both. And aggravating the problem further, this chaotic situation becomes a breeding ground for divisiveness, indifference, and even hatred as more people and economies compete for fewer jobs and dwindling resources.[13]

As it is increasingly more evident that the dominant culture of madness can be curtailed neither by science nor economics, we've become desperate to maintain the delusion of *ad infinitum* prosperity and security, even though it is obvious that neither is possible.

❀

Politics plays a crucial dual role in both domestic and international relations. In addition to attempting to ensure the establishment of peaceful collaborations among citizens, peoples, nations, and a variety of different perceptions of cultural identification, politics also attempts to quell the potential for eruption of violence, although often times it becomes the instigator of hostility. Ideally, it should function as a catalyst for peace, which is preserved through the establishment of laws, regulations, and a specific social code of ethics that citizens must abide by in order to maintain domestic and international harmony. Historically, however, it has been validated in mainly two ways: authoritarian and democratic, the former imposing the will of special interests, and the latter supposedly enforcing what Jean Jacques Rousseau termed the "general will."[14] Controversially, authoritarianism and democracy seem to have blended into mutually deceiving stand alone principles; that is, authoritarianism can display signs of democracy and democracy can hide authoritarianism in its nature. Propaganda, marketing, and the broad communication apparatus available make this effortless merging of opposites an alarming occurrence in modern day politics.

Governments are the physical manifestation of politics. Either a monarchy, dictatorship, democracy, or any other form of representation of authority, they all must be validated by a covenant that is accepted— by force or voluntarily—to the legitimacy of its ruling. Monarchies rely on the God-given right to rule over the people. Dictatorships purport that they rule because it is in the best interest of the people who presumably do not know what's best for them. And in a democracy, the majority of the people rules through an open and free plebiscite in which citizens select those who will represent the "general will" in the public forum. However, these are only the original theoretical concepts; but they have changed significantly over the years. Today, monarchs are either symbolic government figures (Great Britain) or iron-fist rulers (Saudi-Arabia). Dictators can exhibit either a monarchical trend (North Korea) or camouflaged under a democratic cloak (Russia). Democracy, too, has suffered an unwelcomed mutation from its original Greek etymological roots (*demos*, "common people," and *kratos*, "rule and strength.") With the infiltration of private interests in public affairs and through the dissemination of distorted perceptions of cultural values, democracy has long been held hostage by the falsehood of the "inalienable" rights and moral virtues of free market societies," which turns individual freedom into a trite word bereft of meaningful significance. In this mutational process, the meaning of *demos* has been replaced by *ploutos* (wealth), and *kratos* (rule and strength) has turned into sheer power. Plutocracy, a society ruled by the small minorities of the wealthiest citizens, is the new king of government; the monarch and the dictator disguised as a sovereign representation of the common people.

❀

Within the current discordant sociological and political climate, the social science of madness is in dire need of reform. But as long as pseudomoral economic values are extrapolated into the social norms arena, we will continue to associate by default the theories of free enterprise with the principles of a free society, which are not by any means interchangeable; to the contrary, they can be fundamentally opposed. While the interests of free enterprise narrow down to the selfish pursuit of profit, the interests of a free society is anchored on the common good of a free citizenry. Free enterprise constantly attempts to influence, finance, and corrupt all levels of government for its own self-interest. A free society, however, strives to remain vigilant against outside influences in the people's affairs. In a sense, a free society is, indeed, the antithesis of free enterprise, because the latter takes neither the "general will" nor the common good as even remote objectives of its practices.

If we are to reverse the deadly course of the science of madness, political science is perhaps the most important science with which to instigate the transformations we desperately need, if the human species is going to survive in the twenty-first century. And as time travels at an inexorable pace toward the future, everything must change along the chronological journey. But from an anthropocentric point of view, among all that changes none is more important than empowering human transformation, both individually and collectively. And from the collective standpoint, if we were able to overcome the limitations of greed, selfishness, unrestrained competition, divisiveness, gratuitous hatred, and everything else that is corrosively self-destructive, then, perhaps, the human journey will continue to be an awe-inspiring adventure for centuries to come. Conversely, if we choose to maintain the vicious cycle of contemptuous indifference fuelled by arrogant ignorance that we are more capable than we actually are, then all science and technology will prove to be nothing but the greatest curse of humanity; the Pandora's Box we wish we'd never opened.

Therefore, time is of the essence. The sooner we learn that what brings us together is where the answer of our troubles lies, the sooner will be able to turn around from the fast-paced race toward self-annihilation. As for science, the truth is that there is no science of madness, but only mad scientists who haven't realized yet that they are mad—and science in their hands is like an ax in the hands of a mass murderer. Conversely, science wielded by self-realized men and women who are aware of their inherent ecological connection with all that live can, indeed, exert impactful beneficial contributions to the evolution of the human species.

Unfortunately, the blinding factor that does not allow man to see that he is gone mad is his own ignorance. The Russian esotericist P.D.

Ouspensky (1878–1947) peeked through the chinks of the wall of self-limitation when he pointed out:

"Man does not know himself. He does not know his own limitations and his own possibilities. He does not even know to how great an extend he does not know himself."[15]

And not to know one's own ignorance while believing to be knowledgeable is the most dangerous madness of all. Such a man engaged in the pursuit of knowledge will most certainly unleash the madness of science.

NOTES

[1] Theunis Bates, Managing Editor, "Editor's Letter," *The Week*, February 10, 2017, 3.
[2] Ibid.
[3] Ibid.
[4] Fritjof Capra, *The Turning Point* (New York: Bantam Books, 1983), 54.
[5] William Shakespeare, *The Complete Works of William Shakespeare*, (New York: Outlet Book Company, Inc., 1975), 1085. "What a piece of work is man! How noble in reason! how infinite in faculties! in form and moving, how express and admirable! in action how like an angel! in apprehension, how like a god! the beauty of the world! the paragon of animals! And yet, to me, what is this quintessence of dust?" Hamlet, Prince of Denmark, Act II Scene II.
[6] In a *Time* magazine cartoon about the difference between science and religion, it refers to science's perspective that God is man-made, whereas religion proclaims that man is God-made. I add a third alternative that technology has become the man-made god. See *Time*, August 28, 2017, 20.
[7] Erich Fromm, *The Revolution of Hope: Toward a Humanized Technology* (New York: Bantam Book, 1968), 1.
[8] Edith Hamilton, *Mythology* (New York: Back Bay Books/Little Brown and Company, Inc., 1998), 88.
[9] Thomas Robert Malthus, *An Essay on the Principle of Population* (New York: Penguin Books, 1985), 28.
[10] For a brief explanation of David Suzuki's postulate on the nature of economics refer to https://www.youtube.com/watch?v=4NiauhOCfsk
[11] Environmental science is, by definition, an interdisciplinary study that incorporates ecology, biology, physics chemistry, zoology, geology, among other natural science disciplines. Studying it as a social science has become imperative due to the sociological crises that accompany the environmental crisis.

[12] Paulo Freire, *Pedagogy of the Oppressed* (New York: The Continuum Publishing Company, 1996), 37.

[13] The catchphrase "America First" greatly contributed to the election of the United States President Donald Trump in 2016. As more competition for available resources merges with fewer employment opportunities, this kind of economic protectionism is bound to proliferate in years to come.

[14] Rousseau's famous notion of the "general will" reflects the expression of the will of the community, which is to be the determinant of justice and social control. See Jean Jacques Rousseau, *The Social Contract and Discourse on the Origin of Inequality* (New York: Washington Square Press, 1967), xv.

[15] P.D. Ouspensky, *The Psychology of Man's Possible Evolution* (New York: Vintage Books, 1973), 11.

The Madness of Science

O ne of the most astonishing pieces of literature to come out of the twentieth century is Aldous Huxley's *Brave New World*. Published in 1932, the futuristic novel is set in London in the year A.D. 2540, which in the book is presented as the year 632 A.F., or After Ford, when the madness of science achieves the ultimate perfection: an artificial society composed of artificial individuals enjoying artificial happiness. Through high scientific advancements in reproductive technology, sleep learning, psychological manipulations, and mind conditioning par excellence, Huxley engineered a literary representation of how science and technology were capable of altering the essence of our humanity. As science took the reins of life, mankind developed a soulless existence of fabricated contentment in a materialistic utopia. And should negative human emotions arise from the bottom of a mirthful artificial existence, the magical wonder drug, soma, was readily available for consumption offering "all the advantages of Christianity and alcohol; none of their defects."[1]

Another remarkable fictional portrayal of the madness of science is George Orwell's (1903–1950) dystopian novel, *1984*. It is a terrifying sociopolitical account of an omnipresent dictatorial government that keeps citizens under continuous surveillance. The powerful state is under the control of privileged political elites where the tyranny is overseen by Big Brother, the leader who enjoys adoration and popularity, though he might not even exist. The controlling elites of the party have absolutely no interest in the welfare of the population, for power for its own sake is the only thing that matters. This autocratic government even has its own Ministry of Truth, which is in charge of propaganda and historical revisionism to enforce the dominant values of the despotic political state of affairs.[2] It is a nightmarish political scenario that not even Huxley's artificial utopian society might have been able to endure. Fiction aside, what is most alarming is the fact that we've already been experiencing the reality of Huxley's and Orwell's prophetic imagination; in both scientific laboratories and sociopolitical innovations as well.

From the failed experiment of the Soviet Union to the out of control—and equally failed—*laissez faire* capitalism, societies have been grappling with the possibility of establishing a sustainable, just, and meaningful socioeconomic system that will endure the test of time. But as geometric population growth escalates at unprecedented levels, which makes the political management of the masses with divergent point of views an extremely challenging task, we seem to be slipping farther down the path of similar terrifying societies that Huxley and Orwell depicted in their writings. Indeed, from the communist Stalin's Soviet Union to the capitalist Trump's America, there has been a nefarious tendency around the world toward authoritarianism and demagoguery. Either the government is elected, selected, purchased, or usurped, there seems to be a common pattern of governing that neglects fundamental interests of the people they are supposed to serve. And in today's world, the problem has been aggravated by scientific and technological developments that favor manipulation and control. In fact, Huxley observed the dangers of evolving social engineering some 26 years after writing *Brave New World*:

> "If the first half of the twentieth century was the era of the technical engineers, the second half may be the era of the social engineers—and the twenty-first century, I suppose, will be the era of the World Controllers."[3]

By observing a world that is economically bound by globalization in which both societies and individuals are connected through electronic devises, the signs of control and manipulation of peoples and socioeconomic structures have been evident for a long time. And in order to legitimize the process, the tactic is carried out under the righteous banner of freedom, liberty, and justice—an emulation of the rhetorical political legacy of the French Revolution—though they are seldom present in the reality of most of the world's population. In my turn, I would argue that freedom, liberty, and justice are but reveries of a yet to happen utopian society.

Nevertheless, like in the fictional works of Huxley and Orwell, the political propaganda machinery and the relentless promotion of alienation through small-minded cultural interests, mawkish patriotism, sanctimonious religiosity, and mind-numbing entertainment, they all pave the way for the deliverance of the desired outcome: indifference, acceptance, and subservience of the masses of alienated citizens that give way to the ultimate madness of social and political science.

※

When I was in high school I had a nutty teacher whom I thought had lost his marbles. He taught physics and mathematics, two subjects that by themselves can cause a few screws to loosen up in the brain. But the day he predicted that within a century people would be talking on pocket size telephones while seeing each other's face on tiny screens, I determined on the spot that he had, undoubtedly, lost his mind. After all, this was the mid-1970s, a time when mobile phones had just been invented.[4] And yes, a hundred years is a long time, but it still seemed like a technological quantum leap for such a science fiction-like gadget to become a reality. Perhaps there is something to be said about being eccentric, for in a matter of a few decades my teacher's prediction came to fruition in astonishingly premature fashion. In the end, I was the mad one who could not see it coming; but in my defense, I was mostly interested in the arts and the humanities.

Today, the scientific and technological achievements we've accomplished are nothing short of remarkable—and they continue to evolve at an extraordinary pace. However, with advancements in technology come the gargantuan challenges associated with it. From the telegraph (the Victorian era internet) to the telephone, and then to the World Wide Web of the late twentieth century, science and technology have changed; not only modern societies but individual citizens as well. In fact, the world's entire socioeconomic infrastructure utterly depends on it. And people's reliance on the dominant role that technology has in all facets of life—and the nature of the relationship they've been compelled to forge with their personal electronic gadgets—have had a most significant impact on the very nature of the human species. The German-American social psychoanalyst Erich Fromm, like my high school teacher, saw the new trend coming decades earlier. He wrote in the afterword of George Orwell's novel *1984*:

> "George Orwell's 1984 is the expression of a mood, and it is a warning. The mood it expresses is that of near despair about the future of man, and the warning is that unless the course of history changes, men all over the world will lose their most human qualities, will become soulless automatons, and will not even be aware of it."[5]

Watching people eat holding a fork in one hand and a smartphone in the other; or walk about while babbling nonstop; and most dangerous of all, operating motor vehicles while staring at small screens as their nimble thumbs type on tiny keyboards has become routine sights. The visual evidence that people are constantly glued to their inseparable electronic devices is an indication that the alienation brought about by the madness of science is here to stay. Alas, the warning Fromm issued in the quote above has fallen in deaf busy ears, as people gradually lose their most inherent human qualities and become soulless automatons. And this is not by any stretch an exaggeration. The cell phone, which is a peculiar denomination for a handheld computer that, incidentally, also serves as a telephone, has become much more than a mere tool with utilitarian functions. It has turned into a serious pathological addiction leading to legitimate electronic-driven alienation. Seemingly, the growing numbers of people afflicted by this troubling condition have their will power hijacked by their inebriating devices. The problem has reached such a high level of emergence that it has significantly compromised public safety. Indeed, it has become a matter of life and death.

In spite of several studies and numerous fatal crashes attesting to the obvious (texting while driving can be lethal), the compulsive electronic disorder continues unabated—and so do the related daily traffic accidents. There have been countless cases of mostly young drivers swerving onto upcoming traffic lanes and causing critical and often times fatal accidents. The case of Amanda Clark in Oakdale, California, is just one among thousands of occurrences over the years that illustrates the point. Amanda never doubted her ability to use her phone while driving until she rolled her car and survived to tell the story. She wrote in her diary and told her family and friends that she would never do it again. One year and one day after her first crash, she drove off a freeway embankment while texting and would never have another chance not to do it again.[6] Unfortunately, she's just one among thousands of victims. According to statistics compiled by the Department of Transportation, 3,154 people died and another 424,000 were injured in motor vehicle crashes caused by distracted drivers who were texting or using cell phones—and that happened in the year 2013 alone![7] And the casualties have been growing steadily ever since. As a norm of the new culture of madness, younger generations growing up with this electronic compulsive disorder expect to reply to an incoming text message within minutes of receiving it. The urge to use the cell phone is as insidious as it is uncontrollable. It has become a portable artificial appendage of the human body.

When the level of addictive alienation seems to reach a high plateau, a new gimmick comes up to enhance the estrangement of people from nature, others, and themselves. It seems that the madness of science is like a progressive disease that consumes the one who consumes its ever changing innovative products. And because science is controlled by powerful economic forces, the fruits of its creations are always geared toward the single most important objective of capitalism: profit, even if it's at the cost of selling our humanity cheap to electronic alienation.

Take for instance the worldwide phenomenon of *Pokémon Go*, an augmented reality (AR) video game that has become a bizarre international sensation. The game, which is played by distracted dumb people on their smartphones, makes use of GPS (Global Positioning System) technology and camera in the handheld computers (aka cell phones) to hunt for cute cartoon critters that pop into existence alongside real-world physical objects. It has become the biggest mobile game in U.S. history to date. And of course, it's a highly addictive electronic escapism that offers brief respite from the nonstop broadcasting of worldly tragedies and looming fears, as a self-confessed addict admitted to *The New York Times*.[8] And like other distracting time-consuming activities that keep throngs of people constantly staring at the tiny screens in their hands, *Pokémon Go* has caused its share of accidents. Among many reported incidents, two men suffered injuries when they followed their smartphones off a cliff in Encinitas, California while in the pursuit of their nonsensical *Pokémon Go* critter.[9]

Perhaps, instead of augmented reality, what we really need is a return to simplified reality; a reconnection to the Earth and the life that surrounds us, including our own.

❊

Contrary to unfounded religious beliefs based on mythological narratives about the creation of the world, a plethora of scientific evidence undeniably asserts that it took some 4.5 billion years for the Earth to come into being.[10] After the Sun impregnated the planet with the semen of life some 3.2 billion years ago, a most unique abode of creation gradually developed into the cosmic home of the human species, which has been inhabiting it for approximately 4 million years. Putting it in a comparative mathematical perspective, the human species has existed for about 0.1% of Earth's age; and civilization, which is only 6,000 years old, for less than 0.0001%. And yet, in spite of the extraordinary miracle of life that took billions of years to evolve, humans have managed to imperil both the survival of the Earth and their own in a mere 200 years plus. Having been trashing the planet since the Industrial Revolution in the late 1700s, now we rely on the madness of science to discover another planet where we can move to—and trash.

Today, as the world has entered the Anthropocene era,[11] we've embarked on what is arguably the most critical exploration in the history of human civilization: the final frontier of the cosmos in search of a new habitat. Having managed to inflict irremediable damage to our home planet, our high scientific knowledge is now invested in finding another cosmic habitat in an unimaginably infinite Universe. However, the challenge is proving to be as immense as the outer space itself—and the madness associated with it is equally colossal.

Firstly, there is a most serious misperception of identity that has confounded human discernment. Although it is blatantly obvious—and scientifically proven[12]--that the Earth, or Gaia, the Greek name for goddess, is a sovereign living organism that nurtures a multitude of life forms, some skeptical humans seem to have a different interpretation of this (alternative) fact. Haughtily convinced that we are independent from the Earth, which we regard but as a basic reservoir of resources to supply our industrial civilization's economic needs, we developed a truly delusional idea that we can survive and thrive in other planets. Thus, we've entrusted our naïve scientific ingenuity to find another cosmic home in a boundless Universe. However, being bona fide creatures of the Earth, the possibility of finding a suitable planet to inhabit—much less the possibility of surviving on it—is not only infinitesimally slim but also pathologically insane.

The third planet orbiting the Sun, the Earth is unique in the Solar System and possibly one of a kind in the Universe. With an ideal range of temperatures that permit liquid water to exist to sustain a myriad of life forms, the Earth is the only planet known to science that has developed an oxygen-rich atmosphere. These two factors have enabled the rocky planet to evolve and give birth to a complex array of life not known to exist anywhere else.[13] Nevertheless, both the unfettered destruction of the Earth and the desperate search for its replacement continue unabated—with plenty of hope and zilch success.

At the time of this writing, the latest discovery announcement came out in the media with much fanfare. According to news outlets, for the first time, astronomers have discovered seven Earth-size planets that could hold life orbiting a single nearby star (a meager 40 light years away, which is the equivalent of 235 trillion miles away). The excitement is validated by the fact that astronomers have confirmed close to 3,600 planets outside our Solar System since the 1990s, but barely four dozen are in the potential habitable zone of their star; and of those, only 18 are approximately the size of the Earth.[14] As we can see, in spite of the billions of dollars spent in the exploration of the Universe in search of a new planetary home to replace the one we're destroying, science has nothing to show for but occasional enthusiastic discoveries that have yielded no practical results thus far. In contrast, if those billions of dollars were invested in solving the countless grave problems we have right here on Earth, perhaps we wouldn't need to search for another home planet in the first place. Analogically speaking, to search for another habitat in inhospitable faraway environments is like looking for a spouse on dating websites when one's been happily married for decades. It just doesn't make any sense; except if it is business sense, for exploration of outer space is becoming a promising profitable entrepreneurial investment.

As it's been unmistakably demonstrated throughout its degenerative history, in the capitalist system everything becomes an opportunity to accrue profit—and space exploration is no exception. A new class of "astropreneurs" has been engaged in fierce competition among themselves for the lead in this fledgling business arena. Several wealthy entrepreneurs such as Amazon's Jeff Bezos (1964–   ), Microsoft co-founder Paul Allen (1953–   ), British Virgin Group's Richard Branson (1950–   ), and the current leader in the great billionaire space race, Tesla's CEO Elon Musk (1971–), all have been jockeying for an advantageous competitive position in the promising industry of the future[15]— if the future can be taken for granted. Either the objective is to have millions of people living and working in space, as Bezos envisions for his company, or the more immediately feasible field of space tourism, the floodgates of opportunities for profit in space exploration are wide open. Of course, neither the Earth nor humanity at large has anything to do with this venture. To the contrary, the primary goal is the same as the one that has been causing most of our problems on our planet in the first place: the unrestrained pursuit of profit.

❀

The madness of science has been blending effortlessly with the madness of the war industry—and it's been going on for a long time. In the late twentieth century, it was estimated that out of every 1,000 scientists all over the world, 200 were occupied with research into arms technology.[16] In those days of the Cold War between the two ruling superpowers, the price of a new nuclear submarine was equivalent to the education budget of 23 developing countries with 160 million children of school age.[17] Once Third World countries got a glimpse at the gravy train of destruction, they jumped onboard to capitalize on a booming profitable industry (Brazil is a good example of developing nations that became major arms exporters). The profits with the tools of death have been greatly increased with the assistance of scientific research in the profitable business of science.

In essence, science is not only a systematic approach to further the pursuit of knowledge, but also a most important intellectual tool with which to produce a large array of consumer goods for a profit (the pharmaceutical industry is a classic example endorsing this claim). But the most disturbing customer of the business of science is the military, which has many implications in government administration and the setting of national policies. On January 17, 1961 in his sobering farewell address to the nation, the 34th President of the United States, Dwight Eisenhower (1890–1969), warned the nation of this danger on national broadcast television.[18] In what he termed the military-industrial complex (MIC), he warned the nation that an informal alliance existed between the business of armaments and the government, and it posed a grave risk that the nation should guard against very closely:

> "We must never let the weight of this combination endanger our liberties or democratic processes. We should take nothing for granted. Only an alert and knowledgeable citizenry can compel the proper meshing of the huge industrial and military machinery of defense with our peaceful methods and goals, so that security and liberty may prosper together... Akin to, and largely responsible for the sweeping changes in our industrial-military posture, has been the technological revolution during recent decades... The prospect of domination of the nation's scholars by Federal employment, project allocations, and the power of money is ever present—and is gravely to be regarded."[19]

The military-industrial complex term Eisenhower coined has become a dictionary entry meaning "an informal alliance of the military and related government departments with defense industries that is held to influence government policy."[20] Thus, with this definition in mind, it would behoove the citizens of the United States to be leery of political rhetoric and policies aimed at increasing the military's budget under the guise of national security. Besides the fact that it takes much more than weapons to build national safety—high level diplomacy being one of them—it is important to bear in mind that the corporations that participate in the military-industrial complex (MIC) are for-profit enterprises with lucrative government contracts. This is the reason Eisenhower stressed that "...the power of money is ever present—and is gravely to be regarded."

❀

Science, be it biological, social or any other variation of its many fields, must be freed from economic ambitions that risk entrapping it in the web of corruption of selfish interests. Indeed, if science is to recover its fundamental purpose of striving to improve the quality of life and comprehensive human development of individuals and societies—instead of the special interests of corporations, governments, or agencies—it must sever the ties that bind it to commercial activity. In addition to carrying out its investigative endeavors based on empirical observations, when it comes to social science, it must also question sociological circumstances that are accepted by cultural traditions as the norm. Thus, one of the most basic roles of science is to debunk myths and prejudices that do not reflect the best interest of humanity and our life-sustaining environment.

Nevertheless, in a society brainwashed by patriotic fervor, religious convictions,[21] and stubborn obsession with obsolete cultural traditions, treating the madness of science is a tall order. As French social scientist Emile Durkheim (1858–1917) established in his renowned body of work, people in society are glued together by belief systems, which he viewed as an entity larger than the sum of its parts. He conceived society as an integrated whole, each part contributing to the overall stability of the system. Indeed, society is something larger than the sum of its parts.[22] Taking Durkheim's reasoning for granted, then, change cannot happen unless the belief systems that bind us together are revised to address new social standards. However, change must begin with the individual who, in turn, will impart revamped beliefs based on revitalized social awareness. But considering the many deep-seated convictions our society harbors, this is a challenging undertaking—but not an impossible task.

Perhaps, the first step of this thousand-mile journey begins with redirecting scientific interest to human development. For instance, instead of devoting so much time and resources to outer space discoveries, it may be time to launch a new era in the exploration of the human inner Universe. Since we seem to understand the realm of our inward nature even less than we do the far-flung galaxies of the infinite cosmos, maybe the time has come to turn science as a tool for self-discovery, which shall pave the way to self-development. But how can scientific investigation lead to self-discovery? The same way it has led to pharmacological alienation, but with truly life-changing results.

❀

William Blake (1757–1827) was a great visionary poet. At a time of moralistic oppression of the human flesh and spirit, Blake advocated for freedom in all aspects of life. His poetry reflected his concerns of the poor and the exploitation of working classes that persists to this day. He anticipated the challenges, conflicts, and anxieties of the modern world with remarkable precision, which his contemporaries viewed with disdainful suspicion, for they could neither understand nor see the far-off scope of his vision. Believing in the possibility of a new kind of man of the future, in his poem, *The Marriage of Heaven and Hell*, he hinted to the extraordinary possibilities hidden within the human species:

"If the doors of perception were cleansed, everything would appear as it is—infinite. For man has closed himself up, till he sees all things thro' narrow chinks of his cavern."[23]

Although Blake never suggested how the doors of perception could be cleansed, the man of the future he envisioned in his poems peeked through the "chinks of his cavern" and saw the infinite possibilities within his own limitations. By the time the German pharmacologist, Louis Lewin (1850–1929), published his study of the potent cactus *Anhalonium Lewinii* (named after him) in 1886, he unlocked the doors of perception to be wide open.

Worshipped in religious ceremonies as a quasi-god by indigenous peoples for millennia, hallucinogenic substances like the psychoactive alkaloid peyote and psilocybin infused fungi have been used as a bridge to connect with the mysterious realm of the human mind. However, it was not until the mid-twentieth century that powerful mind-altering drugs were recognized as a viable psychiatric treatment for conditions ranging from alcoholism to schizophrenia. The turning point in the modern history of psychedelic development occurred on April 19, 1943, when Swiss chemist, Doctor Albert Hofmann (1906–2008), unwittingly created LSD (lysergic acid diethylamide) in the laboratory of Sandoz, the pharmaceutical company he worked for in Basel, Switzerland.[24] Then, throughout the 1950s and 1960s, LSD and other psychedelic drugs were used in clinical studies as potentially valuable medications in psychotherapeutic treatments. But with the advent of the countercul-ture movement of the rebellious youth of the 1960s and the widespread consumption of psychedelics, President Richard Nixon (1913–1994) signed the Controlled Substance Act (CSA) in 1970 making the drugs illegal, even for therapeutic purposes. Eventually, MDMA (methylenedioxymethamphetamine), commonly known on the streets as the recreational drug Ecstasy, was abruptly banned by the U.S. Drug Enforcement Agency in 1985, despite its effectiveness in the treatment of depression and other illnesses. Alas, politics and religion often get in the way of science.

The real motivation behind the prohibition of psychotropic drugs, I suspect, has more to do with trepidations related to social sciences than health science concerns. The timing of the implementation of the Controlled Substance Act of 1970, signed by a conservative president, leaves no speculative room for second guessing. Apparently, a consciousness-changed youth decrying the values of capitalism was too much of a risk for the status quo to endure. Furthermore, when a Harvard University scholar (Timothy Leary (1920–1996)) becomes a popular apostle for the consumption of psychedelic drugs wanting to bring the establishment down ("turn on, tune in, drop out"), the threat to the prevailing dominant culture was undeniably real. But now, at the dawn of the twenty-first century when we face the much more serious risk of survival, the time to revive psychedelic drugs research for the purpose of changing consciousness is ripe, needed, and urgent. This is not only our opportunity to cleanse the doors of perception, but more importantly, set the madness of science in reverse mode.

The evidence supporting the effectiveness of psychedelic drugs as therapeutic tools is well documented. Today, for the first time in more than 40 years, there is a revival of the use of psychedelic drugs in the medical community to treat a vast array of mental ailments. From treating war veterans suffering from post-traumatic stress disorder (PTSD) to abating the terror of end-of-life anxiety, these wonder mind-altering drugs are experiencing a revival in therapeutic treatment.[25] Despite this rebirth of acknowledging psychedelic drugs as valuable tools for therapeutic purposes, the greatest challenge—and opportunity, too—we have before us at this juncture in human history is how to make responsible use of these extraordinary consciousness-changing drugs to treat the most dangerous illness of our time: the sociological madness triggered by blind ignorance.

Although the reactionary voices of standardized social normality might reverberate in the canyon of my unorthodox madness, the undeniable fact is that we have an extraordinary pharmacological product that, if used with methodical scientific discipline, has the potential to alter the evolutionary path of both the individual and human civilization. A drug like LSD, in spite of the undeserved reputation it has received due to indiscriminate recreational abuse, has proven to be lifesaving and even an inspiring wonder drug, as the case of the late actress Betsy Drake (1923–2015) demonstrates. Seeking to ease the emotional turmoil in her acrimonious marriage to Hollywood superstar, Cary Grant (1904–1986), Drake started seeing a therapist who administered LSD--then a legal drug that Grant also would embrace. She credited LSD with giving her the confidence to leave Grant and pursue a career in psychotherapy.[26]

Today, the challenge is to make use of drugs like LSD in widespread psychotherapeutic strategies to alter the consciousness of the masses and as a pathway to the exploration of the human inner Universe. Is it a farfetched, utopian, or even a plain mad idea? It all depends on who answers the question.

Many renowned scientists, intellectuals, and artists have experienced and given testimony to the transformative power of psychedelic drugs. Swiss scientist and discoverer of LSD, Albert Hofmann, who purported to have used the drug for decades—and he lived to be 102-years-old—was confident of its potential to open up the mind. However, as it is the case with technology or anything else abused or misused, it runs the risk of being detrimental rather than beneficial to the user. Based on his own experience with mescaline, British writer Aldous Huxley alludes to this concept in his essay *Heaven and Hell*, a title he derived from William Blake's poem *The Marriage of Heaven and Hell*:

"Heaven is merely a vintage point, from which the divine Ground can be more clearly seen than on the level of ordinary individualized existence."[27]

The enigmatic American author Carlos Castaneda (1925–1998), who experimented with hallucinogenic cacti and mushrooms under the guidance of a Mexican shaman by the name of Don Juan, also relates to Blake's vision of a portal to higher awareness that can be seen "thro' narrow chinks of his cavern:"

"The particular thing to learn is how to get to the crack between the worlds and how to enter the other world. There is a crack between the two worlds...There is a place where the two worlds overlap. The crack is there. It opens and closes like a door in the wind."[28]

Just as Albert Hofmann is the "father of LSD," Alexander Shulgin (1925–2014) is the progenitor of Ecstasy (MDMA). Sasha, his endearing nickname, was a highly respected chemist and pharmacologist who created more than 100 molecules that produce altered states of consciousness that are conducive to new ways of thinking, feeling, and seeing the world. He's been called the Einstein of pharmacology.[29] Like Hofmann, whom he befriended (Shulgin once asked Hofmann what he thought of MDMA and Hofman replied, "Finally, something I can do with my wife."[30]), Sasha was an obstinate advocate and consumer of psychedelics for self-development purposes. He admitted to self-testing many of his chemical experiments totaling more than 4,000 psychedelic experiences.[31] Like Hofmann, he strongly believed in the power of psychedelic drugs to unlocking the human mind to new perspectives and experiences of living. However, he also regretted that his extraordinary mind-altering scientific discovery was misused and abused in trivial recreational raves. Incidentally, like Hofmann, Shulgin lived a very long, healthy, and productive life until he died at the age of 88.

Albert Hofmann and Alexander Shulgin are among many other luminaries in the field of transpersonal psychology through psychedelic experimentation. Czech-born Stanislav Grof (1931–   ) was also a pioneer in the early studies of LSD and its effects on the psyche. For more than 50 years he researched non-ordinary states of consciousness and developed his own innovative approaches and theories, Holotropic Breathwork[32] being one of the most popular, especially among New Age groups. And of course, there is one of the most controversial scientists of the mind, the Hungarian-born Dr. Thomas Szasz (mentioned earlier in this book) who became famous, not for his experimentations with psychedelic drugs, but for his adamant denial of mental illness as a bona fide disease. Nevertheless, he, too, suggested that cocaine (Freud's therapeutic drug of choice), marijuana, psychedelic mushrooms, and poppies are plants that, along with their by-products, have been used since time immemorial. These substances had always been at people's disposal, showing that to prescribe medicines for oneself, just like choosing one's own diet, must be among the most basic of human rights.[33]

Perhaps the seeds planted by the progressive men of pharmacological science will eventually blossom in the fertile soil of the human mind. Although I maintain optimistic confidence that humanity will awaken from the slumber of self-destructive ignorance that has led to collective madness, I also acknowledge that the urgency of the human condition does not allow us to afford taking the time to take action. This might well be our greatest—and likely last—opportunity to apply the science of chemistry to cure the madness of science. But with so much prejudice, backward thinking, selfish economic interests, and many other hurdles standing along the way of individual and social transformation, the communication of what is truly important to human needs must overshadow the insipid messages coming out of the dominant communication of madness.

NOTES

[1] Aldous Huxley, *Brave New World* (New York: Harper & Brothers Publishers, 1950), xv.

[2] George Orwell, *1984* (New York: Penguin Publishing Group, 1977).

[3] Aldous Huxley, *Brave New World Revisited* (New York: Harper & Row Publishers, Inc., 2000), 27.

[4] Motorola was the first company to produce a handheld mobile phone. On April 3, 1973, Martin Cooper, a Motorola researcher and executive, made the first mobile telephone call from handheld subscriber equipment, placing a call to Dr. Joel S. Engels of Bell labs, his rival.

[5] Orwell, *1984*, 313.

[6] Erin Tracy, "She survived her first distracted driving accident—but not her second," *Merced Sun-Star*, April 10, 2016.
http://www.mercedsunstar.com/news/nation-world/national/article71022122.html

[7] Detailed information and additional statistics are available at
http://www.personalinjurysandiego.org/topics/facts-about-texting-driving/

[8] "*Pokémon Go:* Why it's a worldwide craze," *The Week*, July 29, 2016, 17.

[9] Ibid.

[10] J.D. Macdougall, *A Short History of Planet Earth* (New York: John Wiley & Sons, Inc., 1996), 16.

[11] The Anthropocene is a proposed epoch marking the beginning of time since humans began exerting a significant impact on the Earth's geology and ecosystems. The previous epoch, the Holocene, began some 12,000 years ago as the Earth thawed from the ice age.

[12] James Lovelock, *The Ages of Gaia: A Biography of Our Living Earth* (New York: Bantam Books, 1990).

[13] Carole Stott and Clint Twist, *Space Facts* (New York: DK Publishing, Inc., 1995), 80.

[14] Marcia Dunn, "7 Earth-size worlds could sustain life," *Corvallis Gazette-Times*, February 23, 2017, A1.

[15] "The great billionaire space race," *The Week*, September 23, 2016, 11.

[16] Willy Brandt, *Arms and Hunger* (New York: Pantheon Books, 1986), 50.

[17] Ibid., 48.

[18] For the original complete President Dwight Eisenhower's farewell address to the nation see https://www.youtube.com/watch?v=CWiIYW_fBfY

[19] Eisenhower's Farewell Address to the Nation, January 17, 1961. http://mcadams.posc.mu.edu/ike.htm

[20] *Merriam-Webster's Collegiate Dictionary*, Eleventh Edition (Springfield, MA: Merriam-Webster, Incorporated, 2007), 788.

[21] "Convictions are more dangerous enemies of truth than lies." Friedrich Nietzsche, *Human All Too Human* (Lincoln, Nebraska: University of Nebraska Press, 1986), 234.

[22] Andersen/Taylor, *Sociology: Understanding a Diverse Society*, Second Edition (Mason, OH: Cengage Learning, 2008), 15.

[23] William Blake, *The Essential Blake*, Selected by Stanley Kunitz (New York: MJF Books, 1987), 74.

[24] Albert Hofman, *LSD My Problem Child* (Los Angeles, CA: J.P. Tarcher, Inc., 1983), 16.

[25] Steven Kotler, "The New Psychedelic Renaissance," *Playboy Magazine,* April 2010, 51.

[26] "The actress who quit her career for Cary Grant," *The Week*, November 27, 2015, 35.

[27] Aldous Huxley, *The Doors of Perception, Heaven and Hell* (New York: Harper & Row Publishers, Inc., 1956), 138.

[28] Carlos Castaneda, *The Teachings of Don Juan* (Berkeley, CA: University of California Press, 1998), 149.

[29] Mark Boal, "The Agony & Ecstasy of Alexander Shulgin," *Playboy Magazine*, March 2004, 86.

[30] Ibid., 158.

[31] Jason Szep, "Dr. Ecstasy laments the rave drug's notoriety," *Yahoo! News*, December 2, 2005. http://www.news.yahoo.com/s/nm/20051202/hl_nm/life_ecstasy_dc

[32] For information about Holotropic Breathwork visit http://www.holotropic.com/about.shtml

[33] Martin Broussalis, *Castaneda for Beginners* (New York: Writers and Readers Publishers, Inc., 1999), 7.

The Communication of Madness

T
he first time I gave a serious thought about the communication of madness was when I heard a millennial refer to it as "the media we consume." Suddenly it dawned on me that, like everything else in modern capitalism, communication, too, is an item of consumption. And since the advent of the internet and the World Wide Web that proliferated in the early 1990s, communication has become a powerful tool with which to ignite widespread misinformation, factoids, gossips, lies under the guise of "alternative facts," and all sorts of useless trivialities. Although the technological advancements that has brought about worldwide connectivity and access to information at our fingertips is a most valuable tool, in the hands of underdeveloped human beings enslaved by the dictatorship of free enterprise (an intentional and legitimate oxymoronic association of words) has turned into a dangerous weapon—like an ax in the hands of a mass-murderer. Thus, an invention that in the hands of a self-realized freeman would be an extraordinary device for continuous improvement, in the tyrannical claws of capitalism became but a useful instrument for the profitable consumption of madness of an economic system that thrives in the unrelenting madness of consumption.

In the Electronic Age, technology is typically perceived as a sophisticated gadget, a piece of hardware designed to serve a particular purpose. In regards to communication, as I writer I think of the typewriter or the word-processor as important technological devices. However, the pencil is also a technology, for what determines the status as technology is the deliberate and conscious use of it by human agents.[1] Hence, more than just a machine that does not depend on the human user either for its power or operation, technology as a tool is entirely controlled and operated by human factor, which validates the argument of the importance of human development in the wielding of powerful technological tools. Consequently, neither the radio, television, nor the internet is the culprit of creating the communication of madness. Instead, it's the human factor influenced by dominant cultural principles within a socioeconomic and political environment that determine the use—or misuse—of the technology at hand.

From the time when the first successful trans-Atlantic radio-telephone conversation took place between New York and London in 1926, to the first email sent by computer engineer Ray Tomlinson (1941–2016) in 1971, the world of communications has changed dramatically. Indeed, the first half of the twentieth century heralded the coming of a revolutionary era in broadcasting. The Morse code, the electrical telegraph, and Alexander Graham Bell's (1847–1922) grand invention were relegated to such inferior means of transmitting data that, except for the telephone, they've completely vanished. The difference, however, is that the earlier communication tools were used for very specific purposes, whereas the electronic devices are meant to cover a much broader spectrum of interests.

☯

I surmise that the original intent of developing radio and television in the early decades of the twentieth century was to dissimulate information. Of course, it would be a matter of time for entertainment and advertisement to conflate into a perfect economic partnership. It started out in innocent fashion: serial westerners, mysteries, sci-fi, comedies, and an array of simple family-oriented entertainment that assuaged the tension and anxieties of everyday living. But culture changed, and people changed accordingly; and within the individual and collective transformation of society, the nature of entertainment adjusted to new tastes and trends. However, based on the current dominant genres of broadcasting programs, it seems evident that the cultural and individual transformations society is undergoing is dysfunctional at best.

One evening, days after reading an excellent book about the corrosive effects of electronic media on society,[2] I decided to carry out an informal investigation of the many outlandish forms of entertainment on television. I went to the gym determined to walk on the treadmill for an hour and surf all the TV channels at primetime (between 8:00 and 9:00 pm). With a voice recorder on the equipment's dashboard, I surfed the channels taking notes of the details of the shows I observed. I was flabbergasted with the outcome of my methodical observations. A great number of the mind-numbing—and in some cases offensive—entertainment is clearly geared toward the least educated and most uncouth segments of society. Also, I noted how the type of advertisements sponsoring specific programs promoted demographic-related products: beer commercials and military recruitment ads in contact sports shows (boxing, mixed martial arts, football, etc.); beauty and anti-aging products in gender specific shows (romantic comedies, celebrity news, etc.), among other categories. Incidentally, I must stress that I was not in the least surprised to notice the number of anti-depressants, sleep medications, and a slew of pharmaceutical drugs commercials and their dreadful side effects ubiquitously present across the entertainment genres. What stunned me, however, was the coarse nature of several television programs that exemplify the communication of madness.

Among the most hideous television shows available to a population in desperate need of comprehensive education (mind, heart, and spirit), there are some that boggles the mind how they can be remotely regarded as entertainment. What they reveal about the (lack of) awareness of the masses is the crux of the issue—and the challenges that unawareness poses to society is detrimental to social stability. It is as though people lived in a perpetual state of sleep utterly unaware that they are asleep,[3] while influenced by the dreams and nightmares of their daily experiences. Thus, at the end of a long day of drudgery at work, they bring their depleted minds, exhausted bodies, and empty pockets to the living room couch and prostrate, mindlessly, in front of the television set to consume madness that will make them forget their own. And here is where the real threat to human development lies: the consumption o a daily mental diet of violence, hatred, terror, contempt, envy, fear, and a barrage of negative emotions triggered by the highly lucrative television industry. Meanwhile, the most intellectually vulnerable citizens fall deeper into the black hole of ignorance and insensitivity.

As I flipped through the television channels in my casual research that evening, I realized how everything is fair game to capture susceptible audiences. It is a no-holds-barred competition for advertisement monies in which crime, stupidity, and violence are most valuable commodities, regardless of the negative effects they exert on the already fragile mental and emotional stability of the general population. It's a smorgasbord of dumbing down entertainment: reality shows about the miserable daily life of incarcerated inmates; detailed murder investigation cases; sickly obese people indulging in gluttonous appetites; police officers in brutal live action; and even parodies of the judicial system (Judge Judy, Judge Joe, etc.) are just a few of repugnant forms of entertainment in modern consumerist society.

In addition to barbaric videos of graphic violence, as it is the case of the Spanish language television Univision show *Al Extremo*, in which gruesome footages are preceded by tantalizing headlines, there are also lighter versions of utterly mindless distractions: from the counterfeit world wrestling entertainment to the circus of suburban dwarf ladies engaging in petty disputes, there are options galore for the hoi polloi to squander precious limited free time with wasteful thoughtless leisure.

After an hour of researching the madness of communication, I realized that I was more fatigued by the exposure to the television wasteland than the actual physical exertion of walking on the treadmill. But by the time I watched a video clip of a young man hanging himself in the Univision show *Al Extremo* (To the Extreme) as he dedicated his suicide to his father as a form of punishment for not having helped him with his pain, I realized that I couldn't take it anymore—and I wondered how many people derive pleasure from such degraded forms of distractions. At that moment I realized that television has become the ultimate vehicle to schadenfreude. And when the craving for horrifying information can't be satiated, the deeply disturbed human being can sign up to receive "breaking crime news" in his inbox with headlines like "N.C. Teen Allegedly Found Carrying Mom's Head After Decapitating Her in 'Gruesome Scene'."[4] I never thought I'd live to read headlines like this one; and yet, they've become the norm in the madness of communication.

❀

The underlying truth about communication and madness is that they are both lucrative commodities. And while madness is a free for all that is aggravated by the circumstances of free enterprise economic culture, the business of communications is privately owned and controlled by a selected few. In fact, most of the media in the United States is proprietary, incorporated, organized, and managed as a business entity. The natural inference from this fact is that their primary objective is to generate handsome profits for their shareholders. Therefore, if the culture adjudicates the consumer marketplace to welcome murder and mayhem as mundane forms of entertainment, these commodities of leisure will be profitably sold without compunction. But there is also a secondary function of mass media: to influence and manipulate public opinion.[5] Be it through omissions, inaccuracies, prejudices, or outright lies, it makes difficult—if not impossible—to deliver uncorrupted information independent from political and economic self-interests. And because the media (TV, radio, movie studios, publishing houses, recording companies, and all their subsidiaries) are mostly large corporate conglomerates, some of which are owned and controlled by individual billionaires, their political affiliations turn them into powerful propaganda machineries. Perhaps the most notorious example of this trend is Rupert Murdoch's (1931–   ) News Corporation.

In order to accomplish the essential economic and political objectives of the media, facts, evidences, and even observable reality itself have become irrelevant in the communication of madness. The fundamental importance of honest and unbiased dissemination of information in a free democratic society has been gravely compromised; and often times with serious implications. This is particularly concerning at a time when two-thirds (67%) of Americans get at least some of their news on social media. According to a Pew survey, the percentage rises to 78% of citizens under the age of 50.[6] Furthermore, across the partisan and educational spectrum, Americans seem to have succumbed to the deleterious cultural conditioning of dumbing down the perception of reality. And yes, even the so-called liberals and white-collar working bees have slipped into the crevices of media falsehoods, or what has become popularly known as "fake news." However, among the conservative, religious, and uneducated populace the situation is much worse (no wonder the 45th President of the United States is on record saying that he "loves the poorly educated"[7]). In fact, it has been reported that nearly half of Donald Trump voters believe the bizarre theory that the president's former political nemesis, Hillary Clinton (1947–   ), helped run a child sex slave ring in a Washington D.C. pizza parlor.[8] Despite the absurdity of such an unfounded tittle-tattle, millions of citizens participating in the democratic process seem to be afflicted by an endemic case of idiocy, which is not only troubling but also disturbingly dangerous.

Indeed, there is an epidemic of willful ignorance that continues to spread across the country like an out-of-control wild fire. And as an aggravating factor, political, religious, and cultural convictions have become integral components of individual identity. This personal self-characterization is so profound that any opposition to the fundamentals of these deeply ingrained values is perceived as an imminent threat to the insecure self. It is as though an aggressor attempted to take away the crutches that keep the intellectually disabled citizen upright. It is not about thought-out opinions based on ideas or concepts; it's a psychological dependence to believe in something in order to adapt to the ongoing cultural conditioning to madness. As Bertrand Russell (1872–1970) pointed out, this has been the enduring pattern of societal development:

> "The whole problem with the world is that fools and fanatics are always so certain of themselves, and wiser people full of doubts."[9]

When Kellyanne Conway (1967–), one of President Trump's top advisors, participated in a popular political show, she unwittingly inaugurated a new post-truth era by referring to absolute lack of evidence as "alternative facts." It was a matter of time for the two-word statement to make into the lexicon of the modern communication of madness—and the statement extrapolated into an even more radical proclamation that "there is no such a thing as facts," as another Trump surrogate stated publicly:

> "Well, I think it's also an idea of an opinion. And that's—on one hand, I hear half the media saying that these are lies. But on the other half, there are many people that go, 'No, it's true.' And so one thing that has been interesting this entire campaign season to watch, is that people that say facts are facts—they're not really facts. Everybody has a way—it's kind of like looking at ratings, or looking at a glass of half-full water. Everybody has a way of interpreting them to be the truth, or not truth. There's no such thing, unfortunately, anymore as facts."[10]

Now, there is not an announcement of economic or political nature that does not call for verification. In the face of "alternative facts"—and worse yet, no facts at all—individuals and organizations are coming together to challenge these most deceiving concepts. In the midst of this bizarre communication crisis where democracy is threatened by uninformed and misinformed citizens victimized by purposeful disinformation, exposing fake news has become a civil duty of conscientious citizens. Among the resources available is FactCheck, a project of The Annenberg Public Policy Center of the University of Pennsylvania.[11] A nonpartisan, nonprofit "consumer advocate" for voters, the organization aims to reduce the level of deception and confusion in U.S. politics. Despite its commitment and efforts to monitoring the accuracy of disseminated information, the words of William H. Whyte (1917–1999) hovers in the airwaves like a ghost haunting the truth: "The great enemy of communication is the illusion of it."

Alas, fake news can trigger unexpected confrontations that can lead to major international conflict. In an apparent response to a fake story claiming Israel's former defense minister threatened a nuclear attack against Pakistan if it sent troops to Syria, Pakistan Defense Minister Khawaja Mohammad Asif (1949–   ) reminded Israel that Pakistan is a nuclear state, too.[12] And considering that Pakistan and Israel do not have diplomatic relations, a potential nuclear crisis could have been ignited by totally fictitious news, which is an issue of great concern if the pattern of making up news continues.

❀

One of the greatest tragedies of communication today is that it's been degraded to sheer noise—lots of it! In technical terms, noise is anything that distorts or interferes with message reception, be it physical, psychological, or semantics.[13] It has become so loud and ubiquitous that is stifling the sounds of common sense under the clamor of mindless trivialities, intentional deceptions, and outright lies. It is as though the voice of reason wants to be heard in a crowded room (the world) where thousands of frivolous voices screech louder for attention. Unable to make itself heard, eventually the voice of reason retrieves and the communication of madness takes over.

Since the beginning of the twentieth century, the means of communication have been diversifying in order to keep up with the increasing economic demand to disseminate information. Either it's the commodity of news or the ballyhoo of marketing, the bombardment of information has become so insidious that it seems impossible to evade it, as communications theorist Neil Postman (1931–2003) remarks:

"From millions of sources all over the globe, through every possible channel and medium—light waves, airwaves, ticker tapes, computer banks, telephone wires, television cables, satellites, printing presses—information pours in. Behind it, in every imaginable form of storage—on paper, on video and audio tape, on discs, film, and silicon chips—is an ever greater volume of information waiting to be retrieved...Information has become a form of garbage, not only incapable of answering the most fundamental human questions but barely useful in providing coherent direction to the solution of even mundane problems...the tie between information and human purpose has been severed, i.e., information appears indiscriminately, directed at no one in particular, in enormous volume and at high speeds, and disconnected from theory, meaning, or purpose."[14]

In the midst of continuous onslaught of information coming to us copiously and at very high speeds, something important has been lost in the gargantuan amount of unremitting data that intrudes in our everyday life; and that important element is the connection with our own selves. We've reached a point in the communication of madness in which we don't even seem to consume information anymore; instead, we're consumed by it, daily. Because information is such a valuable commodity in the free market of consumption, there is a ravenous economic need to generate more of the same trite data nonstop. It seems like the same sound bites are hammered into our brains on a moment-to-moment basis; the same depressing news, celebrity gossips, sports thrills, fear mongering, and a vast array of loud noise that completely muffles the voices of wisdom that desperately attempt to be heard to no avail. We've become lost in our distractions—and we lost ourselves along the way. Unfortunately, since we began traveling on the information superhighway, we've missed the exit sign leading us back to common sense.

The turning of communication into a commodity has engendered an unprecedented crisis of fusing inner being with outer reality—some sort of a virtual perception of existence. Just as the stock market reacts to the whims of external conditions—be it economic rumors, political events, or presidential tweets—individuals, too, respond to information they absorb in the wide network of virtual connections in their cyber communities. This phenomenon is particularly observable in the "wired up" generations virtually growing up in virtual reality, and whose virtual world has become more meaningful than the natural world.

As the world becomes increasingly more dependent on technology, it is impossible to imagine communication being dissociated from it. In fact, it has become an indispensable appendage of it. And with the widespread propagation of social media, both business and personal connections are initiated and developed completely independent from human contact. In a sense, the internet has become a relationship surrogate that has been gradually replacing the need for any one-on-one interaction at all. Many if not most people seem to be agreeable with the new trend—and some might even prefer it. This self-inflicted human crisis caused by the preeminence of technology is arguably one of the major challenges of the first-half of the twenty-first century. As people become alienated from one another and nature, the possibility of a significant negative transformation of both the individual and society is perilously real. Furthermore, the unholy triumvirate of automatization, population explosion, and economic expansion threatens to bring about socioeconomic and political crises of apocalyptic proportions, as Erich Fromm warned us almost half a century ago:

> "We do not have much time left. If we do not begin now, it will probably be too late."[15]

As it is, we are running 50 years behind.

If we are to rehumanize the human species before it turns into an unrecognizable technological android, the road ahead is steep and long—and we're lagging 50 years behind schedule. Some contend that we'll be able to humanize technology before the manifold damages become irreversible. But technology is not the issue, for it is merely a tool that we allowed ourselves to misuse while corrupted by economic motivation. Like all the superfluous goods that inundate the market of consumption, there are way too many technological devices that were born from the copulation of greed and profit. Indeed, there are way too many social media, blogs, online businesses, video games—some of which are nauseatingly sick—and countless other activities and gadgets that are posing a legitimate threat to human societies.

Perhaps, the first step we ought to take is to recognize the problem as a veritable challenge that must be addressed. However, if we fail to communicate the importance of making changes before the window of opportunity closes and time expires, then we might be doomed to succumb into a madness of communication in which the voice of reason will be perpetually silenced by the desperate rumbling sounds of our own madness.

NOTES

[1] John Street, *Politics & Technology* (New York: The Guilford Press, 1992), 8.

[2] Neil Postman, *Amusing Ourselves to Death* (New York: Penguin Books, 2005).

[3] P.D. Ouspensky, *The Psychology of Man's Possible Evolution* (New York: Vintage Books, 1974), 33.

[4] "N.C. Teen Allegedly Found Carrying Mom's Head After Decapitating Her in 'Gruesome Scene,'" *Yahoo! News,* March 7, 2017. https://www.yahoo.com/celebrity/n-c-teen-allegedly-found-212757332.html. On the page of the article there is a paragraph that reads: "Want to keep up with the latest crime coverage? Click here (a link) to get breaking crime news, ongoing trial coverage and details of intriguing unsolved cases in the *True Crime Newsletter.*"

[5] For a comprehensive list of articles about media in the United States visit http://www.globalissues.org/article/163/media-in-the-united-states

[6] *Time* magazine, September 25, 2017, 13.

[7] For a 16-second clip of Donald Trump's boasting about winning votes and saying that he loves the poorly educated, see the following URL https://www.youtube.com/watch?v=4QwCeh5s9s8

[8] "Misinformation: Why facts are now irrelevant," *The Week*, January 13, 2017, 17.

[9] Ibid.

[10] Jack Holmes, "A Trump Surrogate Drops the Mic: 'There's No Such Thing as Facts,'" *Esquire Magazine*, December 1, 2016. http://www.esquire.com/news-politics/videos/a51152/trump-surrogate-no-such-thing-as-facts/

[11] For detailed information about this project visit www.FactCheck.org

[12] "Fake story splits Israel, Pakistan," *Corvallis Gazette-Times*, December 26, 2016, B6.

[13] Joseph A. DeVito, *The Interpersonal Communication Book*, Fifth Edition (New York: Harper & Row Publishers, 1989), 7.

[14] Neil Postman, *Technopoly: The Surrender of Culture to Technology* (New York: Vintage Books, 1993), 69-70.

[15] Erich Fromm, *The Revolution of Hope: Toward a Humanized Technology* (New York: Harper & Row Publishers, Inc.), 168.

The Madness of Communication

lthough it is conveyed through multitudinous means, the foundation of communication is language. The use of language is an integral part of being human and it's what distinguishes us from the rest of the animal kingdom. And like the human species, language evolves and changes with the passing of time. There have been hundreds of languages in the course of human history, and there are currently more than 7,000 living languages[1]—and that's not counting technical and technological languages. Thus, it's not surprising that linguistics (the systematic study of language) is one of the fastest-expanding branches of knowledge.

But what exactly is language? By definition, it is a set of symbols and rules that, put together in a meaningful way, provides a complex communication system.[2] And yet, in spite of—or perhaps because of—its complexity, it remains a most imperfect vehicle of communication that often leads to frustration and misunderstandings, even among those communicating in a common language. Since language, like technology, is merely a tool with which to deliver specific objectives, the meaning of a message can only be determined by the interaction between sender and receiver. Meaning, therefore, is not established in the words used, non-verbal expressions, or any other means of delivery, but in the intricate interaction of the involved parties and their own individual idiosyncrasies. For instance, someone who is self-conscious about his body image might respond negatively to a sincere compliment about his looks. The misinterpretation of a message can also occur in both cross-cultural and cross-gender communication.[3] But the thorough nature of communication changes significantly when it's carried out in the obscurity of the internet, for both the message and the parties involved do not have to be authentic if it doesn't suit the purpose. The ability to create a quasi-online avatar alters the rules of the communication game—yes, communication has become a sort of a game in which people play with words, facts, images, and anything else that cannot be verified.

But before exploring the nature of online communication and how it's been transforming language as we know it, it is important to remark that computer technology has a language of its own. From the earliest Egyptian writing that dates back to approximately 3100 B.C.E. to the programming language designed to communicate instructions to a machine, the written code of communications has come a long way. What English, Spanish, Chinese, and Arabic are to humans, ALGOL, BASIC, COBOL, AND FORTRAN are to sophisticated computer systems. Through these sets of characters that can be used to form a meaningful codes and symbols in writing instructions for a computer, a whole new universe of communications has been established—and it has changed forever the way people communicate and interact with one another.

In addition to affecting traditional patterns of communication, the English language is undergoing unprecedented changes in the way it's used in electronic communication. Because of the extraordinary amount of data that is disseminated at increasingly fast-pace, electronic language is abbreviated to a point in which it has become an independent linguistic code in its own right. Unless you're familiar with what I call the EECS (Electronic English Code System), you are bound to be lost in a succinct lexicon that can make lawyers legalese sound like crystal-clear prose. Here are a few examples of IM (instant messaging): TTYL (talk to you later), BFN (by for now), GTG (got to go). You get the point. There are a growing number of similar abbreviated codes that is transforming, not only the English language, but the way people communicate in an ever-growing dominant electronic environment. But that should be the least of our concerns. The real problem is the way human interactions are disadvantageously affected by the madness of communication.

$$❧$$

Even a madman would admit that communications technology has been an exceptional boon to humanity. The opportunities and possibilities for accumulation of knowledge, self-development, getting information at your fingertips (Google is so commonly used that has long been listed as a verb in the dictionary,)[4] connecting with people worldwide, among other benefits of communications technology are, indeed, remarkable human accomplishments. Unfortunately, we have misused, abused, and mishandled technology so poorly that it has turned into a cyber weapon that may well be already killing us piecemeal. The problem as I see it through the lenses of my anomalous mind is of dangerous disrupting imbalance. As humans exist within the universal duality of life (positive and negative, male and female, yin and yang, etc.), whenever one element distances itself from the other, the unit becomes unstable and collapses within itself. In the case of the human species, our dominant intellectual capabilities have evolved at such an extraordinary pace, but regrettably left behind the neglected development of our inherent emotional nature. This imbalance is what has allowed the mind to expand while the spiritual heart withered. And this disparity between the two is what turns our scientific and technological accomplishments into weapons of self and mass destruction.

In addition to the adverse consequences created by the discrepancy between the highly evolved intellect and the under-developed state of human empathy, the insidious tendency of the dominant economic system to convert everything—literally everything!—into a commodity for profit has denied communications technology its potential to transform both the individual and society in constructive fashion. The greedy Midas touch of capitalism can turn even the most ingenious invention into a self-defeating model. As new resourceful tools emerge, they're immediately replicated and repackaged as new products. This pattern has been evident since the beginning of the twenty-first century when the "Golden Era" of social media promised a lucrative future. Suddenly, like the output of a technological assembly line, a large number of social media sites were introduced to a ravenous market ready to devour them. From *Six Degrees*, the first social media site to appear in 1997, to Facebook, the behemoth that monopolizes the social media market today, much has changed. Now, along with Twitter (a presidential favorite), YouTube, and a couple of other social media sites prevailing on this niche market, a radical utilitarian change has taken place. What was originally created to be a practical tool for connecting with people and making friends (MySpace in the early 2000s is a classic example), soon became a major online marketing billboard that draws billions of customers who are often cynically called friends and fans. In fact, many pundits claim that no marketing campaign is comprehensive enough without a Facebook presence. But business' interests aside, even at the impersonal individual level social media has developed into an addictive habit with some damaging side effects.

With the proliferation of social media, it became obvious that sometimes—as it is the case of human beings on Earth—there is just too much of a good thing. Although the potential benefits of social media are undeniable, the wicked marriage of individual alienation and the profit motive has begotten dysfunctional users. The fact that you can connect with a childhood friend whom you haven't seen in decades via social media is a gift of friendship. Or the 46 percent of elders in America who use social networking to build social connections with people they care about is gift of both friendship and good health.[5] But when it turns into an addictive time-killing activity, or a superficial and insincere way to make friends with people you either don't know or even care to know, then it turns into a self-destructive habit that sucks the life out of the unwitting user.

✺

The most concerning element of this widespread trend is the young growing up on this pernicious electronic compulsion. In addition to the incessant use of cell phones, texting, emails, and surfing the internet at will, social media has become the virtual reality living room where people gather but never really get together. Like a cocktail party where invitees roam about holding their champagne flutes while boasting about their lives' achievements, many social media sites—most notoriously Facebook—serve this purpose as well as for marketing and advertisement. And considering that the bulk of users are younger people, the harmful habit-forming of trading the irreplaceable precious commodity of time for low-value entertainment and useless information should be an issue of serious sociological concern. According to the Pew Research Center's Internet & American Life Project, about 65 percent of kids age 12 to 17 (and 37 percent of adults ages 18 and above) used a social networking site in 2010.[6] Today, nearly eight-in-ten online Americans use Facebook.[7] With billions of users around the world, what could have been an extraordinary tool for education and genuine long-distance human bonding has turned into a powerful means of disseminating lies, falsehoods, bullying, violence, hatred, and, ultimately, alienation.

The electronic addiction in general and the social media obsession in particular have become critical psychological and social problems, both of which carrying serious political implications, as the United States presidential elections of 2016 evinced. In addition to the obsessive compulsion to look something up constantly, update profile information, reply to instant messages, or take the sweet time to harass, bully, and threaten others for the sheer satisfaction of the engagement—schadenfreude at its best—the once promising World Wide Web has turned into a tyrannical technological device. Because of the anonymity, invisibility, and the opportunity to create an online identity as one wishes, the web has become a sort of amusement park for sociopaths. In fact, they even have a name. The people who relish this online freedom are called trolls, a term that originally came from a fishing method online thieves use to find victims.[8] However, it was a matter of time for it to morph into an impersonal thug hiding in the dark alley of anonymity ready to pounce on vulnerable transients. From bomb threats to *doxxing* (publishing personal data such as Social Security numbers and other compromising private information), the web has become a dangerous place to roam about. In fact, the scope of the threat is spreading so rapidly that a multi-million dollar internet protection industry continues to thrive offering various products and services: anti-virus software, malware protection, identity theft firewalls, etc. It is a brave new world of unrivaled madness.

According to a Pew Research Center survey published in 2014, 70 percent of 18-to-24-year-olds who use the internet had experienced harassment, and 26 percent of women that age said they'd been stalked online.[9] But this is just one facet of a much bigger problem emerging from a new culture of intimidation that found its perfect venue on the internet, which is like an electronic dais capable of reaching an audience of billions. Therefore, homophily (love of the same)[10] networks have spawned in a swamp of hatred and anonymity. White supremacists, neo-Nazis, misogynist, religious fundamentalists, and terrorist organizations of all kinds of inklings have found an ideal vehicle for spreading their gospel while recruiting new members to their causes. The situation has become so treacherous that the social media Twitter has been expanding efforts to protect users from abuse and harassment (Twitter banned the controversial conservative provocateur Milo Yiannopoulos (1984–   ), an editor of the right-wing news site Breitbart News, for "participating in or inciting targeted abuse of individuals."[11]) However, this is but a symbolic action, for neither the culture of hatred can be curbed nor the voice of violence be silenced by muzzling a vile mouth or two. After all, this is not about quieting a few troublemaker individuals or groups; this is about human madness that has gone out of control.

With approximately 3 to 4 billion internet users worldwide, the possibility of reaching out large audiences is unprecedented. Roughly 500 million tweets are sent each day. Nearly seven hours of footage is uploaded to YouTube each second, in up to 76 different languages. With 1.7 billion active accounts, Facebook is the largest "cyber country" in the world. According to Pew, clear majorities of American Twitter and Facebook users now get their news from these platforms. Fifty-nine percent of American Twitter users rely on the service to follow news events as they happen in real time. The problem is particularly disturbing because of another feature of social media: its users are not passive consumers, like TV viewers or radio listeners or even early internet users. Now, we are all information creators, collectors, and distributors.[12] Thus, alternative facts have become conventional news that, with a modicum of skills and chicanery, anyone can become a convincing broadcaster of falsehoods.

The skyrocketing numbers of internet and social media users is proving to be an unprecedented challenge to both individuals and societies. As people become increasingly connected with the virtual communities of anonymous peers, the problem of alienation from self, nature—and in many cases reality—is snowballing down the mountain of tribulations in the horizon of our historical time. In 1995 there were 39.6 million people in the world with internet connectivity. A mere 10 years later, the number had ballooned to 1 billion. By the year 2020 the number of people connected to the internet is projected to jump to 7.6 billion.[13] And the real time speed in which data is being transmitted is absolutely staggering. In 1995 it took 540 seconds (9 minutes) to download a 4-minute song. By 2015 it took a measly 2 seconds. And when it comes to the amount of data transmitted per second, the numbers are mind-boggling. Every second there are approximately 7,173 tweets, 53,766 Google searches, 120,607 YouTube videos viewed, 2,481,685 emails sent, and 35 million megabytes of internet traffic.[14] With this much activity taking place in the virtual world, the rise of banditry in the information superhighway has put everyone at risk of being robbed;

of personal identity, valuable information, business records, and even national security secrets.

❊

In the 1800s, before the Industrial Revolution had wreaked havoc on the environment and the Earth had not been plastered with asphalt yet, the fear of travelers on the wagon trail roads of America—other than being attacked by Native Americans fighting against the theft of their homeland—was bandits lurking in the shadows of the path. Today, as billions of people travel through the information superhighway of the World Wide Web, the most feared thug prowling the internet is the hacker; the modern version of the highway robber.

In the United States alone, hundreds of thousands of hacking attempts happen every hour.[15] Individuals, businesses, organizations, and government agencies are all targeted for all sorts of reasons. In addition to the common crook and thief trying to steal personal financial information, there are well organized mobs of hackers—many of whom are directed and sponsored by nation states—ready to launch devastating cyberattacks on what was previously believed to be impervious targets. In fact, cyberattacks have breached the Pentagon, the State Department, and the White House, among other high security agencies. An estimated one half of Americans have had their personal data stolen, as financial institutions, high tech companies, among other prominent channels have had their database compromised by hacking activities. But when the cyberattacks are aimed at socioeconomic infra-structures we depend on, the consequences have the potential to be devastating. Had one of the 79 cyberattack attempts to the electric grid that took place in 2014 succeeded, the outcome would have been nightmarish.[16] And as hackers improve their technological arsenal while the attacks continue unabated, it seems it's a matter of time for one of them to pan out; unless cybersecurity firms and their army of cyber-detectives can interfere in a timely fashion to avoid a cyber-catastrophe.

Besides the mainstream cyberattacks that usually begin with a phishing strategy to download viruses, malwares, among other less known intrusion devices, we have now ushered a new era of cyberwars, which has been escalating rapidly. From the interference in the United States presidential election of 2016 by Russia to North Korea-directed attack on Sony Pictures Entertainment, which unleashed a stream of embarrassing company memos, destroyed its computers, and caused an estimated $100 million in damages,[17] the signs of upcoming widespread cyberwars with significantly more serious consequences are out in the open. The power grid, communication devices, transportation systems, water supplies, and a plethora of crucial components of society's infrastructure are all at risk.

In this new electronic superhighway we travel, an assailant can do more serious damage with a keyboard than a mugger could possibly do with an automatic weapon. And as Americans we ought to be seriously concerned, for cyberwar is the only field of warfare in which the United States doesn't have advantage over its enemies.[18] As the era of cyber-conflict is upon us, the danger of extrapolating to physical (nuclear) warfare escalates concomitantly.

Among the armies of hacker groups marauding the internet, there is a wide variety of purposes motivating their actions, some of which have made a name for themselves. Groups such as WikiLeaks, an international non-profit organization that publishes secret information and news leaks from anonymous sources, has established itself as a player in the world of international political meddling. During the heated 2016 U.S. presidential election, it published tens of thousands of hacked emails from the Democratic National Committee. Also, there is the mysterious Anonymous, an international network of "hacktivists"[19] committed to internet activism with a political agenda. With its own website[20] and a peculiar logo of a headless man that represents a leaderless organization and anonymity, it acts like a sort of digital freedom fighters. These and a slew of like-minded internet organizations focusing on social, economic, political, and environmental agenda are not to be regarded as the vulgar greedy thief selling his honor for a handful of bitcoins.[21]

The latest achievement in technological crime that has been sweeping the World Wide Web is ransomware, a computer malware designed for extortion. Although the online criminals use this weapon mostly against businesses and corporations, individuals, organizations, and local governments have been targeted as well. In the United States alone there were an estimated 1,000 ransonware hacks every day in 2015. Just a year later the number jumped to 4,000 per day.[22] This is how the whole scheme works: a gullible—or inattentive—internet user opens an infected attachment that looks legitimate. Then, the malware program downloads the ransomware bug, which encrypts database files that incapacitate the user to access the information, unless they pay a ransom to decrypt the files. The payment, of course, is made in bitcoins. The online thug provides written instructions on establishing a bitcoin account within a specific timeframe; otherwise all files and data will be lost forever. The FBI believes that as of the time of this writing there are 17 major ransomware viruses, and that the majority of hacks originate in Russia and Eastern Europe.[23]

Unfortunately, the madness that has been spreading through electronic means of communication is rampant—and often times utterly senseless. Massive mailings of attachments infected with viruses that impair computer hardware serve no other purpose other than doing harm to strangers. Oddly, the wicked villains engaging in such an irrational malicious act don't even get to enjoy schadenfreude, for they'll never know whether or not the unknown recipient was victimized. But who knows, maybe their mentally disturbed state of being is assuaged by committing a pointless misconduct. Perhaps, they should try some of the many electronic palliatives to counteract their neurotic dysfunction.

✿

After reading the newspaper, I have the habit of checking out the comic strips in order to mollify the tension intrinsic to the news stories. However, one time I came across a cartoon that was as depressing as the news, for it was based on everyday reality of modern time. An overweight old man with a dejected expression stamped in his face stared blankly at a computer screen with his wife standing next to him. She remarked: "How is it possible that you have hundreds of Facebook friends but no one to talk to?"

The number of alienated online loners seems to be growing at exponential rates across the generational spectrum. From toddlers to octogenarians, people are losing themselves in virtual reality that is but an illusion of impersonal connections in the phantasmagoric realm of cyberworld. Indeed, it can be haunting, especially when electronic entertainment addictions take over a person's life; and there are options galore: news, videos, music, porn, or simply web surfing, the internet can be like a colossal black hole that sucks the living light out of addicted users, many of whom are youngsters. As the youth of the Baby Boomer generation in the 1960s and 1970s experimented with mind-altering drugs to expand consciousness, today's electronic drugs of choice are the pathway to complete alienation—and sometimes even murder and death.

The news media has published numerous stories about the deleterious effects of video and computer games. Often times, when the addict also happens to be a loner, the blending of social inadequacy and cultural alienation can beget a murderer. Teenagers obsessed with playing "killer" video games run the risk of succumbing to the temptation to carry out the deed, especially if isolated and alienated from support groups (family, friends, community, etc.). And to make matters worse, it usually produces a domino effect of negative influence. To illustrate the argument, there is the case of an 18-year-old German who turned into a devoted player of group internet "killer games" and became fascinated by mass shootings, which likely inspired him to go on a murderous rampage killing nine people and leaving dozens wounded in the city of Munich.[24] And then there are the cases of lethal overdose when game addicts can play for excessive consecutive hours and die in virtual action. The BBC reported a particular case in which a "twitcher" (Twitch is an internet gaming platform where 2 million subscribers play every day with an additional 10 million watchers) died of gaming overdose.[25] In fact, the World Health Organization (WHO) has recently included gaming disorder in its list of mental health conditions. The WHO characterized a gaming disorder as a "pattern of persistent or recurrent gaming behavior, both on and offline."[26]

As the problem of gaming addiction has been escalating since the latter years of the twentieth century, detox centers to treat video games addicts have been expanding along with the growing rates of addiction. Like gambling or drugs, gaming indulgence is a serious condition that is very difficult to overcome without treatment. If that were not disturbing enough, signs of addiction have been detected in children as young as 8-years-old, some of whom grow up to play for 14 hours a day, often times to eschew personal problems.[27] But even more worrisome is the content of some of these games—the equivalent of the potency of an addictive chemical drug.

Since the 1990s a number of obscenely violent video games have inundated the consumer marketplace. More than two decades ago, one sadistic video game (Mortal Combat) was estimated to generate more than $100 million in business during the Christmas season alone. The game features two martial arts warriors pounding away at each other amid much sputtering of blood. Then the game instructs the players to choose between two forms of murder: ripping the heart out of the victim or removing the head and spinal column in one blow. And as if it were possible, some other games are even more gruesome. Night Trap, for instance, features a gang of black-hooded thugs entering a bathroom where a scantily clad young woman is helplessly captured and a hook is attached to her neck in order to suck out her blood. The software for the game includes images from scenes filmed with real actors, with vivid high-pitched drilling noises and a desperate screaming victim.[28]

This is how entertainment copulates with alienation to give birth to madness.

✿

The madness of communication is often characterized by blatant contradictions, some of which can make you scratch your head wondering about the absurdity of conflicting messages. Take for example the State of Oregon where gambling is a legal economic activity that bolsters the state's budget. At any given evening, primetime television broadcasts are sponsored by advertisement promoting the entertainment value of gambling, including the many casinos luring gamblers to their venues. The number of commercials encouraging Oregonians to buy lottery tickets and play slot machines is high and matched only by another contradictory message: advertisements urging citizens to seek help for gambling addiction. Sometimes during the evening newscast both types of advertisement run intermittently in different advertisement slots. First the encouragement to gamble, then the plead to call a toll-free number to get help for gambling addiction. It's absolutely mind boggling that two opposing messages are coming from the same source of encouragement. Alas, there are several other paradoxical pronouncements in the madness of communication.

By the 1980s when the illegal drugs use seemed to have reached its zenith, the then First Lady of the United States, Nancy Reagan (1921–2016), launched a national campaign aimed at curbing the looming drug crisis with a platitudinous slogan: "Just say no." Although it may have worked as a favorable political marketing tool for her husband's presidency, the cultural lure to consumption of drugs was ubiquitous in most segments of society, particularly in the entertainment industry.

However, as the conservative First Lady entreated youngsters to say no to drugs, the zeitgeist of the 1980s was characterized by drug use in popular culture. In music, arts, movies, literature, among other expressions of culture, the appeal of drugs exceeded a trite plead for restraint. But the contradiction and irony of this case lies in what's been happening in the early decades of the twenty-first century.

Today, the multi-billion pharmaceutical industry bombards consumers to say yes to all sorts of drugs, some of which the side effects are more devastating than the illegal recreational drugs of yore—and significantly more expensive as well. Once the profitability of the drugs marketplace switched from the hands of drug lords to the grip of corporations, "just say no" to drugs became obsolete. Incidentally, the alarming opioid addiction crisis—and the countless lawsuits related to deadly side effects of dangerous legal drugs—have sparked an unspoken need for just saying no to (legal) drugs; an unlikely case against a powerful lucrative industry.

And then, of course, there are the numerous contradictory messages we observe in everyday life. For instance, in spite of the many awareness campaigns alerting to the dangers of drinking and driving, it seems incongruous that alcoholic beverage companies sponsor race car teams that display their logos on the speeding cars and on the drivers' outfit. And despite the speed limits enforced on every highway and road, automobile manufacturers advertise their motor vehicles stressing how much faster they can drive far beyond the speed limit.

Meanwhile, the social outrage with excessive violence in the world goes hand-in-hand with the entertainment value of violence in television shows, movies, video games, and the news; all of which are consumed with a sickly insatiable appetite for belligerent behavior. Concurrently, the pious conservative appeal to sublimate the sexual drive of the youth runs juxtaposed to an incessant commercialization of sex in every segment of society, which is ubiquitous in marketing strategies applied to a variety of economic activities, particularly the entertainment industry. As for good health, the cautions against unhealthy habits and lifestyles are nullified by a slew of advertisements for junk food, alcohol, gambling, among other unwholesome products, behaviors, and patterns. Indeed, the manifold contradictions of the madness of communication are noticeable everywhere, even—or perhaps especially—in human relations.

At a time when technology is redefining the nature of socialization, meaningful personal relationships seem to be transforming at a staggering pace. Social media, dating sites, eLearning, remote work, online meetings, and everything else that technology has made possible present opportunities laden with unprecedented challenges; none of which is more pressing than what's been happening to the essence of human nature.

Unless we monitor the use of technology and do not allow it to control us unwittingly, we might end up turning Aldous Huxley's dystopian fiction of a Brave New World into a dismal superficial reality; an existence in which the only love we may experience is the love of madness.

NOTES

[1] Ethnologue Languages of the World, https://www.ethnologue.com/
[2] Anderson/Taylor, *Sociology: Understanding a Diverse Society Update* (Mason, Ohio: Cengage Learning, 2008), 59.
[3] There are several idiomatic expressions in the same language that carries radically opposite meanings in different cultures where the same language is spoken. As for cross-gender communication, Deborah Tannen's book *You Just Don't Understand: Women and Men in Conversation* exemplifies the point in case.
[4] "To use the Google search engine to obtain information about," *Merriam-Webster's Collegiate Dictionary*, Eleventh Edition (Springfield, MA: Merriam-Webster, Incorporated, 2007), 539.
[5] "Seniors network from the heart," *USA Today-Statesman Journal*, March 4, 2017, 6B.
[6] Marco R. Della Cava, "Social Networking: Too much of a good thing?" *USA Today, Statesman Journal*, February 15, 2010, 2D.
[7] Pew Research Center, Internet, Science & Tech, http://www.pewinternet.org/2016/11/11/social-media-update-2016/
[8] Joel Stein, "Tyranny of the Mob," *Time*, August 29, 2016, 27.
[9] Ibid., 28.
[10] Homophily ("love of the same") is the tendency of individuals to associate and bond with those sharing similar points of view, as in the proverb "birds of a feather flock together."
[11] "Twitter expands hate, abuse fight," *Corvallis Gazette-Times*, February 8, 2017, A10.
[12] Emerson T. Brooking and P.W. Singer, "War Goes Viral: How Social Media is Being Weaponized," *The Atlantic*, November 2016, 73-74.
[13] "A Peek Beneath the Hood of the Internet," *The Week*, April 29, 2016, 18.
[14] Ibid.

[15] "The hacking epidemic," *The Week*, November 4, 2016, 11.

[16] Ibid.

[17] Ibid.

[18] Ibid.

[19] Hacktivism is the subversive use of computers and computer networks to promote a political agenda.

[20] www.anonofficial.com

[21] "Bitcoins a new currency that was created in 2009 by an unknown person using the alias Satoshi Nakamoto. Transactions are made with no middle men—meaning, no banks! There are no transaction fees and no need to give your real name. More merchants are beginning to accept them. Bitcoins can be used to buy merchandise anonymously. Several marketplaces called 'bitcoin exchange' allow people to buy or sell bitcoins using different currencies." For more information visit http://money.cnn.com/infographic/technology/what-is-bitcoin/

[22] "Brownsville averts ransomware hack," *Corvallis Gazette-Times*, December 1, 2016, A2.

[23] Ibid.

[24] George Jahn and David Rising, "Munich shooter called a loner," *Corvallis Gazette-Times*, July 25, 2016, B6.

[25] BBC World News, *Oregon Public Broadcast*, March 12, 2017 at 1:35 am PST.

[26] "Gaming addiction set to be recognized as a mental health disorder," CDC Gaming Reports, Inc. https://www.cdcgamingreports.com/gaming-addiction-set-to-be-recognised-as-a-mental-health-disorder/

[27] Fia Curley, Associated Press, "Video game addicts can go to 'detox'," *Statesman Journal*, June 12, 2006, 1D, 6D.

[28] Sebastian de Assis, *rEvolution in Education* (Lanham, Maryland: The Rowman & Littlefield Publishing Group, 2003), 137.

The Love of Madness

L ove is a mighty force of nature. It manifests itself in a variety of expressive forms ranging from deep feelings to complex attitudes toward the meaning of affection. The Greeks called it "the madness of the gods" and classified it into six categories: *Eros* (sexual passion), *Philia* (deep friendship), *Ludus* (playful love) *Agape* (unconditional love), *Pragma* (longstanding love), and *Philautia* (love of the self).[1] In ancient Chinese culture (Confucianism) love was referred to as *Jen*, the Confucian ideal of cultivating humanity, or what Chu Hsi (1130–1200 A.D.), a famous Confucian scholar of the Sung Dynasty, defined as "the virtue of the soul, the principle of love, and the center of Heaven and Earth."[2] But regardless of definitions or cultural interpretations of what love means, this potent emotion exerts an enormous influence in human behavior—and there is plenty of both scientific and observational evidences that love affects other members of the animal kingdom as well.

As humanity and culture evolve, the nature, meaning, perception, and even the experience of love seem to change, too. The ineffable ecstatic feeling of affection and kinship may turn into something as mundane as casual fondness, which is exemplified in everyday statements such as "I love ice-cream," or "I love going to the coast." In reality, however, what's meant to convey is enjoyment and appreciation, which is not the same as the cascading emotions that come from the experience of love. But like everything else in the dysfunctional and self-consuming economic system we are enslaved to, love turns into a valuable emotional commodity that can be associated with products (jewelry, roses, etc.), marketing (advertisement, slogans, etc.), and manipulation (love as a tool of influence and control). Let's take a look at these different categories.

One of the most popular—and frivolous—holidays is Valentine's Day; the day to celebrate romantic love. Every year weeks before February 14, a wave of advertisements promoting the symbolic material representations of Eros love-mode crashes onto the helpless consumer. From expensive jewelries in heart-shaped designs to romantic dinners at the local restaurant, the commodity of love generates hundreds of millions of dollars in a single event alone. And of course there are numerous other occasions (weddings, anniversaries, birthdays, etc.) when love is commercially celebrated. I do not mean to disparage the material expression of love, but instead, to emphasize the economic function aspect of a potent human emotion. And because of the power and universality of this coveted experience, its marketing appeal can be as enticing as love sex appeal. In fact, it is compelling enough to drive even the motor vehicle industry.

After the Great Recession of 2008 when the tax payers of the United States bailed out the collapsing auto industry, car sales soon picked up again in unexpected fashion. By early 2016, the consulting firm IHS forecasted global vehicle sales to grow some 89.8 million, doubling the pace of 2015—and in the U.S. sales rose 5.7 percent to a record 17.5 million in 2015.[3] Amidst this great consumer market expansion, marketing experts decided to tap on the appeal of love to sell motor vehicles. Corporations like Subaru and Toyota jumped ahead of the competition with advertisements and slogans that capitalize on the commercial value of love. On a Subaru television advertisement, following the visual and narrative description stressing the car's features, the ad ends with the company's latest slogan: "Love is what makes Subaru a Subaru." Toyota is even more ingenious in developing its commercial love appeal. The car manufacturer runs a T.V. ad in which a family driving in a Toyota vehicle picks up a stranded man on the road in a rainy evening. It happens that the man is the referee whose incorrect decision had just cost the teenage boy riding in the backseat a game victory a few moments earlier. The ref sits in the back right next to the teen who seems to give in to forgiveness after his father's eyes showing on the rear mirror entreat the boy to let go of resentment. As the boy silently acquiesces, the slogan pops up on the screen: "Let's go compassion."

Evidently, the emotional appeal of love and its various ramifications (compassion, empathy, etc.) have proven to be effective in marketing strategies. And the scope of commercial campaigns ranges from trivial statements such as a soft drink's slogan "taste the feeling"[4] to egregiously deceitful claims, as it was the case of a bakery that claimed love as an actual ingredient to its granola bars.[5]

Then, there is love as a tool of influence and manipulation of individuals and groups in more personified manner—as distinct from marketing, which is a commercial form of manipulation. Both people and organizations—particularly of religious and political nature—make use of love to achieve desirable goals without any qualms. They play the love card as if it were the ace that gives them a winning hand. Either at the personal or organizational level, the strategy often involves imparting a slew of negative feelings such as guilt and fear in order to get results. An individual may invoke the infamous accusation "if you loved me you wouldn't do this" in an attempt to manipulate someone. A religious group is likely to question one's love of God—and the fear of His wrath—to keep the believer under control of the sect. And at the political level, the plea for unconditional love of country, regardless of the circumstances of national affairs, has proven to be disastrous in world history as it continues to pose a threat today. In fact, the surest way to becoming an abominable social pariah is by questioning or denying love of country.

Thus, love loses its spontaneous emotional nature and turns into a psychological subterfuge with which to manipulate as necessary. And when this powerful human emotion is removed from the metaphorical heart and shoved into the rationalizing head where it cannot empirically exist, the love of madness erupts with a vengeance.

❄

At the half-time show of the fiftieth Super Bowl on February 7, 2016, the most important sports event in the United States, three popular artists sang to a jubilant crowd the following lyrics: "we're gonna get together right now; we're gonna get together somehow." As they finished singing, words appeared in the back of the stadium that read: "Believe in love." It was at that moment that I wondered: what does it mean to believe in love without experiencing it within?

Psychologists, psychiatrists, sociologists, anthropologists, and educators have suggested in countless studies and numerous research papers that love is a "learned response, a learned emotion."[6] However, love is a type of learning that cannot happen in the mind, for it is impossible to experience love from an intellectual perspective. When someone says "I think I love Mary," you can rest assured that love is not what this person is questioning, because the potency of this human emotion is undeniably recognized whenever it is present, and therefore it leaves no room for intellectual doubting. Although love does not belong to the realm of the mind, many people "think they love," or perhaps they just wish they could. Many a religious person claims "to love the Lord," though the manifestation of misperceived love is purely intellectual; that is, based on the scriptures and the idealized concept of a Heavenly Father that is undetectable, unverified, and unreachable. In fact, in the dominant Western religious system, the love of God is essentially the same as the belief in God, in God's existence, God's justice, God's love. The love of God is essentially a thought experience.[7] And yet, despite professing to love an unidentifiable God, a significantly large number of believers seem indifferent and incapable to experience love for their struggling fellow-citizens. But if love is a "learned response, a learned emotion," how do we go about learning matters of the heart without engaging the mind in the process?

The German-American social psychoanalyst, Erich Fromm, offered a very reasonable answer to the conundrum of love as a teachable discipline. He identified it as an art form:

> "The first step to take is to become aware that love is an art, just as living is an art; if we want to learn how to love we must proceed in the same way we have to proceed if we want to learn any other art...What are the necessary steps in learning any art? The process of learning an art can be divided conveniently into two parts: one, the mastery of the theory; the other, the mastery of the practice... the practice of an art requires discipline. I shall never be good at anything if I do not do it in a disciplined way...If one wants to become a master in any art, one's whole life must be devoted to it, or at least related to it."[8]

Whether love is an art that can be learned or a spontaneous human emotion, the object of love is a fundamental element of the experience. And since we cannot give what we do not have, self-love, which is the opposite of love of self,[9] is the first step toward the experience of love. However, if the individual is corrupted by the external conditions of his environment, the object of love can transform the very nature of love itself. In fact, it may become an obsession cultivated by the mind instead of a genuine independent emotion; like the love of God as a thought experience. Thus, in a chaotic metamorphic process, self-love turns into selfishness as the individual becomes incapable of loving others, and they are not capable of loving themselves either.[10] The object of love becomes the centerpiece of an obsessive experience.

Selfishness, which is significantly magnified by the economic principles of capitalism, becomes both the source and object of a distorted perception of love as an intellectual experience. Whatever enhances the motivations of self-interest becomes the recipient of "love" attention; a narcissistic obsession with anything that aggrandizes the assessment of selfhood. At the societal level where individual selfishness is aggregated into a collective selfish unit—be it a family, community, nation, or even the human species at large—the misconstrued concept of love turns into a self-centered objective; like human fascination with science and technological developments that validate our hubris as intelligent animals. Thus, like the myth of Narcissus beholding his own beautiful reflection in a pool of water, humanity has fallen in love with its own achievements and abilities to conquer the natural world, albeit we've failed miserably to conquer ourselves. And like Narcissus whose obsession with his own physical attributes led him to his death, humanity's excessive enchantment with our god-like characteristics of dominating the environment, subjugating people, developing powerful technology and artificial intelligence is leading us to our own demise.

Alas, the self became the madness we fell in love with.

As the unrestrained pursuit of self-interest becomes the center of Western civilization's socioeconomic and political culture, the most powerful symbolic expression of its system of belief is money. Money is the hub that all the spokes of society latch on to, and without which nothing can be done. No wonder there are several popular sayings expressing both the importance and reverential attitude toward this indispensable economic tool: "money makes the world go around; money talks; made of money; show me the money;" among other idioms that reveal the vital importance of monetary power. Indeed, money is the indispensable must have, without which survival is compromised.

Considering the crucial role of money in modern industrial societies, people depend on it for their financial survival as much as they need oxygen to maintain the physical body alive. But while breathing is a natural spontaneous biological function that occurs effortlessly, the pursuit of money has become a maddening strenuous endeavor that engenders all sorts of stress, struggles, conflicts, betrayals, crimes, and wars. Money is the key that opens the iron door of the cage of daily labor drudgery; the passport to the coveted realm of financial freedom. Therefore, because of the imperative nature of its actual and symbolic value, money has become the foremost object of love. Whether it is explicitly acknowledged or not, money is the ultimate ambition of most people in the world, for it represents the materialization of the inherent human love for (financial) freedom.

From an economics standpoint, money has become a sort of a god that is worshipped by the disciples of the capitalism doctrine. The imbued power in its pragmatic value to acquire desired goods and services has transcended even the importance of religious beliefs in people's lives, for it is neither religion nor philosophy but money that is the barrier to human freedom, as Marx pointed out:

> "Money is the universal, self-constituted value of all things. Hence it has robbed the whole world, the human world as well as nature, of its proper value. Money is the alienated essence of man's labor and life, and this alien essence dominates him as he worships it."[11]

As the pursuit of money becomes the preeminent factor in socioeconomic life, unprecedented consequences have followed suit, both at the individual and societal level. Collectively, nations struggling to pay their debts to multinational financial institutions are compelled to allow their natural resources to be impounded by international banks. In order to pay just the interest on their rapidly growing debt, Third World countries mortgage their future by selling off their natural resources to greedy and unscrupulous creditors. For example, the largest South American nation—and ironically the ninth largest economy in the world—Brazil has been pressured to surrender much of its unique and irreplaceable national treasure to meet its financial obligations with the

International Monetary Fund and the World Bank. The renowned scientist and activist, David Suzuki, exposes this travesty of equating the ecosystem as disposable capital:

> "To keep up with a massive international debt, the country (Brazil) is destroying a unique world treasure: its rain forest. It is the richest ecosystem on Earth, home to much of the biological diversity of the planet and affects the atmosphere, soil, water cycles and climate in ways we don't understand. It is criminal to destroy those forests merely to service the interest on international debt, for when they are gone, Brazil will still be mired in debt."[12]

Functioning as the heart of the socioeconomic organism, money pumps the blood of prosperity into the lives of individuals and communities everywhere. Without the nutrients it supplies, the scourge of poverty takes over and miserable conditions ensue. Thus, because of its intrinsic and imperative necessity, money has become the most common object of love, obsession, and even idolatry. In most cases, it is the primary motivation in decision-making regarding education, employment, and in some cases marriages. And despite the unfavorable reputation attributed to money as a materialistic evil, its vital importance to survival may be equated to a sort of "economic Darwinism" in which money is what determines who's the fittest to survive in a highly competitive economic environment. There is no escaping the lure of money; and even sanctimonious moralists succumb to its irresistible temptation.

The holy book of Christianity abounds with passages referring to the deception of infatuation with money. In his first letter to his young disciple Timothy, the apostle Paul had this to say:

> "For the love of money is the root of all sorts of injurious things, and by reaching out for this love some have been led astray from the faith and have stabbed themselves all over with many pains."[13]

After such a stern warning, you would think that people everywhere—especially the cleric class—would heed these words with undivided attention and willingness to action. There would be an international movement to reevaluate the legitimacy of an economic system that is founded on the love of money. Questions would be raised about the "inalienable right" of unlimited accumulation of wealth of a few individuals who infringe on the inalienable rights to a dignified life for millions of others. People would realize at last that unfettered accumulation of wealth inevitably generates massive poverty to a vast majority that cannot compete against stronger contenders in the free marketplace. But like the young merchant who walked away after hearing Jesus' suggestions to dispose of his belongings and follow him on the path of genuine love,[14] we, too, have eschewed apostle Paul's warning as an unbearable inconvenience to our way of life. The love of money cannot be superseded—not even by the love of God.

❀

Whether the object of love is money, God, or a romantic liaison, love itself has its own inherent characteristics. This noble human sentiment—and there are countless evidences that animals are capable of experiencing it, too—has such a transformative power that might as well be the last hope for the survival of our industrial-technological civilization teetering on the edge of a self-destructive precipice. However, if love is to be considered as the only reasonable answer to the problem of human existence, then we must realize that radical changes in our socioeconomic structure will be required, if love is to become a social and not only a highly individualistic marginal phenomenon.[15] Perhaps, if we were to disregard the object of love and only focus on developing the ability to experience it at an expanded level, then we might be able to reverse—or at least mitigate—the impact of our self-inflicted tragedy. But considering the current state of indifference to our fellow brothers and sisters and our Mother Earth, which is amplified by the very tenets of capitalism (greed, selfishness, competition, etc.), the endeavor might prove to be rather daunting; unless, the art of loving can be taught.

According to Friedrich Nietzsche, learning to love is not only possible but necessary, especially at a time when divisiveness, hatred, and xenophobia are spreading like a wild fire across the political world:

> "We must learn to love, learn to be kind, and this from earliest youth; if education or chance give us no opportunity to practice these feelings, our soul becomes dry and unsuited even to understanding the tender inventions of loving people. Likewise, hatred must be learned and nurtured, if one wishes to become a proficient hater: otherwise the germ for that, too, will gradually wither."[16]

And learn to love we must, indeed, lest the demagogues and preachers of hatred take over the world stage to convince the uncouth masses that the enemy is "them," whoever they happen to be at the time. In the meantime, the self-serving politicians and preachers of religious dogmas continue propagating an unforgiving message of divisiveness with those who oppose or disagree with their creeds. Their intolerance and utter disregard to forgiveness contradict the very tenets they're supposed to observe; be it as a nation's values or the moral principles of religious sacred texts. It is what Wilhelm Reich called the "emotional plague of mankind,"[17] which has ravaged humanity from time immemorial and documented ever since the inception of written history. The innumerable contradictions reflect the madness of the human condition plagued by underdeveloped emotions:

> "One thinks himself the master of others, and still remains a greater slave than they...Man is born free, yet he goes through life as a slave...Man is born equal, but he does not grow equal. Man has created great teachings, yet each simple teaching has served his oppression. Man is the 'Son of God,' created in his image; yet man is 'sinful,' a prey of the 'Devil'...Humanity has developed many kinds of religions. Every single kind of religion turned into another way of suppression and misery...After thousands of years of concentration upon the riddle of the nature of man, humanity finds itself exactly where it started: with the confession of utter ignorance."[18]

The more I think about the madness that has taken over industrial-technological societies—and the love of this madness—the more I agree with Erich Fromm's conclusion that "love is the only sane and satisfactory answer to the problem of human existence."[19] Perhaps, if we were to effectuate the true meaning of our national values we'd be able to see through the fabric of the flag what it really represents: our people, without whom there is no nation. Thus, when citizens recite the pledge of allegiance in rote memory mode, if they were to be mindful of what "one nation, under God, indivisible, with liberty and justice for all" means, they'd be able to experience the indivisibility as an oneness with all citizens whose liberty and justice cannot be sustained without the basic needs of life. They'd understand the meaning of empathy and compassion; not through the analytical mind, but with the simple wisdom of their hearts; effortlessly.

As for religious morality, one single passage from a holy text should suffice to validate Fromm's claim that "love is the only sane and satisfactory answer to the problem of human existence," if only we could abide by the principle in earnest practice:

> "If I speak in the tongues of men or of angels, but do not have love, I am only a resounding gong or a clanging cymbal...Love is patient, love is kind. It does not envy, it does not boast, it is not proud. It does not dishonor others, it is not self-seeking, it is not easily angered, it keeps no record of wrongs...Love does not delight in evil but rejoices with the truth. It always protects, always trusts, always, hopes, always perseveres. Love never fails."[20]

If love never fails, then, perhaps, it has the potential to be the sane and satisfactory answer to an insane world in chaos. And yet, even the language of love seems incomprehensible and utterly impractical in a society characterized by all sorts of divisiveness and hatred. The hopeful aspiration is for love to become a form of emotional madness that is infectious and potentially become endemic. Maybe the satisfactory answer to the problem of human existence rests on the madness of love.

NOTES

[1] http://greece.greekreporter.com/2014/01/09/the-ancient-greeks-6-types-of-love/

[2] Ch'u Chai with Winberg Chai, *The Story of Chinese Philosophy* (New York: Washington Square Press, Inc., 1961), 24-25.

[3] "Global car sales pick up," *Corvallis Gazette-Times*, March 4, 2016, A8.

[4] On paper napkins handed out with drinks on United Airlines flights, a logo of Coca-Cola appears on the bottom left corner and underneath it reads: "taste the feeling."

[5] Eric Boehm, "FDA Warning to Bakery: You Can't Say There is 'Love' in Your Granola," October 3, 2017. http://reason.com/blog/2017/10/03/fda-warning-to-bakery-theres-no-love-in

[6] Leo Buscaglia, *Love* (New York: Ballantine Books, 1972), 55.

[7] Erich Fromm, *The Art of Loving* (New York: Harper & Row Publishers, Inc., 1989), 72-73.

[8] Ibid., 5, 98, 100.

[9] The distinction that Jean Jacques Rousseau makes between *amour-propre* and *amour de soi*. See Leo Damrosch, *Jean Jacques Rousseau, Restless Genius* (New York: Houghton Mifflin Company, 2005), 238.

[10] Erich Fromm, *The Art of Loving*, 55.

[11] Peter Singer, *MARX* (Great Britain: The Guernsey Press Co. Ltd., 1980), 18.

[12] David Suzuki, *The David Suzuki Reader* (Vancouver, British Columbia, Canada: Greystone Books, 2003), 96.

[13] Timothy 6:10, *The New World Translation of the Holy Scriptures* (New York: Watchtower Bible and Tract Society of New York, Inc., 1984), 1482.

[14] "Jesus said to him: if you want to be perfect, go sell your belongings and give to the poor and you will have treasure in heaven, and come be my follower," Matthew 18:21. *The New World Translation of the Holy Scriptures*, 1241.

[15] Erich Fromm, *The Art of Loving*, 119.

[16] Friedrich Nietzsche, *Human All Too Human* (Lincoln, Nebraska: University of Nebraska Press, 1986), 251.

[17] A plague indicates a highly contagious disease that can become epidemic (rapidly widespread) or pandemic (an epidemic throughout many countries). Thus, the emotional plague of mankind that Reich alludes to is driven by intolerance, hatred, and a maddening compulsion to control and manipulate people's lives.

[18] Wilhelm Reich, *The Murder of Christ* (New York: Farrar, Straus and Giroux, 1971), 1-2.

[19] Erich Fromm, *The Art of Loving*, 120.

[20] Corinthians 13:1-8

The Madness of Love

D espite its undeniable reputation as the most transformative sentiment human beings can experience, there is an inherent element of madness to love. Indeed, this most powerful emotion can literally drive a man mad. Like hunger or thirst that must be satiated in order to ward off a complete breakdown of the physical body, the irrepressible need for love must be attended to, lest it can wreak havoc with the well being of the individual. But unlike the biological necessity for food and water, the absence of the essential emotional nutrient of love can have devastating consequences to both individuals and groups, be it families, communities, nations, or the human population at large. Perhaps, the sanity we've been so desperately looking for may lie dormant in the madness of love.

Considering the nefarious characteristics of human nature, it is astonishing that people are capable of loving; not love in the selfishly limiting romantic experience or love of close family members—or even love of pets for that matter—but the ability to expand the emotional ripples of love to the outer circles of the self. It seems like an almost impossible task, for in a socioeconomic culture that fosters selfishness and incites the pursuit of self-interest, it is absolutely remarkable that some people are capable of caring for their fellow humans beings with genuine spontaneity. In fact, when taking into account how much the tenets of capitalism aggravate the wicked nature of the human species, the ability of people to love outside their private sphere indicates an abnormality that can only be identified as madness: a state of extreme folly; a bona fide psycho-emotional illness.

Therefore, it is understandable that a traditional conservative citizen would ridicule someone afflicted by the madness of love. After all, how could a "normal" mainstream person whose values are buttressed on economic principles even attempt to fathom the actions of a loving tree hugger? In the eyes of a businessman, trees are but raw material to be plucked out of the Earth as fast as they can build houses in the sprawling suburbia of megalopolises. It means development, expansion, and of course, profit. Conversely, a tree hugger doesn't see a tree—he feels it. Both cognitively and emotionally, he understands that a tree is a live being whose roots spread underground as its branches reach out to the expansive blue sky. Some of them, like the giant sequoias at Calaveras Big Trees State Park in Northern California, are more than a thousand-years-old. And the tree hugger knows that they are the habitat to numerous species that depend on them for their survival; birds, beasts, and bees that have the same inalienable right to exist as we all do. And tree huggers may be mad but they are not stupid. They understand the importance of harvesting trees for human needs; they only wished it would be carried out with a great deal of ecological responsibility. But from the logging industry standpoint, anything that hinders or curtails the harvesting of timber is an affront to the basic principles of free market economics.

It is true that in our industrial-technological society the act of hugging a tree—or any other display of affection toward a non-animal species—is looked down upon according to the rationality of our cultural norms. Perhaps the only exception to this habitual judgment is when illustrious members of society publicly acknowledge complicity to the "folly" of communicating with nature. The likes of Hermann Hesse (1877–1962), the German author and Nobel Prize winner for literature, or the transcendentalist writer Henry David Thoreau (1817–1862), they can get away with making statements like the ones below:

"Trees are sanctuaries. Whoever knows how to speak to them, whoever knows how to listen to them, can learn the truth. They do not preach learning and precept, they preach undeterred by particulars, the ancient law of life"[1] –Hermann Hesse

"I frequently tramped eight or ten miles through the deepest snow to keep an appointment with a beech-tree, or a yellow birch, or an old acquaintance among the pines."[2] –Henry David Thoreau

Yes, these remarkable men of letters can pen words of madness without being ridiculed by mainstream society. But if an idealistic young woman resolutely sets camp on an ancient redwood tree to draw attention to the preservation of old growth forests, she is portrayed in the media as an oddity, albeit she accomplished her goal.[3] For the rest of us, however, expressing feelings for a tree, plant, or flower will likely be deemed as an act of mild insanity. After all, there is an irrational component to the madness of love.

As it was observed in the previous chapter, there are several types of love. Although each is distinct in nature, they all share a common characteristic: irrationality, which makes sense since love is not governed by reason; instead, it is an ineffable sentiment ruled by the realm of human emotions. The illogical aspect of love can be clearly observable in three specific domains where it manifests its fervor: romantic, patriotic, and religious.

Just as the human body operates mostly in involuntary biological functions (breathing, heartbeat, etc.), so is love an involuntary reaction of the figurative emotional body. In evolved individuals—or what in Eastern thought is called enlightened—the manifestation of love is expressed in a broad scope of feelings ranging from empathy for the suffering of others to devotion to a worthy cause.[4] But in romantic love, the unrestrained passion turns into a neurological condition that showers the brain with all sorts of chemical reactions. It becomes a veritable biological function in which nature ensures the continuity of the species through an uncontrollable desire for deep union, therefore triggering an irresistible craving for sexual intercourse and gratification. Contrary to Aristotle's popular quote that "love is composed of a single soul inhabiting two bodies," in the physical manifestation of love, two independent individuals connect as one body. And because of this soul and physical connection, the intertwining nature of romantic love generates a great deal of separation anxiety, fear of loss of love, among other potentially obsessive reactions that, depending on the intensity of the fixation, may easily be characterized as obsessive compulsive disorder, an addiction, or a plain mental disorder.[5] It legitimizes the popular expression "falling madly in love."

Similarly to the devotional nature of romantic love in which two people surrender their beings to the other, patriotic or nationalistic love is a quintessential manifestation of the madness of love. While in romantic love two separate individuals become one, in patriotic love one lonely citizen merges with a national collective identity that empowers his isolated existence within the society he belongs. Also, like in romantic love, people who give in to nationalistic affection tend to disregard all the imperfections, faults, and blemishes of their country without questioning the morality of their government and politicians' actions. They pay homage to the symbols of the nation, sing the national anthem with utmost reverence, and pledge allegiance to the flag without any concerns about who or what represents the banner at a particular time. Patriotic love, then, is but idolatrous love; a hollow and mawkish feeling bereft of genuine sentiments of love; love for the nation and its people. Thus, if romantic love is *folie à deux* (madness of two), patriotic love is *folie à beaucoup de monde* (madness of the crowd). This insane collective psychosis is fostered by powerful special interest groups lurking behind governmental infrastructures that manipulate the masses' instincts and emotions at will—as Joseph Goebbels did for Nazi Germany as its minister of propaganda. Today, the dissimulating apparatus of propaganda has become an essential tool with which to imbue citizens with a maudlin sense of patriotism:

> "Media domination and massive propaganda is an absolute necessity for the government. The government could have all the bombs and money in the world, but without control of the public mind they could not behave as they do. If the general population were to become of the true motives and outcomes of the actions of corporations and politicians, the greed and corruption would be extremely minimized."[6]

And what better way to manipulate hearts and minds but through the irrationality of blind patriotism. You don't have to be a genius like Albert Einstein (1879–1955) to figure out what he did—or at least acknowledge the truism of his words:

> "Private capitalists inevitably control, directly or indirectly, the main sources of information. It is thus extremely difficult, and indeed in most cases quite impossible, for the individual citizen to come to objective conclusions and to make intelligent use of his political rights."[7]

Indeed, in the bogus irrational love for the "fatherland" lies one of the most serious dangers to authentic national interest. A purported love of country that does not involve love of its people is nothing but a *folie à beaucoup de monde* (madness of the crowd); an overly used—and highly successful—tool of manipulation of the intellectually maladroit masses. It is akin to the irrational religious love of God whose most believers seem neither to embrace nor take into account the love of His children.

The madness of love reaches its pinnacle in the love of an impersonal God who abides in the invisible realm of heaven. The mighty—and wrathful—numinous being is the figment of humanity's terrified collective mind tormented by the insecurity of the unknown. In fact, it's not even love; it is an irrational desperate drive triggered by a bewildering fear of abandonment, like a child's sense of helplessness.[8] The overwhelming anxiety that the prospect of death generates demands a support system; and God, the Heavenly Father, is the stalwart figure people can lean on for solace and safety. As Voltaire (1694 – 1778) said, "If God did not exist, it would be necessary to invent him."

❧

By definition, love is a "strong affection for another arising out of kinship or personal ties."[9] Thus, it seems that in order to develop a strong affection, the object of the projected emotion must be at least remotely real, which the rationalization of an impersonal God does not substantiate. It is this adulterated concept of love—one that cannot be experienced in earnest—that makes it irrational. If a psychiatric patient were to proclaim to love someone he does not know, can't see, and never met, he would be medicated for whatever medical condition is causing his delusion. Perhaps this is the reason behind Marx's notorious quote referring to religion as the opium of the people. But on the other hand, if we take into consideration the "kinship or personal ties" aspect of the definition of love, we realize that the only way we can love the idea of God is through His creation; the only feasible kinship in the process. Either is love for nature, animals, or our fellow humans—the latter being the unfeigned possibility to experience unadulterated love—it allows for loving God in a vicarious and yet tangible experience. But unfortunately, as Ludwig Feuerbach (1804–1872) astutely observed, the concept of God became a delusional palliative for human imperfection:

> "We project all our own unrealized perfection onto an imaginary non-human entity, God, instead of concerning ourselves with the realizable improvement of our fellow human beings."[10]

If loving an impersonal and invisible figment of imagination were not disturbing enough, when this object of love is an almighty wrathful entity that a God-loving nation claims to be "God's own country,"[11] the consequences can be literally explosive. This association with imaginary divine power bestows the rights and responsibilities to wield that power according to the needs and conveniences of "God's chosen nation." The following excerpt from the *Operation Crossroads* in 1946 (the code name to the U.S. military nuclear test of two atomic bombs in the Bikini atoll) illustrates the point:

> "Having found the atomic bomb, we have used it. It's an awful responsibility that has come to us. We thank God that it has come to us instead of our enemies. And we pray the He many guide us to use it in His way and for His purpose...The United States wants to use this great destructive power for the benefit of mankind."[12]

Alas, with so much destructive power in the hands of such a psychologically and emotionally unstable species, it is no wonder that the God-loving people also purport to be God-fearing. However, what at first seems to be a farfetched duality (why would one fear a loving being?), the madness of love is strangely characterized by suffering, therefore the association of love and fear; fear of pain and punishment, which generates dreadful anxiety for those who venture to love.

⚬

There is no way around it: the relationship between love and pain is as real as it is inevitable. Many poets at different times and places have stressed the agonizing experience that love—mostly the end of it—exerts in the human being. Although these sensitive artists of letters tend to refer to romantic love when alluding to the sorrow it creates, I hypothesize that the fear of love has infiltrate all other possibilities of the experience. Because love is such a powerful emotion that we cannot control, the vulnerability it creates becomes a clear and present danger to the brave souls who venture into this treacherous territory. And to make matters worse, once this inebriating sentiment takes root in the heart, the mind is overridden and rendered futile in any effort to avoid the inevitable. French philosopher Blaise Pascal (1623–1662) illustrated this argument in his famous statement:

> "The heart has its reasons, which reason knows nothing of...We know the truth not only by the reason, but by the heart."[13]

Regardless of the predisposition or courage required to love, the undeniable truth is that love offers an exceptional opportunity for knowledge and growth. It is as though the inherent nature of the relationship between love and pain begot a unique power that wouldn't be possible to acquire otherwise. Indeed, the grief that love engenders can be so poignant that even the valiant adventurers of knowledge can be torn asunder; and yet, they do not shy away from the challenge. It's very likely that they have figured out the underlying truth sustaining the words of English poet Lord Byron (1788–1824):

> "But grief should be the instructor of the wise. Sorrow is knowledge: they who know the most must mourn the deepest."[14]

And despite the pain, the pursuit of comprehensive knowledge of what it means to be human makes it all worth it. After all, love is one of the most demanding teachers of all; and even when it is not present, it has always something important to teach.

❀

It is undeniable by logic, observation, and experience that love is a unifying emotional energy. However, in the absence of it, a vacuum of developmental inertia grows in the symbolic human heart as this most powerful emotional energy becomes inactive. When this happens, the individual becomes indifferent and more selfish in his life's pursuits; except when his interests extend to the few in the inner circles of his concerns. At the collective level, patriotic fervor runs ablaze among love-starved citizens whose emptiness needs to be filled with an adulterated concept of love, which in reality is but an irrational drive disguised as an emotion. It is the madness of love when love is in absentia.

As the love-deprived individual imprisons himself behind the bars of selfishness, the group coalesces into Collective Solipsism[15] (extreme egocentrism). It becomes a disjointed aggregation of isolated egocentric selves forming a dysfunctional social entity with collective personality disorder. Deluded into believing that the self is the only existent thing, the hundreds of millions of demented egocentrics continue on their desperate search for unity. Thus, they reach out to all sorts of affiliations, which patriotic and religious are the most common, influential— and dangerous--of them all. But they still come out short, for the love of country, God, ideology, or any other element that does not involve a tangible object of love that does rely on the realm of the intellect is insufficient to fill in the emptiness of being. The unity that begs to be fulfilled can only be achieved in the connection with the whole of life. It is the key that unlocks the door of the imprisonment of an egocentric self. Albert Einstein demonstrated this concept in a simple statement:

> "A human being is a part of a whole...[but] he experiences himself, his thoughts and feelings as something separated from the rest...This delusion is a kind of prison for us, restricting us to our personal desirers and to affection for a few persons nearest to us. Our task must be to free ourselves from this prison by widening our circle of compassion to embrace all living creatures and the whole of nature in its beauty."[16]

Perhaps the art of music can best illustrate the process of finding, fostering, and fulfilling the experience of wholeness with the higher object of love; in this case music itself. First, the musician falls in love with an instrument that he becomes agog to be proficient. He dedicates himself to daily practice of his art until he's mastered all of its cadences and nuances. After learning how to get the most out of his musical tool, he is able to create and perform beautiful music. Then, once this necessary individualistic goal is achieved, he's now ready to join a band or orchestra, and he will play for the sake of experiencing the collective joy of harmonious interaction with fellow musicians. The ultimate objective, however, is to deliver an outstanding performance for the listening pleasures of the audience while consumed by the joy of being—a musician.

A similar process to this analogy of music as love itself can be reflected in human societies. First the individual must find, cultivate, and excel in the art of loving (borrowing Erich Fromm's term). Once he's mastered the art within himself, he'll be eager to express it in the community where other likeminded people long for the same, which is to create a harmonious performance that demonstrates how the music of life ought to be composed, performed, and, of course, enjoyed by all the participants. It may sound utopian and perhaps even maudlin, but if we are to be liberated from the prison of selfishness the collective action is imperative. No matter how masterful a musician may be, it is impossible for him to produce orchestral music alone; and life is one ginormous ensemble.

However, because of the inherent connection between love and pain, performing the music of love requires a great deal of courage.

Firstly, it is important to understand what courage is and what it is not. According to some illustrious philosophers such as Kierkegaard, Nietzsche, Camus and Sartre, courage is not the absence of despair, but the capacity to move ahead in spite of despair. Courage is not mere stubbornness either. Neither is it a virtue or value among other personal values like love or fidelity, but the foundation that underlines and gives reality to all other virtues and personal values. Without courage our love pales into mere dependency, and our fidelity becomes mere conformism. In human beings courage is necessary to make being and becoming possible.[17]

Courage is a matter of the heart, as the etymology of the word indicates (it derives from the French word *coeur*, which means heart). Conversely, what triggers the need for courage is rooted in the mind, mainly fear and anxiety. Analogically speaking, fear and anxiety are like Siamese siblings who are not separated but each has his own individual characteristics. There is, indeed, a subtle and yet distinct difference between these two destructive mental processes. While fear has a definite object that can be rationalized, confronted, and endured through courage, anxiety is a mind-generated feeling of helplessness that has no particular object (you can be anxious about something, but not of something). In essence, anxiety is but fear of the unknown,[18] which cannot be counteracted by courage, but only through resilience, self-discipline, and determination. Courage can meet every object of fear, but this is not so with anxiety.

Thus, the question of love as an act of courage lies between what is a matter of the heart (courage) and the mind (fear and anxiety). In the same token, love is also a matter of individual and collective experience, both of which requires the courage to accept the pain that love brings, as well as the mentally-produced anxiety of the anticipation of the eventual loss. This seems to be quite clear when it comes to the individual experience of love: the heart expands in the surrendering to the emotion while the mind recoils in fear. But what does it mean when it refers to a collective experience of love?

According to renowned Brazilian educator, Paulo Freire, it all begins with dialogue. He observes that dialogue is a unique human phenomenon whose purpose in the experience of love is to transform the world. He cautions, however, that dialogue cannot exist in the absence of a profound love for the world and for people:

> "Because love is an act of courage, not of fear, love is commitment to others. No matter where the oppressed are found, the act of love is commitment to their cause—the cause of liberation. And this commitment, because it is loving, is dialogical. As an act of bravery, love cannot be sentimental; as an act of freedom, it must not serve as pretext for manipulation. It must generate other acts of freedom; otherwise it is not love. Only by abolishing the situation of oppression is it possible to restore the love which that situation made impossible."[19]

That situation meaning indifference, which is fomented by the absence of love; love as a commitment to others. Only when the apathy toward the welfare of every person, nature, and the reverence for life itself is overcome will love as an empathetic force be restored. And because the oppressors who dehumanize others and violate their rights become dehumanized themselves by default, it is only the oppressed who by freeing themselves can free their oppressors from being dehumanized[20] by the sordid actions they carry out against love, freedom, and the dignity of justice.

In the end, the ultimate essence of the madness of love is its digression from the norm. After all, caring and compassion do not go well with a socioeconomic culture that promotes excessive egoistic individualism. Empathy is not good for business—greed is! To love as a higher manifestation of the intelligence of the evolved human is not something the alienated masses and their oppressors can fathom. Worse yet, love as a condition in which the happiness of another person is essential to your own, as American writer Robert A. Heilein (1907–1988) suggested, is an utterly incomprehensible experience for those consumed by their own selfishness. They are capable of loving only those within the narrow confinements of their troubled hearts, narrowed minds, and small circles. However, they are very much capable of pretending to care, granted that the caring yields handsome financial returns. And when love mingles with riches the consequences can be disastrous.

Undoubtedly, one of the most brilliant literary examples of such a tragedy is the story of King Lear. Through the inspiration of his genius, Shakespeare created the monarch who after reigning for many years gets ready to retire. In an act of supreme foolishness, King Lear decides to divvy up his kingdom into three parts, giving the largest share to the daughter who convinces him she loves him the most. Lear's two oldest daughters, the selfish, greedy, and untrustworthy Goneril and Regan, do everything in their power to convince their father of their abiding love. The youngest girl, Cordelia, the one who genuinely loves her father "as a daughter should," refuses to participate in this thoughtless game of display of affection. Displeased with her lackluster but honest retort, King Lear cuts Cordelia off without a dime and divides his kingdom between the oldest daughters. But as soon as he signs off his realm to Goneril and Regan, they team up to deprive him of his courtiers, servants, his dignity, and eventually his sanity. Mad, alone, homeless, and helpless, he dies of a broken heart while cradling his youngest loving daughter's lifeless body in his arms. Alas, in the throe of his sorrow he learns that love of wealth can be a treacherous dagger that kills authentic love. "Oh, that way madness lies: let me shun that,"[21] Lear whimpered in disgrace as he realizes that dwelling on the injury (the treachery of his two elder daughters) would drive him mad.

Perhaps if it were possible to teach love as an experience, instead of having to rely on the rationalization of this powerful emotion, King Lear and all non-fictitious characters in the world would recognize love without needing intellectual or rhetorical validation. They would be able to exercise the experience of love as a natural expression of their humanity, either they're giving or receiving love. One can only imagine how many Shakespearean-like tragedies caused by the absence of love could be avoided—and how many people could be spared from the madness of not knowing how to love. But unfortunately, the educational system has become an indispensable appendage of the economic system. It does not exist to educate and empower students, but to train and prepare them to fulfill an economic function.

Alas, the ultimate purpose of modern education is to promote the education of madness.

NOTES

[1] Lisa Purcell, Editor, *Trees, A Photographic Celebration* (New York: Metro Books, 2007), 59.

[2] Ibid., 494.

[3] Activist Julia Butterfly Hill lived in a canopy atop an ancient redwood tree for 738 days to call attention to save the redwoods in Humboldt County, California. From December 10, 1997 to December 18, 1999, Julia "perched" on Luna, the name given to the tree, as she succeeded to gain international attention for the cause of old growth forest preservation. She chronicled her activism in her book *The Legacy of Luna: The Story of a Tree, a Woman, and the Struggle to Save the Redwoods.*

[4] A typical example of love to a worthy cause is illustrated in Ernesto "Che" Guevara's quote: *"Déjeme decirle, a riesgo de parecer ridículo, que el revolucionario verdadero está guiado por grandes sentimientos de amor."* (Let me say, at the risk of seeming ridiculous, that the true revolutionary is guided by great feelings of love.)

[5] Tara Parker-Pope, "Is It Love or Mental Illness? They're Closer Than You Think*," The Wall Street Journal*, February 13, 2007, https://www.wsj.com/articles/SB117131067930406235

[6] Kennie Anderson, *Land of Hypocrisy* (Black Hawk, SD: Progressive Productions, 2003), 10.

[7] Ibid., 10.

[8] Sigmund Freud once told Carl Gustav Jung that he had got the heart of religion: it was founded in the child's sense of helplessness. See Sigmund Freud, *The Future of an Illusion* (New York: W. W. Norton & Company, 1989), xxiii.

[9] *Merriam-Webster's Collegiate Dictionary*, Eleventh Edition (Springfield, MA: Merriam-Webster, Inc., 2007), 737.

[10] For an excellent and comprehensive analysis of the concept of God in particular and Christianity in general, refer to Ludwig Feuerbach, *The Essence of Christianity* (New York: Prometheus Books, 1989).

[11] Sigmund Freud, *The Future of an Illusion*, 24.

[12] Excerpted from Robert Stone's film documentary *Radio Bikini* (Los Angeles: Docurama, 2003).

[13] Blaise Pascal, *Pensées* (London: J. M. Dent & Sons, Ltd., 1960), 59.

[14] Lord Byron, *The Works of Lord Byron* (Denmark: Wordsworth Edition, Ltd., 1994), 380.

[15] Collective Solipsism is a term I coined to describe the disjointed aggregation of egocentric selves forming a dysfunctional group with collective personality disorder and identity crisis.

[16] As quoted in the epigraph of Maia Szalavitz and Bruce D. Perry, M.D, Ph.D., Born for Love: Why Empathy is Essential—and Endangered (New York: Harper Collins Publishers, Inc., 2010).

[17] Rollo May, *The Courage to Create* (New York: W. W. Norton & Company, 1994), 12-13.

[18] Paul Tillich, *The Courage to Be* (New Haven, Connecticut: Yale University Press, 2000), 36-37.

[19] Paulo Freire, *Pedagogy of the Oppressed* (New York: The Continuum Publishing Company, 1996), 70-71.

[20] Ibid., 38.

[21] William Shakespeare, *The Complete Works of William Shakespeare*, King Lear, Act III Scene IV (New York: Outlet Book Company, Inc., 1975), 992.

The Education of Madness

Etymologically, the word education comes from the Latin word *educatio* and the verb *educare*, which essentially means the act to create, to guide and to conduct. But that is in terms of semantics. Some modern educators might argue that education is the art of learning the utilization of knowledge; a pragmatic and functional knowledge that must serve the dominant cultural system. Looking back into history ought to be the first step to take toward understanding how the education of madness developed.

Since ancient Greece, education has been one of the most powerful social forces responsible for forging Western civilization. It has been also a fundamental tool of indoctrination and domination under the control of powerful socioeconomic-political structures such as empires, states, religions, etc. And even though noteworthy progress has been made in field of education, it has mostly been in intellectual and technical knowledge, while insignificant attention has been given to the complex development of the whole human being: mind, heart, and spirit. Thus, the comprehensive evolutionary possibilities of humankind have been considerably hampered by a utilitarian educational system.

After the fall of the Roman Empire, the system of theology and philosophy known as Scholasticism emerged in medieval Europe. This educational system was based on the central idea that reason and faith were compatible; a shrewd maneuver to rationalize the dogma of the Church and authenticate faith as knowledge. It was not until the Renaissance period that the supremacy of Scholasticism was confronted, followed by the economic development of the New World, which opened up educational opportunities once reserved exclusively for the clergy, nobility, and the ruling class.[1] However, it was the advent of the Industrial Revolution that forever altered the meaning, goals, and purpose of education. In fact, the Industrial Revolution set off an educational revolution of its own, as economic expansion demanded the production of qualified labor in "factory schools." It turned education into economic functionalism. It transformed the individual learner into a receptacle of information as part of training to fulfill an economic function. This is what Brazilian educator Paulo Freire classifies as the "banking" concept of education in which the students are the depositories and the teacher the depositor of data.[2] But you don't have to be an expert in education to understand this concept; even poets know about it, as William Butler Yates (1865–1939) expressed: "Education is not the filling of a pail, but the lighting of a fire."

As the Industrial Revolution evolved and merged with the Electronic Revolution, so did the educational system supporting the objectives of a new socioeconomic reality. In this process, education was geared toward the acquisition of specialized knowledge with the purpose of fulfilling economic functions; a materialist concept of education that has led pseudo educationalists to refer to the gains of education as "intellectual capital."[3] In the meantime, as human life becomes more and more centralized in the economic objectives of production and consumption, the comprehensive development of both the individual and society has remained stagnant. Actually, based on the current world situation, it seems that the human spirit has been deteriorating faster than the environment; the latter being the consequence of the former.

In order to keep up with the fast-growing needs of the expanding economic system, the National Society for the Promotion of Industrial Education was organized in 1906 in the United States to advocate for vocational education.[4] However, toward the end of the 1900s the economic-driven focus of preparatory education veered toward the earliest level of schooling, as young children were robbed of the innocence of childhood by the need to prepare for the demanding high-skills necessary to compete in the cut-throat job market awaiting them in the future. Hence, childhood became the collateral damage of the education of madness.

❀

I once saw a cartoon in the newspaper of a mother dropping her child off at an elementary school. Standing on the sidewalk with a disenchanted expression, the child turns to her mother and says: "You can make my body go to school, but my soul will be outside running through sprinklers." I was supposed to laugh at the comic nature of the cartoon; instead, I was saddened by the recollection of my own childhood experiences. I remembered the numerous times in my early "educational" years when I bemoaned going to school against my will. In fact, I still marvel at my resilience to overcome what should have been an utter disgust for education, or as Mark Twain said, "I never let schooling interfere with my education." Therefore, it should not come as a surprise that most children hate going to school.

The cry for help is resonating everywhere. Youngsters seem to be so desperate that they're even reaching out to columnist advisors in the media, as the case below illustrates:

"My life is boring, repetitive and I am often depressed," a 15-year-old wrote to a popular syndicated newspaper advisor. "Every day is the same: Get up, go to a long day of school, come home, do homework, play video games, draw, go to bed...My social skills are borderline nonexistent. My entire life is school...I need help, some advice, something, ANYthing!"5

As it is, children's education is but a tedious preamble of things to come; a preview of what to expect in the grown up years. Indeed, schooling has become an oppressive training for the drudgery that awaits in the future. It's become a factory of functional cogs that will replace the worn out ones in the complex economic machinery. The educational system does not—and cannot—foster independent critical thinking, for that poses a threat to the upper layers of the "mother system" it's meant to serve: the dominant socioeconomic system. Although freedom and spontaneity in education would greatly benefit individual and social development, it is not in the best selfish interest of powerful economic forces dictating the needs of the labor market. To the contrary, an education that operates on the basic assumption that a "man's ontological vocation (a genuine calling of the soul) is to be a subject who acts upon and transforms his world, and in so doing moves toward ever new possibilities of fuller and richer life individually and collectively"6 could not be tolerated by a dull and oppressive educational system, as teacher and writer Grace Llewellyn (1964–) explains:

"If we encourage teenagers to seek visions, democracy would get a boost, but the powers of mass production and rat racing consumerism would take a dive. We would see that far too much of what we accept as 'reality' is a blasphemy against true reality. Since our consumptive culture is out of balance with the rest of the universe, it would look very bad under the inspection of visionary young people. Get it? Western civilization does not invite its young to seek visions, because those visions would force a big change."[7]

Therefore, instead of establishing an educational system in which the fundamental issues of our grave socioeconomic, political, environmental, and existential challenges are openly discussed among the youth—the inheritors of the gargantuan problems left behind by their antecessors—education becomes a powerful tool of manipulation and perpetuation of the defunct status quo. And it starts at very young age.

"Teaching Kids How Business Works." That's the catch phrase of a newspaper advertisement for Junior Achievement, an organization that delivers "educational" materials in work-readiness, entrepreneurship, financial literacy for children from kindergarten to high-school. "The curriculum we've designed teaches children the value of the free enterprise system and helps them understand business and economics."[8] On the organization's website, the students' testimonials reveal the indoctrination strategy of turning youngsters into functional cogs of an exasperating economic system. "Junior Achievement reinforced concepts for me to remember later in life,"[9] says a satisfied student. Underneath the display of fade away students' testimonials, a slew of corporation logos, ranging from ExxonMobil and Fidelity Investment to UPS and Coca-Cola, scroll sideways evincing the backers of this economic training program. And of course, there are many other clever "educational opportunities" for children as young as kindergarteners to become money savvy.

Ally Financial, a large financial services corporation, developed a "teaching kids the value of money program" for little children to learn about money. The book that spearheads the program is titled *Planet Zeee and the Money Tree*, an unimaginative story that takes a "child on an intergalactic adventure with kids from planet Zeee as they learn important money lessons from their Earthling friends." The inert tale is touted as a "tool to help parents and educators to teach children the fundamentals of learning, saving and growing money."[10] And in order to reinforce and validate their initiative, Ally Financial sponsored a survey to back the argument of an unfulfilled educational need. According to the results of their survey, parents want their children to be financially savvy, though they are not doing a good job at it. Those loving and caring parents who are themselves lost in the economic madness that rules the world want their children to prosper financially, too. Thus, they buy into the indoctrinating argument that you should "start young and tell [your children] that the bank is looking after the money you earn. Handing out pocket change starting when children are about 3 can help them understand that money has value and can even be used to buy things they want."[11] If parents manage to do a good job initiating their children to the importance of economics, by the time they are in first-grade they'll be ready to learn how to manage portfolios.

A public elementary school on the South Side of Chicago has turned into an experiment in financial literacy with real-life oomph: each incoming first-grade class gets $20,000 that the children ultimately get to pick stocks for and manage. The Ariel School is the brain child of Ariel Capital Management firm that established the school in 1996 to teach the basics of investing and the fundamental principles of free market capitalism—to 6-year-old children! The rational supporting the initiative is based on the fact that as pensions are being phased out, people must rely on their own investments smarts, and therefore it should become an integral part of the curriculum at schools across the country. The newly formed President's Advisory Council on Financial Literacy is among those advocating that personal finance be required teaching at every elementary school.[12] The concept has gone mainstream education and financial institutions embrace it with unbridled enthusiasm. In fact, it has become so much a part of the educational system that April is now celebrated as the Youth Financial Literacy Month.

In fairness, in a culture in which economics sits at the top of the pyramid of values, preparing young children to manage what their livelihoods will depend on seems like a step in the right direction. But that's exactly where the root of the problem lies. Education is not supposed to be a mere economic development tool; a training program to adjust, mold, and fit children into a machinery of production and consumption. As it is, education has become a mechanistic system of production of workforce-ready laborers. If education will ever reverse from the path of utilitarian madness, it will have to adopt a humanistic educational mod-

el in which the development of humankind—not the economic system--
is the ultimate beneficiary of the educational process. As long as we continue to equate education with profits instead of progress, both our individual and collective development will be severely hampered, which at
this critical stage in human history it may prove to be irreversibly disastrous. And so it might well be, for education is a powerful economic
force in and by itself that shall not relinquish its self-serving objectives.

From kindergarten to graduate school, education is a multi-billion
dollar industry. Considering the great economic influence of the business of education and the extraordinary impact it has on economic development, it is obvious that the educational system is a very well safe-
guarded institution. But by whom? We can dilute the question of whose
invisible hand controls the educational system by eliminating those who
certainly do not: students, teachers, parents, and the general public obviously don't. Neither do scholars, academics, intellectuals, and artists.
We may concur that the Department of Education is the organization in
charge of the educational system. Possibly in charge, but definitely not
in control, which brings us back to the original question.

According to distinguished English philosopher Bertrand Russell,
the wish to preserve the past rather than the hope of creating the future
dominates the minds of those who control the teaching of the young. He
asserted that education was a political institution, which the hope for
social reconstruction depends on.[13] Therefore, he refused to compromise with any restriction in freedom of expression, censorship, persecution, or any other means of control over education, otherwise education
produces belief instead of thought. When education becomes mechanical, stifled, and standardized, there is the risk of "training" youngsters
to understand knowledge from a purely utilitarian point of view. In essence, education becomes a powerful tool for manipulation of ideas;
and that is an egregious violation of the basic principles of freedom,
democracy, and human rights.

❀

On December 10, 1948 the General Assembly of the United Nations
adopted and proclaimed the Universal Declaration of Human Rights.
This document came on the footsteps of one of the most violent times in
human history: The Second World War; the turning point to the awareness that we might not get another chance for human reconciliation.

Although the strong rhetoric in the preamble of the Declaration refers to "equal and inalienable rights of all members of the human family," and "everyone is entitled to all the rights and freedoms set forth in this Declaration, without distinction of any kind," like in other similar documents it falls short in the actualization of the language. In fact, Article 25 Clause 1 of the Declaration reflects the actual discrepancy between the words and the reality of the vast majority of humans:

> "Everyone has the right to a standard of living adequate for the health and well-being of himself and of his family, including food, clothing, housing and medical care and necessary social services, and the right to security in the event of unemployment, sickness, disability, widowhood, old age, or other lack of livelihood in circumstances beyond his control."[14]

It might have been fortuitous that this article is followed by the one dealing with education. After all, you cannot afford to get an education without having your basic needs properly in place, though hundreds of thousands of children heroically endure the challenge every day. Nevertheless, the striking point in Article 26 dealing with education lies in Clause 2:

> "Education shall be directed to the full development of the human personality and to the strengthening of respect for human rights and fundamental freedoms. It shall promote understanding, tolerance and friendship among all nations, racial or religious groups, and shall further the activities of the United Nations for the maintenance of peace."[15]

If education is to fulfill the developmental needs of human beings and further the activities of the United Nations for the maintenance of peace, a radical transformation of the educational system as we know it will have to be effectuated. Schooling as a means of preparing students to fulfill an economic function can no longer continue to be the main purpose of the institution. With so much at stake in this critical historical time of industrial-technological civilization, education must adopt and adapt to its unprecedented role as a leading agent in the renewal of society, for we are in desperate need of an education renaissance. As it is today, the aim of education is to produce well-trained workers for the job market. But at a time when we are facing widespread environmental crises, which is aggravated by unremitting and dangerously high population growth—and an alarming culture of intolerance and hatred— there is little time left on the clock of survival to educate the masses about the gravity of the problems of our time. The urgency of our socio- economic, political, and planetary circumstances demands that we shift the aim of education toward the study of the problems at the core of the current human crises.

Neither education for economic functionalism nor the intrusion of religious pseudo-values in schools shall remain relevant if education is to be transformed. The opposition to—or worse yet, prohibition of— basic humanistic educational principles such as the natural evolution of the human species can no longer be tolerated.[16] The foolish debates on whether or not to display the Ten Commandments in schools, which is supported by the asinine argument that such a move would help stem school violence,[17] must be classified as pathologically insane. It belongs to the education of madness only. Organized religion—any religion—has no place in transformative education in freedom. Religion is a private matter; it's what the individual does with his own solitariness. Thus, indoctrination, either it is religious, political, or otherwise has no place in liberated education; one that is not controlled by special interest groups.

If the aims of Article 26 Clause 2 of the United Nations Universal Declaration of Human Rights are to be observed, education will have to assume a genuine revolutionary role. At a time when there is so much discord, intolerance, mistrust, and hatred, education will have to be- come the vehicle through which to deliver a cure for our social ills, many of which are caused by the disparity between the highly intelligent technician and the underdeveloped human. As science and technology evolve, so must the human being improve, lest we'll be consumed by the madness of our own creation. In the meantime, our highly sophisticated technological society is turning citizens into subjects of consumption, while programming us into conformity to the logic of its system. "To the degree that this happens, we are also becoming submerged in a new culture of silence,"[18] as Paulo Freire warned in his writings. Silence, submission and conformity to the status quo will not get us out of trou- ble; to the contrary, will only shove our heads deeper down the quick- sand pool we're already submerged. If future generations are to escape from going under and drowning in the suffocating drab lifestyle we've created, they'll have to rebel, protest, and make a hell of a lot of noise. Let education be their loudspeaker.

❀

Eleven years after issuing the Universal Declaration of Human Rights, the United Nations General Assembly unanimously adopted the Declaration of the Rights of the Child on November 20, 1959. Besides replacing the Geneva Declaration of the Rights of the Child of 1924, the document outlines 10 principles deemed to be essential for a wholesome childhood. But like all other eloquently written statements in defense of the rights of human dignity, this one, too, fell short of its practical objectives in the general context of humanity. The Declaration proclaims that the child "may have a happy childhood and enjoy his own good and for the good of society."[19] However, more than half a century since its inception, the focus has remained steadily on the good, not of society in particular, but the economic system at large.

It seems like a plausible assumption that only a child can determine what a happy childhood means; and even that will vary depending on the child's idiosyncrasies. Adult bureaucrats, many of whom have lost—and in many cases never had--their connection with this magical time in the human experience, may draft eloquent documents laden with moral principles, but they're likely to miss the point. What do they mean when they profess "the right of the child to a happy childhood?" Does it involve the freedom to enjoy the fleeting years of innocence without the pressure of preparing for adulthood responsibilities? Evidently, that's not the case, for the entire course of the educational system is geared toward economic functionalism. So, what does a happy childhood mean? I checked in with the child still living in the heart of my being to see if he could clue me in to a reasonable answer.

Like the girl in the comic strip that I mentioned earlier, when I was a child all I wanted to do was to let "my soul run through sprinklers" every time I (my physical body) was dropped off at school. The alphabet, numbers, and the panoply of information they wanted to shove into my developing brain seemed untimely. After all, there would be plenty of time for me to learn everything I needed at a later time. All they (teachers and parents) had to do was to impregnate my mind with a passion for learning and I'd pursue it for the rest of my life. But as a pre-middle school age child, I somehow knew that the precious time of carefree innocence would disappear in thin air as fast as a feather vanishes in a windstorm. And there was no recouping it. The reality is that childhood is a once in a lifetime occasion; and like life itself, you only live it once. Unfortunately, because of the way the educational system has been established to support the interests of economic needs, children don't get to take a glimpse at the feather in the windstorm.

By the time I entered middle school the full-court pressure was on: improve academic performance, earn good grades, have acceptable behavior, along with a laundry list of expected conduct and demands to achieve what I wasn't ready to fulfill. To make matters worse, I had to endure the oppressive educational system trapped behind a wooden desk while constantly monitoring the clock eager to hear the recess bell. If it weren't for the pleasant presence of the girl I liked sitting next to my desk, I'd probably have stormed out of the classroom in an open act of bravado and rebellion against educational coercion. Later on in my life, I was glad to learn that Einstein, arguably the greatest scientist of all time, also endured and corroborated what I've always deemed to be a dysfunctional and inefficient educational system:

> "One had to cram all this stuff into one's mind, whether one liked it or not. This coercion had such a deterring effect that, after I had passed the final examination, I found the consideration of any scientific problems distasteful to me for an entire year... It is in fact nothing short of a miracle that the modern methods of instruction have not yet entirely strangled the holy curiosity of inquiry; for this delicate little plant, aside from stimulation, stands mainly in need of freedom; without this it goes to wrack and ruin without fail. It is a very grave mistake to think that the enjoyment of seeing and searching can be promoted by means of coercion and a sense of duty."[20]

As fledgling puberty shifted to overdrive, I got to high school hitting on all cylinders of the engine of revolt. Inspired by the art of my musical idols, I unwelcomed the machine whenever I sang the refrain "you didn't like school, you know you're nobody's fool"[21] while taking a shower. The irony of it, however, is that I've always had a passion and an unquenchable thirst for knowledge, not to mention my unwavering commitment to learning. It was the institution of utilitarian education that I deplored; the establishment whose primary purpose was to mold me into a fitting cog for the machine I wanted to abdicate. Hence, by the time I managed to complete the torturous process of schooling, I decided I was ready to begin my education of higher learning; not at the university level—at least not yet—but traveling around the world carrying my teachers in my backpack: Nietzsche, Rousseau, Fromm, Reich, Chuang Tzu, Huxley, Hesse, Castaneda, to name just a few of my true educators. I've always agreed with Russian-born American writer Isaac Asimov's (1920–1992) conviction that self-education is the only kind of education there is.

After many years on the road and countless hours of reading, as a young adult I realized the education of madness they'd put me through when I was a child. My innermost intellectual and artistic aspirations had been stifled in the interest of preparing me to get a good paying job and become a productive member of the economic community. I was being trained to be a valuable worker, not a worthy human being. And if I happened to feel miserable about the economic function I'd have to fulfill for the rest of my professional life, I should not fret. After all, the pharmaceutical industry produces effective wonder drugs—some with most serious side effects—for the many mental illnesses aggravated by the education of madness.

Therefore, based on my own case scenario, I've concluded that there can never be happiness in an oppressed childhood in which innocence is robbed at will. Children, like all other human beings, have inalienable rights that, in spite of the eloquence of the Declaration of the Rights of the Child and the hypocrisy of pseudo-moralists, are violated rampantly and without resistance. Unfortunately, in the well-intentioned hearts of loving parents, they contribute to the madness that is passed on from one generation to the next. Alas, much harm can come out of misguided love. The number of dysfunctional, unhappy, frustrated, depressed, and unfulfilled adults bears testimony to human tragedies that began in childhood. In addition to the doctor-prescribed wonder drugs that suppress the symptoms of their mental and emotional disturbances, downtrodden adults also have the option to turn to other therapeutic alternatives: indulgence in alcohol, food, sex, and of course, shopping, which deepens both their debt and despair. And as the futile attempt to fill in the enormous crater left behind by the bombardment of cultural insipidities propagated through the educational system, the realization that the emotional hole cannot be filled with ex-

ternalities begets hopelessness; and that is the crux of the human tragedy.

Hence, once desolation sets in and we realize the vainness of our
efforts to become happy and fulfilled human beings, putting an end to
the misery is *sine qua non*. At this point, as Freud observed, even the
prospect of dreadful death can turn into a welcoming relief:

> "And, finally, what good to us is a long life if it is difficult and barren of
> joys, and if it is so full of misery that we can only welcome death as a de-
> liverer?"[22]

As the individual anguish blends in with the collective wretchedness, the need for a new education paradigm is evident. The emphasis
on economic functionalism in education at a time we face multitudinous
unprecedented challenges can no longer be justified; to the contrary, it
ought to be disparaged. Focusing education on teaching children how to
build and manage financial portfolios while their life-sustaining environment disintegrates before their eyes is not only an educational travesty; it is a crime against the future of humanity.

The last and most dreadful event that could possibly happen is already taking place: the continuous unforgiving exploitation of Mother
Earth; the planet that nourishes us while serving as fodder for the economic system. Unless we expeditiously reverse the course of self-
destruction, we might find ourselves reciting the soliloquy that Shakespeare's reckless character, Lord Macbeth, delivers upon hearing of the
death of his beloved wife. In our case, however, it would be delivered as
we commit matricide:

> "To-morrow, and to-morrow, and to-morrow,
> Creeps in this petty pace from day to day,
> To the last syllable of recorded time;
> And all our yesterdays have lighted fools
> The way to dusty death. Out, out brief candle!
> Life's but a walking shadow; a poor player,
> That struts and frets his hour upon the stage,
> And then is heard no more: it is a tale
> Told by an idiot, full of sound and fury,
> Signifying nothing!"[23]

Perhaps individual life is "but a walking shadow that struts and frets his hour upon the stage." However, life itself is enduring; it's a shining light that we must not allow it to be extinguished. But considering the current state of affairs, if we fail to preserve it, there will be no idiots left to tell the tale of the sounds of our fury, for the meaning of life will certainly signify nothing—and that would be a most horrendous Shakespearean tragedy.

Fortunately there is hope; and hope belongs to the future and the youth that will inhabit its chronological domain. The present, which belongs to all of us, is the realm of action through which we build the road to the future where hope's blessings abide. And one of the most important components of the road to the future is education; not utilitarian education, but a systematic educational approach for human development in which we obliterate, once and for all, the madness of education.

NOTES

[1] Sebastian de Assis, *Teachers of the World, Unite!* (Corvallis, OR: The Educational Center Press, 2000), 23-24.

[2] Paulo Freire, *Pedagogy of the Oppressed* (New York: The Continuum Publishing Company, 1996), 53.

[3] E.D. Hirsch, *The schools we need and why we don't have them* (New York: Bantam Doubleday Dell Publishing Group, Inc., 1996), 256.

[4] Sebastian de Assis, *rEvolution in Education* (Lanham, Maryland: Rowman & Litttlefield Publishing Group, 2003), 68.

[5] Dear Abby, "Teen feels stuck in a rut," *Corvallis Gazette-Times*, Saturday, February 11, 2017, B6.

[6] Paulo Freire, *Pedagogy of the Oppressed*, 14.

[7] Grace Llewellyn, *The Teenage Liberation Handbook* (Rockport, MA: Element Books, 1997), 70.

[8] The Oregonian, March 11, 1998, A12.

[9] https://www.juniorachievement.org/web/ja-usa/about;jsessionid=CDE9D80272E16A77C3D7BF28C3A02677

[10] http://www.allywalletwise.com/childrensbook

[11] "Financial literacy: Raising money-savvy kids," *The Week*, April 21, 2017, 33.

[12] Dave Carpenter, The Associated Press, "First-graders learn to manage portfolios," *Statesman Journal*, March 10, 2008, 6A.

[13] Sebastian de Assis, *rEvolution in Education*, 29.

[14] *The United Nations Universal Declaration of Human Rights*, Article 25, Clause 1. United Nations Office of Public Information.

[15] Ibid., Article 26, Clause 2.

[16] In 1925, Tennessee Governor Austin Peay signed the Butler Act, which prohibited the teaching of the Theory of Evolution in public schools. It took 42 years for the State of Tennessee to repeal the law in 1967.

[17] Angie Cannon, "Civics or religion? Commandments clash," *U.S. News & World Report*, February 28, 2000, 36.

[18] Paulo Freire, *Pedagogy of the Oppressed*, 15.

[19] *Declaration of the Rights of the Child* as unanimously adopted by the General Assembly of the United Nations on November 20, 1959, Preamble. United Nations Office of Public Information.

[20] http://www.froebelweb.org/web7011.html. Education Quotes, *Frobel Web*.

[21] Roger Waters, "Welcome to the Machine," *Wish You Were Here*, Pink Floyd (New York: Columbia Records, 1975).

[22] Sigmund Freud, *Civilization and its Discontents* (New York: W.W. Norton & Company, 1989), 40-41.

[23] William Shakespeare, "Macbeth," Act V Scene V, *William Shakespeare The Complete Works* (New York: Outlet Book Company, Inc., 1975), 1068.

The Madness of Education

There should be no doubt that education occupies a prominent position in the development of the individual and society. However, since education became the indispensable tool for economic expansion, it has turned into an assembly line for the production of functional workers who oil the machine with their labor. Meanwhile, a most grievous neglect to holistic human development has contributed to the many social problems we have today. Either it's teachers' training, curriculum development, textbooks, or educational strategies, the entire system is geared toward more and more economic production and consumption of everything; from goods and services to information and dogmas. Indeed, economics has become so entrenched in education that you can no longer discern the difference in their functions.

Seething underneath, like the boiling lava of a volcano about to erupt, the throes of revolutionary education for social change demand to come out by dint of urgency. As genuine education—that most useful art of enriching people's lives, knowledge, and self-development—has been hijacked by the powerful triumvirate of economic, political, and religious forces, education in freedom has turned into training for adaptability to the dominant culture. It's become an indispensable institution for propagating specific cultural values and a most influential tool for propaganda of a culture's legitimacy. And it has been used this way everywhere in the world. From behind the erstwhile iron curtain of the former Soviet Union to the front of the leading nation of free market capitalism in the West, institutionalized education has exercised a fundamental role in the indoctrination of citizens. The Nazis did it, and the communists, capitalists, and religious groups still do. And in order to be most effective, the propaganda must start at very young age, as writer Kennie Anderson points out:

> "It is difficult for people to change their opinions after they've reached a certain stage of development in their experiences and education. Beliefs are too strongly rooted in the foundations of their earlier years. Opinions were molded by early environmental factors and experiences, and many reject anything that does not support the information they were exposed to earlier...even if that information is completely false."[1]

During the Cold War, Western nations consistently criticized the Soviet block of brainwashing their citizens to buy into the communist ideology. However, a similar pattern has been happening in societies sponsoring the values of free market economy, which is conveniently appended to the larger banner of freedom. They, too, distort and manipulate information conveyed to students in order to magnify the authenticity of their pseudo-morality—and programming young minds to allegiances that can last a lifetime. The Pledge of Allegiance is one of the most notorious examples of this political-educational strategy. Ironically, the Pledge of Allegiance was written by a socialist minister named Francis Bellamy (1855–1931) in August 1892 who hoped that the pledge would be used by citizens in any country. In its original form it read: "I pledge allegiance to my Flag and the Republic for which it stands, one nation, indivisible, with liberty and justice for all." In 1923 the words "The Flag of the United States of America" were added to the pledge. Later, in response to the godless communist threat of the time, in 1954 President Eisenhower encouraged Congress to add the words "under God," creating the 31-word pledge widely used today in schools, organizations, and business meetings.[2]

The mind-conditioning and cultural domestication training are evident in the content of textbooks, particularly in the subject of history. Sociologist and historian James Loewen (1942–), who spent two years at the Smithsonian Institution surveying twelve leading high school textbooks of American history, wrote an illuminating book that sheds light on the darkness of American education. Based on the results of his research, he concluded that the content in history books is but "an embarrassing amalgam of bland optimism, blind patriotism, and misinformation pure and simple."[3] Among the many examples of factual distortions and omissions that he cites, one of the most blaring cases is the story of Helen Keller (1880–1968), who at 19 months old suffered a severe illness that left her blind and deaf.[4] While most of the references to her is rooted on her resilience and determination to overcome her handicaps—with the help of her remarkably inspiring teacher, Anne Sullivan (1866–1936)—other significant aspects of Keller's life are blatantly omitted from history textbooks, for they would compromise the "educational" interests of the powers controlling the institution of learning. After all, it is best to focus on a great story of human courage and resolve than political and socially sensitive issues. In spite of the cover up, this is what Loewen unearthed in his research:

"Over the past ten years, I have asked dozens of college students who Helen Keller was and what she did. They all know that she was a blind and deaf girl. Most of them know that she was befriended by a teacher, Anne Sullivan, and learned to read and write and even to speak...A few know that she graduated from college. But about what happened next, about the whole of her adult life, they are ignorant...To ignore the sixty-four years of her adult life or to encapsulate them with the single word 'humanitarian' is to lie by omission. The truth is that Helen Keller was a radical socialist. She joined the Socialist party of Massachusetts in 1909...Keller's commitment to socialism stemmed from her experience as a disabled person...At the time Keller became a socialist, she was one of the most famous women on the planet...She helped found the American Civil Liberties Union."[5]

Convenient omission of facts aside, the fundamental question regarding education is what and whom is it supposed to be for? The individual? Society? Or the economic system? Most people would unreluctantly respond that all three are essential beneficiaries of the educational system, but only a few would recognize that all human endeavors begin with the individual, therefore the purpose of education. Fewer yet would acknowledge that as it is currently established, education is but a socioeconomic-political instrument of labor training and mind control. As special interests have permeated pedagogy, the student is obliged to mold into the educational system, instead of the other way around. Unless it lies within the parameters of an economic function, when has a child or adolescent ever been asked what he wants to study based on his ontological vocation? When has any of the bogus

educationalists ever considered the relationship of a child's unique nature with his learning interests? In the meantime, the pseudo-experts
debate the possible reasons youngsters are depressed, despondent, and
discouraged, as well as the reasons for the high school dropout rates to
be so high. And if the dissatisfaction with schooling were not hard
enough for students to endure, parents add on a great deal of pressure
on the child to excel in what they hate to do. They are coerced to succeed in the most antagonistic fashion.

Alas, in the madness of education the future becomes—as if it were
possible—bleaker than the present reality, for children are not given the
opportunity to explore solutions for the daunting challenges of their
historical time. Anything that deviates from the interests of the economic system is not welcome in the educational system; even what's compromising the very future of children: environmental degradation,
overpopulation, social injustice, criminal economic inequality, among
other transgressions. What a glaring blunder it is to ignore the words of
British philosopher and mathematician, Alfred North Whitehead
(1861–1947):

> "There is only one subject-matter for education, and that is Life in all its
> manifestations."[6]

What a novel idea for an archaic utilitarian educational system: Life in
all its manifestations as the only subject-matter for education. Whitehead envisioned this concept as a protest against dead knowledge; the
superfluous information and factoids that take unnecessary space in the
brain's memory bank. He pleads his case in succinct convincing fashion:

> "Culture is activity of thought, and receptiveness to beauty and humane
> feelings. Scraps of information have nothing to do with it. A merely well-
> informed man is the most useless bore on God's Earth...In training a
> child to activity of thought, above all things, we must beware of what I
> will call 'inert ideas'—that is to say, ideas that are merely received into the
> mind without being utilized, or tested, or thrown into fresh combina-
> tions..Education with inert ideas is not only useless: it is, above all things,
> harmful."[7]

Whitehead's statement resonates the meaning behind Einstein's famous quote: "Imagination is more important than knowledge." But to me, the notion of "Life in all its manifestations" transcends the domain of knowledge or imagination; it crosses over to one of the fundamental purposes in education: responsibility for Life. As the only animal in the kingdom entrusted with refined intellectual abilities, we carry the hefty accountability to be the stewards of the planet and monitors of "Life in all its manifestations." Unfortunately, as it is currently established, the main purpose of education is the production of able workers. As such, education is stymied from fulfilling its genuine function in human development.

Seemingly, the education whose only one subject-matter is "Life in all its manifestations" can only be delivered in freedom; freedom to learn, to choose, and most importantly, to be. Many educationalists have proposed innovative methods of education that promotes human development in freedom. The pioneer of this movement was the Swiss philosopher of the Enlightenment period, Jean Jacques Rousseau. His (in)famous book *Émile*, published in 1762 and still considered one of the most important works on education ever written, is a treatise on the nature of education in relation to the nature of the human being, which to Rousseau was essentially good until corrupted by society. Thus, his educational approach reflects his belief that in exercising education in freedom, the child must learn only what he wants to learn, either because it is useful or pleasing. Growing up in such a freedom, the child not only develops a passion for learning but also deepens his own self-development as a human being. Rousseau maintains that the application of what he has learned to the purpose of life enhances the child's self-worth; and as he extends self-love to others, it transforms education into virtue that has its root in the heart of every one of us. Then, as the illusion of self-interest dissipates, the love for the human race becomes nothing but the love of justice within us. This care of the general well-being is the first concern of the wise man; and the more he bestows upon the happiness of others, the wiser and better he becomes[8]—and so does the society he belongs.

Rousseau's most immediate follower was his countryman Johann Heirich Pestalozzi (1747–1827). He agreed with Rousseau's ideas on the naturally good origin of man and the corrupting effect of society on the individual. Based on the Rousseauian principle and a commitment to aid the education of the poorer classes, Pestalozzi established an experimental school for indigent children. It provided working and learning experiences for approximately fifty boys and girls ranging in age from six to eighteen. They were all fed, clothed, and, especially, nurtured in their emotional needs, as Pestalozzi believed that school should be like a loving family situation where children can feel the security of home life.

"Home is the great school of character and of citizenship. Man is first of all a child, and then the apprentice of his calling."[9]

Pestalozzi's concept of "school as a loving family" is a novel idea that is irreconcilable with the dominant educational system that promotes individual achievements in a highly competitive environment. Incidentally, Friedrich Froebel (1782–1852), the talented educator who developed the concept of kindergarten, was one of the most famous educationalists influenced by Pestalozzi's approach. Yet, visiting a kindergarten classroom today, you would not recognize the influence of Pestalozzi's educational methodology. What you would identify right away, however, is that the preparation of the future labor force must begin as early as possible.

In order to combat the onslaught of childhood in the post-Industrial Revolution era, radical approaches to education came forth under the enduring influence of Jean Jacques Rousseau; arguably the most influential thinker of the Enlightenment era. Therefore, when progressive Scottish educator Alexander Sutherland Neill (1883–1973) founded a school in 1921 in Suffolk, England, many reactionary education theorists viewed his approach as "radical freedom;" a preposterous oxymoron only a moron could come up with. In his Summerhill School, Neill implemented an educational approach based on the "radical" concept of absolute freedom in the development of children. The central idea is based on the principle that school is made to fit the student, instead of making the child to fit the school. He was convinced that in education, intellectual development was not enough, if other relevant aspects of human nature were neglected. Education must be both intellectual and emotional; in fact, the separation between intellect and feeling has led modern man to a near schizoid state of mind in which he has become almost incapable of experiencing anything except in thought, as Erich Fromm writes in the foreword of Neill's book:

"Neill is a critic of present-day society. He emphasizes that the kind of person we develop is a mass-man. 'We are living in an insane society' and 'most of our religious practices are sham...Neill does not try to educate children to fit well into the existing order, but endeavors to rear children who will become happy human beings, men and women whose values are not to have much, not to use much, but to be much... [Neill] has made a decision between full human development and full marketplace success."[10]

Many other educators for human development emerged in the twentieth century to offset the economic development focus of the dominant educational system. Among them, Rudolf Steiner (1861–1925), an Austrian educator, scientist, and artist, created one of the most interesting approaches to comprehensive education. Viewing education as art form that blends in with a non-religious spiritual-philosophical process, Steiner directed his method to understanding the nature of evolving human being, which he called Anthroposophy.[11] His philosophy postulates the existence of a spiritual world accessible through the higher faculties of knowledge latent in every human being—a spiritual version of the Socratic-Platonic view of inherent knowledge. A visionary, Steiner recognized in the beginning of the twentieth century that humanity was undergoing significant transformation in its evolutionary path. Thus, he warned about a one-sided development of intelligence, which undermines the integrity of the education of the complete human person. And when the focus of education switched to economic functionalism, the intellect turned into a tool with which to advance a materialistic culture. In a lecture delivered on August 15, 1919 at Dornach, Switzerland, Steiner cautioned about the changing role of education:

"...the question of education is the most important question occupying people today...education is central to our social problems..Now, our greatest need is to work ourselves out of that materialism and find a path back to a more spiritual attitude...Much of the modern illustrative teaching method results in the death of the soul. Of course, people do not know they are killing the soul; nevertheless, it dies...What we hear time and again is the question of what is carried forward when the human being dies. We rarely hear the question of what is carried forward when a human being is born."[12]

Steiner established an unprecedented methodology in education in which he combined spirituality with the liberation of the individual learner from the shackles of economic and political oppression. He contended that education ought to be a channel whereby active, conscious love can manifest as the principle of Life itself. In social reformation, he called for a "Threefold Social Organism;" that is, socialism in economics, democracy in justice, and freedom in cultural life.[13] He led the way for other progressive educators—like Paulo Freire—to understand education as a critical tool for individual development and social transformation. He insisted that knowledge transcends the existence of the self; instead, it should concern itself with the well-being of others and Life in all its manifestations. In 1919, he indicated that the wheel of change was already turning:

> "If we look at our modern situation—and we must do this to understand these times—the cleft between what we might call a declining society and a rising, but as yet chaotic society is readily apparent...I wish to begin by pointing out the obvious fact that our society, primarily sustained by the middle class, is in the process of rapid decline. It is equally obvious that another society is beginning to dawn."[14]

Nevertheless, almost a century after Steiner predicted the dawn of a new era of social renewal, the Sun is yet to rise on the horizon of social justice—and the role of education in social transformation remains as elusive as ever. As long as economic and political forces control the educational system, the madness of education will be perpetuated for centuries to come.

As education for human development takes the backseat to economic priorities, both the nature and function of education have metamorphosed into a pragmatic workforce training system in which students become passive participants. Since nobody ever asks a youngster what he really wants to learn, instead of what he wants to do for a living when he grows up, he must study to adapt himself to a (lucrative) professional function that is in high demand in the competitive labor marketplace where he'll sell his skills. His innermost talents and inclinations—what

Freire termed "ontological vocation"—will have to be eradicated in order to accommodate the student's future economic needs. Whether he is a gifted musician, an imaginative writer, a natural actor, or simply has an absolute passion for the humanities, his work aspirations must be crushed in favor of a promising field of study that leads to a good paying job. Therefore, he must embark on a long and tedious workforce preparation journey based on an uninspired memorization process (rote memory, logical memory, mnemonics, etc.) that obliterates the joy of learning even among the most studious and capable pupils.[15] Consequently, education becomes but accumulation of data; the capital knowledge to be invested toward a dubiously secure financial future. Alas, students turn into bulimic learners who vomit the information they acquire in inane standardized tests.

The economic pressure to succeed in the job marketplace is fueled by the high speed evolution of technological progress. Not since the Industrial Revolution with its extraordinary achievements at the time (e.g. the spinning wheel, the steam engine, the railway locomotive, etc.) have we seen technology improve at such alarming rates. And just as industrialization drove hordes of people from the countryside to urban centers, the Electronic Revolution of the late twentieth century and beyond has been steering humanity to a cyber-world where people are becoming increasingly more alienated from nature, others, and worst of all, themselves. Thus, as cybernation (the automatic control of a process or operation by means of computerization) has taken over modern industrialized societies, people are becoming more passive, bored, unfeeling, and one-sidedly cerebral while developing pathological symptoms like anxiety, depression, indifference to life, and a growing tendency for violence and hatred. Indeed, the long-range implications of a cybernated world for mental health are disturbing.[16] But that does not seem to be of concern to a maligned educational system.

School districts across the country are committed to expanding programs that supply students—as early as kindergarten—with iPads and other electronic devises. Since a large number of school districts' board members have absolutely no background in education, they vote on implementing programs based on economic functionalism. In my small town of Corvallis, Oregon, the school district recommended spending $1.2 million to expand the instructional technology program for the biennial budget. Although at the time there were nearly 2,000 iPads for students in six elementary schools, and approximately 1,400 for students in middle school grades, the program's goal is to give all students access to information technology.[17] Fortunately, a few enlightened parents became concerned about having their very young children exposed to technology addiction at kindergarten, which ironically means "garden for the children."[18] Parents opposing the expansion of the school district's iPad program voiced their objection. Concerned about the effects of screen time on young children's health, they took matters in their hands and addressed their opposition to the school board's myopic vision of what early childhood education is supposed to be.[19]

The questions that beg to be answered remain unasked: are children benefiting from academic and technological learning at such a young age? Is the early training to improve future economic function worth aborting the innocence of childhood? Has the quality of life of children been enhanced? Or are they merely becoming alienated, controlled, and manipulated as early as possible? Raising these and other similar questions is not a judgment on the values of technology as a tool for human development, but a cautionary alert on its misuse and abuse by invisible economic hands that have a hold on the educational system; a system whose primary concern is to mass-produce capable workforce for the labor market.

However, even in its limited function as an academic assembly line of trained workers, the educational system has failed the children, the young, and the adult learner it is meant to educate. While attempting to fit the individual student to a socioeconomic reality, an inordinate number of people end up doing work they absolutely abhor. Primed from very young age to pursue employment based on quantitative results, which wages sit on the top of the list, the qualitative element of work is completely overlooked; at least until the youngster realizes that he's chosen the wrong path for the wrong reason. How many frustrating careers have been launched by the prospect of a lucrative profession? After all, there's got to be more to work than the amount of money, prestige, convenience, or any other side benefit that does not involve meaningful work. There must be an authentic motivation to work other than to eke out a living. The basic reason people work must lie in their desire to work and their love of work, both of which are nearly non-existent among a large number of average workers in industrialized societies. Steiner observed this phenomenon almost one hundred years ago—and the situation has deteriorated significantly since:

"The most obvious thing in modern life is the many torn human souls, troubled souls who know nothing about how to do anything with life, asking time and again, 'What should I do? What is the meaning of life for me?...Why is that? It arises out of a deficiency in our education...we educate children in a way that does not awaken the inner strength that makes human beings fit for life...If we want to have a truly social future, we must prepare for that through education...We must fundamentally change our principles of education if we are to have any hope of achieving what is right."[20]

Today, the most challenging dilemma is not about having meaningful work, but having any work at all. With the growing automatization of the economic system, the labor force increasingly risks losing millions of jobs to robots who do not get tired, need health care, vacation, retirement, or any other of many human needs. Of course, the main reason for the emergence of robotic work is not practicality but profit. Every time a robot takes your phone call to process a payment, or the many machines that replace human labor in numerous and varied industries (grocery stores' self-service check-outs, automated tellers, online operations, etc.), millions of people's livelihoods are snatched away from the lot of opportunities. Meanwhile, the owners of the means of production with the assistance of their wily robots profit handsomely from the commerce. At a time when the world's population is growing at a frightening pace, the collusion of the economic system with technological development is an extremely dangerous endeavor. And since free market capitalism is buttressed on the principle of the pursuit of profit, unfettered greed, and morbid selfishness, this devious innovative approach to decreasing production cost for the sake of profit is bound to be disastrous for the human species in the years ahead.

If competing with machines were not challenging enough, there are many other disadvantageous aspects unwittingly linked to the skills set of a human laborer. Regardless of how much workforce-ready training you receive from the educational system assembly line, you must be ahead of the human competition with certain characteristics that are mostly beyond your control. In order to sell yourself on the job market, you must bear in mind that unspoken aspects of your visual appearance often play a significant role in the decision-making process of hiring. For instance, if you are of a particular ethnicity, obese, or past a certain age, you are likely to be, in spite of your qualifications and all the laws in the books, silently discriminated for the job you so desperately need to survive. But in the end every worker, regardless of his circumstances, remains in an unfavorable position against the wonders of technology that has seized control of the world, as French philosopher and political activist Simone Weil (1909–1943) observed:

> "To the conflict set up by money between buyers and sellers of labor has been added another conflict, set up by the very means of production, be-tween those who have the machine at their disposal and those who are at the disposal of the machine."[21]

As technology has blended in the production output of the economy, the educational system has become an even more critical tool for human adaptation to the needs of the labor market. Not since the fragmentation of work unleashed by Scientific Management (the theory of management that analyzes and synthesizes workflows) have we seen such a dramatic change in workforce behavior. Just as Frederick W. Taylor (1856–1916), the founder of Scientific Management, managed to break up the work process by dividing workers from one another and from their creativity, modern electronic technology directed by artificial intelligence is alienating even further man from himself, his work, his fellow-humans, and the indispensable natural environment. Indeed, not since Henry Ford (1863–1947) took Taylor's assault a step further by turning workers into human appendages of the assembly line have we witnessed such a large scope of dehumanization in the workplace.[22] In the meantime, the educational system continues focusing on spreading knowledge that is utilitarian in nature and does not adequately address the plethora of critical issues children will have to face in adulthood.

Meanwhile, serious global crises escalate in all fronts: ecological, demographic, economic, political, and at the center of it all, the existential crisis that has been driving people to an uninterrupted state of terror. In the face of so many daunting challenges, the educational system remains as an innocuous, ineffective, and indecent training of students to become productive laborers without engaging them in the pursuit of solutions for the grave problems of their lifetime. And as the ominous clouds of looming environmental catastrophes, nuclear holocaust, and other nightmarish situations unfold, one cannot help but wonder what lies ahead in the future of madness.

NOTES

[1] Kennie Anderson, *Land of Hypocrisy* (Black Hawk: SD: Progressive Productions, 2003), 4.

[2] Historic Documents, *The Pledge of Allegiance*, http://www.ushistory.org/documents/pledge.htm

[3] James W. Loewen, back cover, *Lies My Teacher Told Me* (New York: The New Press, 1995).

[4] For comprehensive details about Helen Keller and her remarkable teacher, Anne Sullivan, refer to Helen Keller, *The Story of My Life* (Mineola, NY: Dover Publications, Inc., 1996).

[5] Loewen, *Lies My Teacher Told Me*, 10-12.

[6] Alfred North Whitehead, *The Aims of Education* (New York: The Free Press, 1967), 6-7.

[7] Ibid., 1-2.

[8] Jean Jacques Rousseau, *Émile* (London: The Guernsey Press Co. Ltd., 1992), 215.

[9] Johann Pestalozzi, *Pestalozzi's Educational Writings* (New York: Longmans Green & Company, 1912), 23.

[10] A.S. Neill, *Summerhill: A Radical Approach to Child Rearing* (New York: Hart Publishing Company, 1960), xiv-xv.

[11] Anthroposophy is a formal educational, therapeutic, and creative system seeking to emphasize natural means to optimize physical, mental, emotional, and spiritual well-being.

[12] Rudolf Steiner, *Education as a Force for Social Change* (New York: Anthroposophic Press, 1997), 54-55, 61.

[13] Ibid., vii.

[14] Ibid., 125.

[15] Albert Einstein's criticism of rote memory education illustrates the point: "One had to cram all this stuff into one's mind for the examinations, whether one liked it or not. This coercion had such a deterring effect on me that, after I had passed the final examination, I found the consideration of any scientific problems distasteful to me for an entire year." http://rescomp.stanford.edu/cheshire/EinsteinQuotes.html

[16] Erich Fromm, *The Revolution of Hope: Toward a Humanized Technology* (New York: Bantam Books, 1968), 97-98.

[17] Anthony Rimel, "District considers tablet expansion," *Gazette-Times*, February 9, 2016, A1.

[18] Friedrich Fröbel's imaginative approach to early childhood rearing is traditionally based on playing, singing, drawing, among other carefree activities

and social interactions. The excessive use of technology poses a hindrance to Fröbel's ultimate objective: allowing a child to experience childhood to the fullest.

[19] Anthony Rimel, "Parents pursue protest against iPads," *Gazette-Times,* March 7, 2016 A1, A3.

[20] Rudolf Steiner, *Education as a Force for Social Change,* 39.

[21] Keith Thomas, Editor, *The Oxford Book of Work* (Oxford, UK: Oxford University Press, 1999), 520.

[22] For an excellent account on the travesties engendered by Frederick W. Taylor's Scientific Management and Henry Ford's assembly line system of production, refer to Bernard Doray, *From Taylorism to Fordism: A Rational Madness* (London: Free Association Books, 1988.)

The Future of Madness

M adness has been part of the human existence since the beginning of time. The manifestations of mental and emotional
disturbances in human behavior have been recorded
throughout the course of history, both at the individual and collective
level. And based on the trends of history, it is safe to expect that it shall
endure in the future, however long the future may be. But considering
the current state of disarray and chaos in the world, the future of madness forebodes the terrifying prospect of self-destruction.

Like a mutating pathogen that overcomes the antidotes attempting
to destroy it, madness has solidified its presence in the social body of
human civilization; worse yet, it has been spreading its infectiousness
through all facets of life on Earth. Climate change, overpopulation, urban sprawling, air, water, and soil pollution; all of it displays the symptoms of the high degree of madness we've managed to pull off as a species. In fact, we've reached the point in which we have become the deadly virus that infected the Earth threatening to obliterate it along with all
the life it sustains. Ironically, the most intelligent animal on the planet
in charge of its stewardship is the one posing the most imminent danger
to Earth. Although, I've never been a religious man, I doubt that the
Christian God that hypothetically created humans in His image envisioned that His earthlings would wreak such havoc to life that took billions of years to develop—a travesty even if the world were created in
only six days. In any case, unless we start acknowledging the inter-
connectedness of all life as one living system we depend on for our survival, we'll likely succumb to the doom of the madness we've embraced
as normality. Perhaps, our best hope lies in the words of artist Roger

Waters (1943–   ) who suggested that "At any moment you can grasp the reins and start guiding your own destiny," while wondering "whether the human race is capable of being humane."[1] But before attempting to figure it out, we must first find the lost reins that fell off the indomitable stallion we rode on the road to progress.

✿

Indeed, madness has been running rampant like a wild horse whose rider has lost control of the unruly equine. Since the early stages of the Industrial Revolution, humanity's obsession with technological, scientific, and economic development has been exacerbated by an uncontrollable impulse to expand every aspect of modern civilization. By the dawn of the twentieth century, the ominous signs of trouble ahead loomed in the horizon like a dark threatening cloud foreboding rain in the parade of progress. As technology evolved, scientific discoveries disclosed possibilities for extended longevity, and economic development improved living conditions of peoples around the world, one of the main culprits of the myriad challenges we face in the twenty-first century became undeniable: overpopulation. It took humanity thousands of years for the world's population to reach 1 billion people in 1804. But the next billion came roughly a hundred years later. In 1997, almost 6 billion people lived on the planet. And as the trend continues, by 2044 the Earth is expected to provide space and resources to a human population of 12 billion.[2] This is an unsustainable growth rate that bodes serious consequences for the future of humanity and the Earth.

Nevertheless, the new religion of science and its technology god reluctantly attempt to ensure us that salvation is within reach. After all, with the growing scientific knowledge and extraordinary technological tools at our disposal, we shall be able to reduce or eliminate altogether the depletion of the Ozone layer, air pollution, scarcity of water, and all the other numerous problems the unfettered population and economic growth entail. And in case this proves to be an unrealizable tall order task, our powerful telescopes will eventually spot a suitable planet that our spacecrafts will transport (a few of) us to. But alas, the asinine idea that the human species is independent from the Earth only reveals the hubris of modern men; an extrapolation of excessive haughtiness that has crossed over to the realm of absolute madness. Perhaps it is just a magnification of the human ignorance that Shakespeare acknowledged centuries ago and revealed through the words of Isabella in his play *Measure for Measure*:

"Man, proud man!
Dress'd in a little brief authority,
Most ignorant of what he's most assured,
His glassy essence, like an angry ape,
Plays such fantastic tricks before high heaven,
As makes the angels weep."[3]

Either it is outright madness, blind naiveté, or mindless stupidity, the delusion that we will find timely solutions for the complex problems we've been creating since the Industrial Revolution is a serious problem in and by itself. But don't take my word for it; instead, heed the message of one of the greatest prophets of the new religion of science, Albert Einstein who asserted in what has become a popular quote that "we can't solve problems by using the same kind of thinking we used when we created them." But the many problems we face are far from being relegated to economic, scientific, and demographic issues only, though the latter is the engine propelling our civilization to the dead end cul-de-sac. Religion, particularly Christianity with its anti-contraceptive dogmas, add an additional aggravation to the already perilous crisis. However, as the rapidly growing world population expands, everyone's quality of life will be significantly affected for generations to come. Ignoring the gravity of population explosion comes with potentially apocalyptic consequences; the Malthusian nightmare discussed earlier in this book.

Despite the ever-looming danger of atomic bombs taking off from their silos toward its destruction target, the population bomb has already left its demographic silo and it's a matter of time until it blasts off its nefarious effects, many of which are already being felt today. Although theoretically both bombs can and should be disarmed, I argue that if overpopulation is curbed, all other socioeconomic and political problems become much more manageable. After all, human conflicts are inescapably linked to battles for resources; and with fewer people competing for them, it can only alleviate the pressure. Understanding this concept, a modern-day version of Thomas Robert Malthus advocated for prompt and reasonable solutions that are not based on long-standing forms of thinking.

Paul Ehrlich (1932–), a biology professor at Stanford University, wrote an important book in 1968 titled *The Population Bomb*. In this work he argues that many dire earlier predictions of Malthus were not farfetched at all. According to Ehrlich, the growth of world population was a time bomb ready to go off in the near future with dismal consequences. Supporting his arguments with solid scientific research, he stated that the sheer mathematics of population growth worldwide were sufficient to demonstrate that world population could not possibly continue to expand at its present rates. In addition to the uncomfortable overcrowding and its impact on the deterioration of the environment, the availability of clean water, air, food, and other critical factors in the health of populations cannot be overlooked, especially in long-term planning. Thus, Ehrlich purported that only limits on population growth can avert disaster; that is, implementing a zero population growth approach. The goal is to reach the *Population Replacement Level*, a state in which the combined birthrate and death rate of a population simply sustains the population at a steady level, called the *Equilibrium Level*.4 However, putting this demographic management strategy to practice requires a number of measures, some of which defy archaic religious dogma that threatens the lives of the nonreligious. Either through various contraceptive methods, education, or medical intervention to prevent child birth, population must be curtailed or human surplus will be eliminated in unnecessarily painful fashion. What cannot continue unabated is the unsustainable trend of adding approximately 270,000 people every day to Earth.5 It has created a demographic imbalance that will likely doom human civilization; perhaps even before a nuclear war breaks out.

❧

"Man, proud man! Dress'd in a little brief authority. Most ignorant of what he's most assured." In my estimation, this is one of the most accurate lines about the human condition Shakespeare ever wrote. The proud man dressed in a little brief authority who is so convinced that he knows it all, is a revelation to the nature of the proud man, who in reality is delusional believing that he knows what he does not know—or as Mark Twain (1835–1910) noted, "It ain't what you know that gets you in

trouble. It's what you know for sure that just ain't so."[6] And this bizarre mental handicap has been present throughout the course of human history. So, when men thought that the Earth was flat and whoever believed otherwise was burned at the stake, it was the conviction of his knowledge that encouraged him to commit such barbaric atrocities. Conversely, the modern man who is more confident than ever before in his knowledge of the cosmos, nature, life, and has all the technological tools to expand his intellectual capabilities, he, too, is convinced that he is most assured of what he is most ignorant. He believes that he can and will find a way out of his life's predicament simply because he thinks he knows. And that is one of the most frightening prospects for the future of madness.

In 1999, Cornell University researchers, David Dunning and Justin Kruger, conducted a study in which they documented the effects of low-ability individuals who suffer from illusory superiority, mistakenly assessing their ability as much higher than it actually is. In essence, they are most ignorant of what they're most assured. Titled *Unskilled and Unaware of it: How Difficulties in Recognizing One's Own Incompetence Lead to Inflated Self-Assessments*, Dunning and Kruger noted that ignorance of standards of performance lies behind a great deal of incorrect self-assessment of competence. It is known as metacognitive[7] incapacity on the part of those with low ability to recognize their ineptitude and evaluate their competence accurately—or the lack thereof. Hence, the little knowledge the incompetent may have becomes a big dangerous thing. But the Dunning-Kruger effect is not a pathological condition. It is the human condition.[8] And that's where the problem lies. Whether you believe the Earth is flat or that you possess the knowledge to solve the grave problems on Earth, your own ignorance becomes your most dangerous enemy, as Mark Twain observed. After all, if you are incompetent, you can't know you are incompetent; and neither will you be able to know a right answer if you cannot recognize what a right answer is.

Unable to identify their own incompetence and ignorance, the proud men of science ventured into emulating God who created them in His image. Thus, he engineered artificial intelligence that is gradually taking over all aspects of modern life; a brave new world that threatens to supersede humanity in the decision-making process of vital issues of life. As organic ignorance is transposed to artificial intelligence, the dangerous future of madness looks increasingly dismal, regardless of the promising perspectives of technological development.

❀

Among all the technological tools ever created by human intelligence, none has been as frightening and increasingly ubiquitous as AI, or artificial intelligence. In a nutshell, AI refers to computer programs that can perform tasks that used to require human intelligence to carry out, e.g. speech recognition and language translations. However, this technology has been evolving at such an astounding pace that's been posing a veritable threat to the future of human civilization.

Generally speaking, technology is the knowledge that allows human beings to develop tools and machines to increase control and understanding of the natural environment. The term is derived from the Greek words *tekhnē*, which refers to an art or craft, and *logia*, meaning an area of study. Therefore, technology means, literally, the study or science of crafting. These innovations of human creativity, be it a hammer or a rocket, are all considered tools with which to transform traditional cultural systems that engender—often times unexpectedly—unpredictable social consequences. Thus, the use of technology can be put to use in both creative and destructive fashions, as a hammer can be useful in building a house that a rocket used as a weapon can destroy it. However, once technology became inextricably involved with science and driven by economic interests, it started spinning out of control in the modern industrial era. And with the continuous advancement of AI fueled by the profit motive, we've reached the apex of a self-inflicted technological danger of unprecedented consequences.

Not since pioneer craftsman Johannes Gutenberg (c.1395–1468) invented the printing press has technology had such a widespread impact as artificial intelligence. You may question this assertion by saying that industrial technology and its machines of mass-production paved the way for the development of modern societies, therefore playing a more fundamental role in our current accomplishments. I'd acquiesce to the argument with a caveat: while Gutenberg's invention endeavored to disseminate knowledge and information, AI envisions manipulating and controlling them, albeit under the guise of doing so in the best interest of society. And while industrialization incentivized by the pursuit of profit has posed a most serious threat to humanity and the natural environment, AI imperils human autonomy as it expands its control of society's functional infrastructure.

In the face of the rapid progress AI has achieved in recent years, some of the brightest minds engaged in technological development have issued dire warnings about its potentially dangerous consequences. In 2014, tech billionaire, Elon Musk (1971–), founder of the famous Tesla series of electric cars and of Space X, which sends rockets to the space station, warned that the rise of artificial intelligence was "potentially more dangerous than nukes." He added:

"I think we should be very careful about artificial intelligence. If I were to guess like what our biggest existential threat is, it's probably that...You can have AI which [sic] is much smarter than the smartest human on Earth. This is a dangerous situation."[9]

Many other scientists and experts in the field of technology have expressed similar concerns. In an interview with BBC News on December 2, 2014, famous British astrophysicist Stephen Hawking (1942–2018) stated that "The development of full artificial intelligence could spell the end of the human race."[10] And Bill Gates (1955–), co-founder of Microsoft Corporation, has sided with Elon Musk's warnings of the dangers of AI when he said:

"I am in the camp that is concerned about super intelligence...I agree with Elon Musk and some others on this and don't understand why some people are not concerned."[11]

Indeed, the great computer revolution of the 20th century has unleashed an extraordinary transformation, not only in the realm of technology but in individual and societal life as well. Back in 1969, the IBM 360 computers used by NASA could hold approximately six megabytes of data. By today's standards, an inexpensive 32-gigabyte memory card available for less than $20 stores more than 5,000 times the data of those huge IBM 360 computers, which in their day were worth more than $3 million each. Notwithstanding, today's average smartphones have at least 16 gigabytes, or more than 2,500 times storage capability than those IBM computers NASA used in the exploration of outerspace.[12] And in order to better understand the astounding evolution of electronics technology, those giant IBM 360 computers of 1969 morph in comparison to what the company is producing today. Watson, the IBM supercomputer that combines artificial intelligence and sophisticated analytical software for optimal performance, is capable of answering all sorts of questions and process information more like a smart human than a smart computer. Its advanced cognitive system has been raising anxiety among many professionals who feel threatened by the implementation of this cognitive technology in the workplace.

An Associated Press analysis of employment data from 20 countries found that millions of mid-skill, mid-pay jobs already have disappeared in recent years, leaving a growing number of technologists and economists wondering whether this is a new trend of the global economy.[13] As smarter machines and niftier software continue to replace more and more mid-pay jobs, businesses are reaping a double harvest: increased productive at lower cost, which translates into swelling profits. The electronic automatization of an economic system that is stimulated by the pursuit of profit has been casting a most somber cloud on the horizon of employment for a fast-growing world population. As Automated Teller Machines (ATM) gradually dislodge the bank teller, or the self-service check-out supermarket machines oust the clerk, or the online travel agencies replace travel agents, among numerous other instances in which human labor can be easily substituted by technological devices, the future of work as a means of earning a living is in serious jeopardy.

Although every time technological inventions in the past two centuries stirred outcries against potential employment losses (the locomotive, the telegraph, the telephone, the automobile, etc.), for the first time we are seeing machines that can think--or something very close to it. Thus, the rise of computer technology poses a threat that previous generations of machines did not: The old machines replaced brawn but created jobs that required human intelligence to operate. The new machines, however, are a menace to both.[14]

The observable and undeniable fact is that the world economy is becoming increasingly more dependent on machines than humans. Millions of jobs worldwide have been disappearing at an astonishing pace. Although it is true that technology also creates jobs to a few beneficiaries such as software engineers or app designers, in most fields of work technology is eliminating far more jobs than it is creating, particularly in the low-skill level. For instance, Webb Wheel Products, a company based in Cullman, Alabama, that produces wheel-end equipment (break drums, hubs, rotors, etc.) has been using robots in its assembly line to paint brake drums. Despite making 300,000 more drums annually—a 25 percent increase in output—as of 2013, the company had not added a single factory worker in three years, because the robots were delivering the expected results.[15] The reality is that technology has been reducing the number of jobs in manufacturing at drastic rates—and this pattern is likely to accelerate in the years to come.

⚛

In his inspiring book addressing the issues of economics as if people mattered, German economist E.F. Schumacher (1911–1977) stated that—for humane, aesthetic, moral and political reasons—the overwhelming nature of modern technology threatens a quality of life that has meaning, freedom of choice, a human sense of scale, and an equal chance for justice and individual creativity.[16] A large silent group of supporters of Schumacher's approach have proposed a value system in which all people recognize that the Earth's resources are finite and that human life must be structured around a commitment to control growth of industry, the size of cities, the use of energy; and of course, population explosion. But unless, these principles are observed, technology may turn into the dagger that we forged in the fire of progress, and with which we shall commit *seppuku* (the samurai ritual of noble suicide) of our civilization.

Alas, the dangers that technology pose to humanity are not limited to economics. Surely, the automatization of the economic system in an overpopulated world bodes a nightmarish scenario of millions of unemployed people. However, this is just one of the tentacles of the electronic octopus that has gotten a strong hold on every single aspect of modern civilization. From delivery of water and power to communications and financial services, industrial societies have become utterly dependent on computer technology for nearly every significant facet of the social order. This vulnerability has turned technology into a potential weapon of destruction in the hands of those wanting to do harm, whatever their motivation may be. A clever thief can steal more money with a computer than with a handgun; and a wily terrorist can unleash more chaos with a keyboard than a bomb. And if that were not treacherous enough, the spread of malicious software known as ransomware extort victims who must pay with the crypto currency bitcoin in order to restore their electronic files, as a recent global cyberattack froze more than 300,000 computers in some 150 countries in a single day.[17]

Unfortunately, there are even more significant daunting threats, such as potential cyberattacks that can cripple the power grid of nations, which could paralyze the functioning of societies for an extended period of time. These are legitimate concerns that shall distress the world for years to come. As it is, the future of madness promises to be like a titillating wicked videogame, except that it doesn't happen in the delusion of a cyber reality, but in real time and to real people.

At a time when people are becoming increasingly alienated and disconnected from the natural world, the future of humanity looks as precarious as the outlook of the Earth. The electronic dependence and addiction plaguing modern societies augurs to get worse in the course of the twenty-first century. We live in a time when handheld electronic devices have become appendages of the human body; a vital part of it that sometimes can be deadly as well. It seems like every day there are stories in the news media relating to fatal accidents caused by electronic distractions that are developing into flagrant crisis of attention. In one of the most egregious cases ever reported, a 26-year-old Oregon woman was hit by a train while distracted by her cell-phone. Although multiple visual and auditory warnings were all functioning on the rail tracks— and the conductor climbed onto a walkway on the front of the engine screaming and yelling at her trying to get her attention—she remained completely oblivious to the fast moving locomotive. The bizarre detail of the incident is that the seriously injured woman is neither deaf nor was she wearing headphones at the time she was struck.[18] Then, how could she have not heard the blaring warning sounds? Or seen the flashing lights on the crossroads? The only feasible explanation for such a glaring distraction is that technology has consumed people's attention to a state of self-oblivion. Lost somewhere amidst electronic chips lies the alienated modern man's soul.

There is no denying that the future of madness is already present. As countless, unprecedented, and life-threatening crises challenge the ever-growing human population in the twenty-first century, the demise of the planet Earth is, without a modicum of doubt, the most urgent predicament for the survival of the human species. After all, without unpolluted air, potable water, fertile soil, and all the environmental conditions necessary for the sustenance of billions of human beings, nothing; absolutely nothing is of any importance. And even though the men of science who in their own state of alienated knowledge ("man, proud man, dressed in a little brief authority, most ignorant of what he's most assured") continue searching for another habitat for the selfish human species, though the prospects for such a finding is unrealistic at best. Besides, time is running out for this outer space Columbus-like exploration to succeed. According to British physicist Stephen Hawking, humanity has approximately 100 years to find another planet to live on before global warming renders Earth uninhabitable.[19] Perhaps, we'd be better off if we could rediscover our lost selves instead.

Until we realize that we are neither a superior species nor independent from the Earth—we are but a sophisticated manifestation of the planet's complex life forms—we shall be doomed to experience a terrifying ecological nightmare in the offing. Unless we expeditiously reverse the undeniable negative circumstances that our civilization has inflicted on the planet, we'll be most certainly heading toward the madness of the future.

NOTES

[1] Roger Waters, *The Dark Side of the Moon Documentary* DVD (London, UK: Eagle Rock Entertainment, Ltd., 2003).

[2] Data from membership mailing materials of former Zero Population Growth, rebranded as Population Connection. For more information about the organization visit http://www.populationconnection.org/. And for a shocking visual impact of population growth per second, visit U.S. and World Population Clock at https://www.census.gov/popclock/.

[3] William Shakespeare, *The Complete Works* (Avenel, New Jersey: Gramercy Books, 1975), 107.

[4] Andersen/Taylor, *Sociology: Understanding a Diverse Society Update, 4/e w/Practice Test* (Mason, Ohio: Cengage Learning, 2008), 570-571.

[5] Ibid., 568.

[6] This quote appears at the beginning of the excellent movie, *The Big Short*, which is based on actual events that led to the 2008 economic collapse of the housing market in the United States that affected the global economy to what's been infamously known as the Great Recession.

[7] Metacognition refers to higher order thinking, which involves active control over the cognitive processes engaging in learning.

[8] William Poundstone, "The Dunning-Kruger President: How did a psychology term become a partisan trending topic?," *Psychology Today,* January 21, 2017. https://www.psychologytoday.com/blog/head-in-the-cloud/201701/the-dunning-kruger-president

[9] Mario Seiglie, "Artificial Intelligence: The Coming Threat," *Beyond Today*, May-June 2017, 27.

[10] Ibid.

[11] Ibid.

[12] Ibid., 26.

[13] Paul Wiseman and Bernard Condon, AP Business Writers, "Will technology create a world without work?" *Corvallis Gazette-Times*, January 25, 2013 A1.

[14] Ibid., A6.

[15] Bernard Condon and Paul Wiseman, AP Business Writers, "Recession, tech skill middle-class jobs," *Corvallis Gazette-Times,* January 23, 2013, A1.

[16] E.F. Schumacher, *Small is Beautiful* (New York: Harper & Row Publishers, Inc., 1973).

[17] "Malware: Ransomware attack roils the globe," *The Week*, May 26, 2017, 20.

[18] "Woman hit by train distracted by phone," *Corvallis Gazette-Times*, April 22, 2017, A10.

[19] *Time*, May 22, 2017, 8.

The Madness of the Future

O n April 22, 1970 the alarm clock of awareness went off. It marked the observance of the original Earth Day. At last, people realized that the Earth was sending distress signals that could no longer be ignored. Gaia, the ancestral mother of life and the primordial deity of the Earth in Greek mythology, was becoming an enraged goddess--and justifiably so. A voracious economic system was consuming the planet and polluting its air, water, soil, and even the stratosphere that has turned into a sort of landfill for space trash, which lingers around the globe as an ominous predicament of the future of the Earth. Perhaps it was coincidental that the first Earth Day celebration began some nine months after the landing on the moon; just enough time to gestate a new consciousness after witnessing the barren wasted land of the nearest cosmic rock. It made us realize that unless urgent measures are taken to abate the assault on Gaia (the concept of Gaia is entirely linked with the concept of life,[1]) the odds of survival in the twenty-first century will be significantly compromised.

After three decades of ongoing consumption binge energized by an economic system with an insatiable appetite for profit—and a rapidly growing world population—the twenty-first century arrived exposing the environment's festering wounds. Indeed, the undeterred burning of fossil fuels has left numerous scars and irreparable damages to the planet. From consequential acid rain[2] to deliberate deforestation, the continuous onslaught on what has become an unwholesome Earth has reached dangerous levels. And yet, the ignorance, negligence, and irresponsibility toward the environment have remained unchecked for centuries. Founded on the principle of domination over nature, the profligate use of resources demanded by the industrial output of consumer goods that keeps the economic system machine churning is unsustainable. Instead of decelerating the excessive exploitation of natural resources, the maddening economic system of consumption has been siphoning as much as it possibly can, until there is nothing left to harvest. Since 1950 more than 25 percent of the remaining forests on the planet have been cut down,[3] and soon the lungs of the planet will be unable to breathe life as we know it. And regardless of the vociferous boasting about technological advancements, scientific discoveries, and free market economic expansion, few people with their common sense still intact would consider a process of environmental deterioration as a legitimate representation of progress; at least not according to Genuine Progress Indicator (GPI), which takes into account social factors and environmental cost of progress. But as the Earth cries out for help, the sounds of urgency falls in deaf human ears. Gaia has been desperately blowing her trumpets to draw attention to her plight—and ours—and yet we've become, not oblivious, but indifferent to it.

In a blatant display of Gaia's omnipotence, the twenty-first century began reassuring the evidence of the human impotence in the face of the power of nature. It started out on December 26, 2004 when an Indian Ocean earthquake with a magnitude of approximately 9.3 in the Richter scale generated a mammoth tsunami. This second strongest ever recorded earthquake (only the 1960 Chile earthquake measured higher at 9.5) killed hundreds of thousands of people, displaced some 500,000 more, and inundated communities in 14 countries with waves up to 100 feet.[4] Less than a year later, Hurricane Katrina blasted through the Gulf of Mexico and on August 29, 2005 struck the Gulf Coast of the United States with a vengeance leaving behind a trail of destruction with hundreds of thousands of people homeless in Louisiana, Mississippi and Alabama and $108 billion in damages.[5] Then, another alarming warning of nature's mighty sovereignty came off the Pacific coast of Tōhoku earthquake and tsunami that caused the meltdown of the Fukushima Daiichi Nuclear Power Plant in Japan. With radiation leaking from the disabled nuclear reactors and flowing through the Pacific Ocean, the world was put on notice of the imminent dangers we face; and that neither technology nor science can bring to a standstill.

Despite human intellectual hubris that relies on technology and science to solve our countless problems, we know, without a shadow of doubt, that we cannot control the forces of nature. This has proven to be an undeniable fact since the dawn of civilization. Conversely, we have demonstrated our ability to impart irreversible damage to the planet with our irresponsible actions, as it is the only way we exert any power over the natural environment. Maybe at a subconscious level, we decided to impose our willpower on Gaia; to show the mythological goddess that we are the sovereigns of the Earth. But as we subjugate the planet to unrelenting exploitation and vicious assaults to the life it sustains, our display of dominance might prove to be more devastating to us than all the forces of nature combined. It is the madness of our arrogance that is paving the way to the madness of the future.

❀

In the millenary course of the development of human history, many civilizations have vanished from the Earth, some without leaving a trace of the reasons for their disappearance. But among the perished societies we've collected reliable historical records, we know that a number of civilizations destroyed themselves by destroying the environment on which their very existence depended. This happened to the Anasazi Indians of Arizona and New Mexico about 700 years ago, and to the Mayan civilization in Guatemala about 1,000 years ago.[6] But an even more famous example is the case of the fall of Mesopotamia (mostly what is nowadays Iraq), a civilization that flourished about 3,000 years before Christ. Advantageously located in the lush river basin of the Tigris and Euphrates rivers, the Mesopotamians developed an extensive irrigation system that provided abundant food supply for their population. This irrigation system, however, had no drainage. The water constantly evaporated, gradually growing saltier. Over the centuries, this saltier water seeped into the ground, the underground water table rose, and the land became too salty to grow crops. Unwittingly, the Mesopotamians destroyed the agricultural base that allowed them to thrive for dozens of centuries. What once was a beautiful, lush, green land producing fruits, vegetables, and grains in abundance is now a barren desert.[7] Thus, the lesson for modern industrial civilization is simple: either by ignorance or abuse, the mishandling of the natural environment paves the way to nature's foreclosure, which creates the conditions for the collapse of developed civilization, regardless of how technologically advanced it may be. After all, without a sustainable environment, disease and famine are most certainly bound to spread—and so will wars in the fight for those dwindling resources.

As we progress through the twenty-first century, the dangers of civilization breakdown is not limited to an isolated country or distant region of the world. The potential for ecological catastrophe—not to mention a total meltdown of the financial system—is a global threat with unimaginable consequences for humanity. We have become so inextricably connected that environmental abuses on one side of the Atlantic Ocean will generate negative effects on the 3,000 mile-distant opposite shore. It affects all hemispheres of the planet and all peoples and life forms everywhere. As far as the environment is concerned, we're on the verge of becoming a "Mesopotamia world community."

Nevertheless, the world community remains lukewarm at best about the gravity and scope of the environmental problems that is deteriorating steadily. By dint of economic demands, we continue carrying on business as usual as though neither time nor resources would run out. Meanwhile, the central and most critical cause aggravating this travesty, the unremitting human population growth, marches on unabated and with no signs of halting its tragic movement. Seemingly, we've reached the point of no return; the moment when we can see the edge of the precipice in the horizon but we cannot stop moving in that direction. And despite all the observable evidences backed up by scientific research, the demands of an absolutely insane economic system of consumption induced by the pursuit of profit cannot allow it to be reversed—and politicians, lobbyists, and special private interests will not allow it either. And yet, the risks we take for not taking action are perilous to the core, as Al Gore (1948–   ), the former Vice President of the United States turned environmental activist cautions:

"The climate crisis is, indeed, extremely dangerous. In fact, it is a true planetary emergency. Two thousand scientists in a hundred countries, working for more than 20 years in the most elaborate and well-organized scientific collaboration in the history of humankind, have forged an exceptionally strong consensus that all the nations on Earth must work together to solve the crisis of global warming. The voluminous evidence now strongly suggests that unless we act boldly and quickly to deal with the underlying causes of global warming, our world will undergo a string of terrible catastrophes."[8]

Unfortunately, like several other civilizations and empires that fell apart because of their negligence, ignorance, or both, modern industrial technological civilization shares a commonality with all of them: we, too, have been consumed by our triumphs and indulgences, and such irresponsible behavior is paving the way to our potential demise. In essence, we have become the victims of our own success.

※

Although the human footprints on the environment have been visible for a very long time, ecological degradation did not begin in earnest until the Industrial Revolution established a deadly partnership with free market economics. Alas, the advantages of industrialization, mass-production and consumption have come with a high environmental and sociological price tag. It's like a Faustian bargain in which we exchanged pristine rivers, clean air, open fields, and clear blue skies for the countless gadgets and conveniences of the modern world. At this point, even if we were to impose regulatory management to avoid exhausting Earth's natural resources, many of them are already so depleted and degraded that will take centuries to restore it to its original state. We've gambled our future for the gain of short-term profits.

The rate of economic expansion, population growth, and excessive output of industrial goods escalated after the end of World War II. At the same time, never in world history had humans imparted as much damage to the environment as we did in the second half of the twentieth century. As wide-scale deforestation, the poisoning of soil, water, and air, and the expansion of cities and industrial complexes around the world wreaked havoc on the environment, the effects of massive fossil fuel burning unleashed a barrage of dangerous side-effects. Greenhouse gases such as carbon dioxide and CFCs (chlorofluorocarbons) from foam containers and refrigerator coolants increase in atmospheric concentration each year. The former affects global warming; the latter depletes atmospheric ozone. In addition, the search for new energy sources has led to the production of 100,000 metric tons of nuclear waste. Millions of tons of radioactive tailings worldwide are left from uranium mining.[9] And in the end, we still have to figure out where to put all the toxic waste; how to nurture eroding soil needed to feed billions of people--and where to shelter them—among countless other challenges that come with the nefarious side-effects of the industrial-technological concept of progress.

However, environmental issues are not limited to ecological misfortunes; to the contrary, it has deep roots in socioeconomic and political grounds. In fact, environmental degradation has a long history of racism and social class discrimination (what is academically termed environmental racism and classism.) Since the earlier stages of the development of industrialization that compelled the migration of millions from the countryside to the cities, the overworked and underpaid working class was confined to the poorest and most inauspicious urban locations. Of course, this hasn't changed through the decades leading to the twenty-first century. In the United States pollution has a racial and social class bias. Because racial minorities and the poor live in cheap dwellings in disadvantages areas of urban centers, they are disproportionately exposed to air pollution, hazardous wastes, and pesticides, among other poisonous elements.[10] Furthermore, the disenfranchised population is significantly more vulnerable to natural disasters, as it was evinced when Hurricane Katrina made landfall in Louisiana. The most negatively affected neighborhoods were the lowest lying ones (some 20 feet below sea level); the ones that were primarily poor citizens of Black or Hispanic descent. In addition, waste is dumped with disproportionate frequency in areas with high concentrations of minorities, particularly Native Americans, Hispanic, Blacks, as well as white people and other ethnic backgrounds of lower socioeconomic status.[11] Hence, environmental racism is but an extension of economic exploitation carried over to the habitat of the segregated poor.

Nevertheless, among all the environmental challenges we face, none seems to overshadow what is arguably the gravest of them all: the shortage of water; the nectar of life without which no living creature on the planet can survive. By its own nature, it's the most precious resource on Earth—and it has been drying up at a frightening pace.

❋

Water is the indispensable resource without which there is no life. Civilization might be able to survive without fossil fuel, atomic energy, or any other necessity of modern life. Water, however, is sine qua non. In his own words, American journalist Alex Prud'homme (1962–   ) corroborates this indisputable fact with the following statement:

"Water is considered an 'axis resource,' meaning it's the resource that underlies all others...So whether you're building a computer chip, or growing crops, or generating power, all these things require lots of water. But there's only a finite amount of water, and now resources are butting up against each other."[12]

Nevertheless, the fundamental function of water is to sustain life; but not only human life, though we've manipulated the use of this most precious resource to our own selfish interests. Endowed with an extraordinary ability to transform our surroundings based on our needs and conveniences, we've engineered behemoth dams to generate energy to our cities. Regrettably, seldom we take into account the ecological impact of such magnanimous engineering projects. But when it comes to water, because of its imperative role in our lives, we have made remarkable efforts to harness, store, and protect this vital resource that enables civilizations to thrive. It is no wonder that all major human societies have developed by large bodies of water.

Since the powerful Roman Empire constructed complex aqueducts some 300 years before Christ, we've been discovering and improving on new ways of delivering water to all necessary purposes of society. In modern times, California's Central Valley is an example of both the creativity and destructive consequences of human's meddling in the natural world. After President Harry S. Truman (1884–1972) delivered his 1949 inaugural address that called for a "bold new program for making the benefits of our scientific advances and industrial progress available for the improvement and growth of underdeveloped areas,"[13] the great California desert project took off in the following decade. From barren desert to fertile farmland, Central Valley California became one of the most important agricultural regions on Earth; a bread basket created by the sophisticated engineering of aquifers that drastically transformed the landscape of the area. Today, however, with severe droughts and critical shortage of water, farmers are destroying their crops and selling their water rights instead.[14] Let others venture in taking the risk of bankruptcy in a region where there is too little water supply to meet demands. According to the American Geophysical Union, the four winters since 2012 have produced the most severe drought in the past 1,200 years. The year 2015 was the driest ever on record.[15]

In the meantime, sprawling urban centers keep siphoning water from nearby rivers, most of which have gotten to critical points. From its origin in the Rocky Mountains, the Colorado River aqueduct crosses the Mojave Desert to deliver 37 percent of Southern California's urban water. Separate canals bring irrigation water to 900,000 acres of productive desert farmland. As a result of such high usage over decades, the past 15 years were the driest in the river's watershed in a century.[16] And considering that Western states have divvied up the Colorado River's water, building dams and diverting the flow hundreds of miles to Los Angeles, Sand Diego, Phoenix, and other fast-growing cities—the river serves 30 million people in seven U.S. states and Mexico, with 70 percent more of its water siphoned off to irrigate 3.5 million acres of cropland[17]—the future doesn't necessarily bode a wave of optimism. Besides, taking into consideration that climate change will likely decrease the river's flow by 5 to 20 percent in the next 40 years, geoscientists' forecast for the future is ominous at best: less precipitation in the Rocky Mountains will yield less water and droughts will last longer; higher overall air temperatures will mean more water loss to evaporation; earlier runoffs and lower flows later in the year; all of it will negatively contribute to water becoming scarcer in the growing season."[18] And considering that 80 percent of the State of California's water goes to agriculture and each of us consumes more than 4,500 gallons of water daily in food,[19] unless urgent measures are implemented, the likelihood that the Colorado River will run out of water within a century is not a farfetched conjecture.

※

Sometimes the best way to grasp the extent of a situation is by delving into the basic facts of the matter at hand. Thus, here are just a few relevant data to shed some light on the water crisis:

- Although we live on a planet covered by water, more than 97 percent is salty and nearly 2 percent is locked up in snow and ice. The world's supply of fresh water is about 9.25 million trillion gallons.
- Nearly 70 percent of the world's fresh water is locked in ice. Most of the rest is in aquifers that we're draining much more quickly than the natural recharge rate.

- Two-thirds of our water is used to grow food.
- With 83 million more people on Earth each year, water demand will keep going up.
- Americans use about 100 gallons of water at home each day, in contrast with millions of the world's poorest who subsist on fewer than five gallons a day.
- Forty-six percent of people on Earth do not have water piped to their homes. And in developing countries, women walk an average of 3.7 miles to get water.
- In 15 years, 1.8 billion people will live in regions of severe water scarcity.
- In Florida, 3,000 gallons are used to water the grass for each golf game played.[20]

The information above represents but the tip of the iceberg of the complexity of the water dilemma around the world. In addition to our civilization's insatiable thirst for a rapidly dwindling fresh water supply, even the 97 percent salty bodies of water are in peril. At a recent United Nations Ocean Conference, the UN Secretary General, Antonio Guterres (1949–   ), issued dire warnings about the deteriorating health of the planet's oceans. As increasingly widespread pollution, overfishing, and the accelerating effects of climate change on the oceans' temperature pose dangerous consequences to the planet's three-quarters dominant space, the critical relationship between humans and the oceans are in jeopardy of stalling. "Oceans are warming and becoming more acidic, causing coral bleaching and reducing biodiversity," Guterres cautioned. "Changing currents will have a serious impact on weather patterns, and we must prepare for more frequent storms and droughts."[21] At this rate of devastation, even the desalination technology that began in the 1970s in the parched Middle East and has since spread to 150 countries will be compromised. Considering that 16 billion gallons are produced daily by the world's 14,450 desalination plants[22]—with Persian Gulf countries relying mostly on seawater for their water needs—the ongoing damage to the oceans pose a serious threat to the already politically unstable region. And with new desalination plants expected to add as much as 13 billion gallons a day to the global water supply—the equivalent of another Colorado River[23]—the current conditions of Earth's oceans amplify the water supply predicament.

But it is not only water shortage that highlights this most consequential twenty-first century crisis. Perhaps even more troubling is the issue of water quality in the limited supply we have. Today, even the lucky few who get their water from mountain springs where the beginning of the flow originates, they, too, have been plagued by water contamination. A routine water quality test carried out in a mountain in Montana proved to be unsafe. The note from the lab evinced the gravity of the problem: "Too numerous to count—background bacteria."[24] Seemingly, few things are as insidious as bad water. Regardless of how clean the water in the glass you hold may look, a myriad of chemicals called "emerging contaminants," many of which are not tested for their toxicity, because there are just too many of them. Then, when you add all the other "regular contaminants," which can range from lead and plastic to narcotics and pharmaceuticals, you have an inauspicious water cocktail that can literally catch on fire; or worse yet, explode.

On New Year's Day 2009, a water well exploded in the small town of Dimock, northern Pennsylvania. The Pennsylvania Department of Environmental Protection determined that methane from a natural gas well had seeped into the water supplies of several Dimock families. In some cases, there was so much gas in the water, people could light it on fire.[25] In a different finding, a U.S. Geological Survey researcher used a substantial array of 10,000 test wells to sample groundwater beneath the Massachusetts Military Reservation on Cape Cod. Because of the contaminants under the site where jet fuel spilled years ago, water collected there could replace cigarette lighter fluid and burned just the same.[26] This became, literally, a burning issue to our already somber water's woes.

As it is with everything else, the free market profit-driven redeemer always comes to the rescue of society, as market forces step in under the guise of offering bogus solutions to the very same problems it creates. Thus, when it comes to shortage of water, privatization has been seen by the World Bank and developed nations as the most effective way to provide clean water to poor countries. However, as it's always the case in most capitalist ventures, the rich have benefited at the expense of the poor. Political resistance and violence have erupted in response to increasingly high cost of water. From Bolivia to Zimbabwe, many demonstrations and social upheavals have occurred in protest against the ownership of water rights by multinational companies. And since profiteering underlines these initiatives, the opposition should not come as a surprise. Sub-Saharan Africa, for instance, received less than 1 percent of all the money invested in water supplies by private companies in 10 years between 1997 and 2007.[27] With such a disparity in place, social unrest is but inevitable.

In September 1998, the International Monetary Fund (IMF) approved a $138 million loan for Bolivia with some very tight strings attached: Bolivia had to agree selling off "all remaining public enterprises, including national oil refineries and Cochabamba's local water agency, SEMAPA. A year later, after closed-door negotiations, the Bolivian government signed a $2.5 billion contract to hand over Cochabamba's municipal water system to Aguas del Tunari, a multinational consortium of private investors. Incidentally, Aguas del Tunari was the sole bidder for the privatization of Cochabamba's water system. Thus, it took merely three months for the population of Cochabamba to shut down the city for four days, going on strike, and erecting roadblocks throughout the city. The local turmoil was fueled by skyrocketing increases in water rates that tripled the water bills since the privatization of the city's water infrastructure.[28] The case of Cochabamba, which entangles profit-seeking ventures with the human need for essential—and rapidly disappearing—natural resources, bodes the coming of potential water wars in the foreseeable future.

❦

In the ill-omened mismanagement of uninterrupted growth—and the continuous decline of vital natural resources such as water—lies the madness of the future. Like the deranged idea that fossil fuel would last forever, the belief that water supply is infinite still prevails in many uneducated factions of society. They take for granted that water flows out of the tap naturally, even though they cannot see the residues of pesticides, fungicides, and herbicides that steeped into groundwater and wells from mechanized agricultural production. Neither can they see the countless pollutants they ingest daily, in spite of the metal-like taste that gives away the fact. Nevertheless, many already know that fresh water is one of the most critical issues of the twenty-first century.

Every day each person drinks approximately 4 to 5 quarts of water in a variety of beverages we consume. However, to produce the food we consume daily—the other fundamental necessity for human survival—it requires more than 2,000 quarts of water.[29] Furthermore, as aquifers run dry in many parts of the world, competition for access and control of water supplies will likely become an even more lucrative corporate investment that will enrich a few at the expense of many. It's estimated that the annual depletion of aquifers worldwide amount to at least 160 billion tons of water per year. And because it takes about a thousand tons of water to produce 1 ton of grain, the water taken each year and not replaced could produce 160 million tons of grain—enough to feed approximately half a billion people at today's average rate of consumption.[30] Thus, by logical inference, shortage of water translates into a complete socioeconomic destabilization. And when survival is at stake, hostility and war always ensue.

As both the world's population and economic output increases at dizzying speed—the pace of change and growth today is faster than at any other time in human history—we are left with the herculean task of balancing the hallowed principle of free market economics: supply and demand. The problem, however, is that we've already passed the point of balancing human needs and economic demands. We've reached the point of crisis, which demands that we supply solutions to immediate problems with an eye in the future. Otherwise, there will be no future at all; certainly not one that we'd want to be a part of.

After analyzing important aspects of what I perceive to be a mad reality, I'm certainly convinced that at the core of the tragic ecological devastation, widespread poverty, human despair and disease, among countless other misfortunes of our highly technological civilization, lies the destructive forces of capitalism. Like a beast that devours everything on its path, the system can only thrive on unfettered exploitation of people and unrelenting exploration of the natural environment.

Now it is clear to me that the madness of the future is nothing but a sequel of the madness of the past. The only way we can possibly regain our life-saving sanity is in the present. But we must act with a sense of urgency, for the present is swiftly slipping into the future.

NOTES

[1] James Lovelock, *The Ages of Gaia* (New York: Bantam Books, 1990), 16.
[2] This type of pollution is a major threat to the forests and wildlife of the northeastern United States and the adjoining areas of Canada. Acid rain is a result of the combination of water and chemicals released into the atmosphere by the burning of fossil fuels. E.D. Hirsch, Jr., Joseph F. Kett, James Trefil, *The Dictionary of Cultural Literacy* (New York: Houghton Mifflin Company, 1993), 496.
[3] James W. Loewen, *Lies My Teacher Told Me* (New York: The New Press, 1995), 260.
[4] http://www.history.com/this-day-in-history/tsunami-devastates-indian-ocean-coast
[5] http://www.history.com/topics/hurricane-katrina
[6] James M. Henslin, *Sociology: A Down to Earth Approach* (Needham Heights, MA: Allyn and Bacon, 1999), 635.
[7] Ibid.
[8] Al Gore, *An Inconvenient Truth* (New York: Rodale, 2006), 10.
[9] Rick Potts, *Humanity Descent: The Consequences of Ecological Instability* (New York: William Morrow and Company, Inc., 1996), 38.
[10] James M. Henslin, *Sociology: A Down to Earth Approach*, 637.
[11] Anderson/Taylor, *Sociology: Understanding a Diverse Society Update, 4/e w/Practice Test* (Mason, Ohio: Cengage Learning, 2008), 579.
[12] Julian Brookes, "Why Water is the New Oil?" *Rolling Stone Magazine*, July 7, 2011. http://www.rollingstone.com/politics/news/why-water-is-the-new-oil-20110707
[13] Tom Athanasiou, *Divided Planet: The Ecology of Rich and Poor* (New York: Little, Brown and Company, 1996), 287.
[14] Steve Burns, Executive in Charge of Production, *Collapse: Based on the Book by Jared Diamond* (DVD), National Geographic Society, 2010.
[15] David Carle, "A Level of Concern," *The American Legion*, July 2015, 33.
[16] Ibid.
[17] Sarah Zielinski, "The Colorado River Runs Dry," *Smithsonian Magazine*, October 2010. http://www.smithsonianmag.com/science-nature/the-colorado-river-runs-dry-61427169/
[18] Ibid.
[19] David Carle, "A Level of Concern," 34.
[20] "Water: Our Thirsty World, A Special Issue, *National Geographic*, April 2010, 52, 56, 150.
[21] Anmar Frangoul, "UN Secretary General Guterres says world's oceans are facing unprecedented threat," *CNBC*, June 6, 2017. https://finance.yahoo.com/news/un-secretary-general-guterres-says-114445465.html
[22] *National Geographic*, 32.
[23] Ibid., 33.

[24] Michael Parfit, "Troubled Waters Run Deep," *National Geographic Special Edition*, November 1993, 78.
[25] David Freeman and Timothy Gower, "Big Gulp," *Reader's Digest*, August 2011, 78.
[26] Michael Parfit, "Troubled Waters Run Deep," 80.
[27] John Vidal, "Privatization Has Failed to Address the Water Problem in Developing Nations," *Will the World Run Out of Fresh Water?* (Farmington Hills, MI: Greenhaven Press, 2007), 73.
[28] Sheraz Sadiq, Associate Producer for Frontline World, "Timeline: Cochabamba's Water Revolt," Public Broadcast System, http://www.pbs.org/frontlineworld/stories/bolivia/timeline.html
[29] James Martin, *The Meaning of the 21st Century* (New York: Riverhead Books, 2006), 66.
[30] Ibid., 67.

Conclusion

As I reach the end of this book, a fundamental question remains to be answered: What is madness?

In the introduction I referred to dictionary definitions of madness, which are varied and inconclusive: rage, insanity, extreme folly, ecstasy, enthusiasm, and ailments characterized by frenzied behavior. However, the pursuit of treatment to any ailment is not based on the symptoms of the illness but the underlying causes. Although the experts in the medical field persuade us to believe that madness—or more scientifically termed, mental illness—is triggered by biophysical imbalances and neurological malfunctions, they can't pinpoint what set off the multitude of symptoms; the root cause, that is. Thus, instead of heeding their systematic speculations based on biochemistry, I've relied on my empirical knowledge of the world to reach my own conclusion: the root cause of mental and emotional disturbances afflicting hundreds of millions of people everywhere sprouts from complex sociological issues. It is the millenary development of a socioeconomic and political culture of madness that has endured the centuries and now pervades in industrial-technological societies. Perhaps there is an element of the egg or chicken-first dilemma to this quandary. In my turn, however, I am convinced that, in spite of an inherent element of insanity in the human species, people go mad because they grow up in a culture of madness; or as Rousseau asserted, "society is the original sin."[1] The anthropological and sociological characteristics of madness can be observed from the very early stages of the human evolutionary process. But it's from the Middle Ages to the present time that a plethora of evidences of inhered human madness emerges to the surface of the muddled waters of our modern industrial civilization.

After ruling the Western World for hundreds of years, the fall of the mighty Roman Empire gave way to what's arguably the darkest time in human history—until now. For a period of a thousand years, between the 5th and 15th century C.E., humanity plunged into an abyss of ignorance and despair. Consumed by fear and insecurities, Christianity stepped in to fill the chaotic emptiness of the human existence. Soon, the Church centralized its government around the triumph of papal monarchy, challenged the sway of emperors and kings, and called forth the crusading movement, one of the most egregious acts of plundering in human history. However, the most important asset possessed by the Church was the governance of knowledge; the supremacy of intellectual authority. Thus, with accumulation of wealth, political power, and control of knowledge, the Christian Church became a dominant empire on its own terms—and its influence remains unabated centuries later. In the United States, as well as in many Western countries, Christianity is much more than a dominant religion: it is an established political force to be reckoned with.

Nevertheless, of all the riches acquired from the plundering of nations and the drubbing of naïve people's mind into submission, one of the most valuable assets of the Christian Church has been the monopoly of knowledge, which it proclaimed as the undeniable "truth" supported by the holy words of sacred scriptures. These words, which the assumed representative of God on Earth never jotted down, not only command respect, but also can be interpreted in convenient ways for the purpose of manipulation. Thus, in a simplistic dialectical process, if knowledge equals God and the Church is the only liaison to this powerful supernatural being, then the Church controls this knowledge. And since Francis Bacon (1561–1626) avowed that "knowledge is power," the inference is that the Church is power. However, its power is as spurious as the knowledge it claims to possess—and most of it is absurd at best.

The intrinsic madness to the fabrication of knowledge is best exemplified in the work of the biblical scholar James Ussher (1581–1656), the Anglican Archbishop of Armagh in Northern Ireland. Computing from the named generations recorded in the Bible, Ussher arrived at the conclusion that creation had occurred in the year 4004 B.C.E. Not to be academically overshadowed, the Reverend Dr. John Lightfoot (1602–

1675), vice-chancellor of the Cambridge University, the renowned institution of higher learning, added the most preposterous assumption of knowledge ever uttered by a member of the Christian Church:

> "...heaven and Earth, centre and circumference, were created all together in the same instant, and clouds full of water. This work took place and man was created by the Trinity on October 23, 4004 B.C.E. at nine o'clock in the morning."[2]

The stupidity, hubris, and insanity of this statement by a religious man of knowledge always made me wonder how in the world he calculated this preposterous data, particularly the precise time of creation. Although today the lunacy of Dr. John Lightfoot's scholarly proclamation is debunked by basic information in a fifth grade science textbook, there are many other equally outlandish religious declarations prevailing in our highly scientific and technological society. Indeed, the fact that puerile religious concepts still exert enormous influence in social and political affairs is an issue of grave concern—and the consequences are hefty.

In addition to misusing the pretentious ownership of truth to manipulate the masses, the Christian Church turned its specious knowledge into a weapon with which to commit horrific crimes against humanity. The burning of human beings at the stake for disagreeing with Christianity's dogma, many of whom were absolutely correct about their proclamation of knowledge, e.g. the Italian Dominican friar Giordano Bruno (1548–1600), is tantamount to the modern abuses of the radicalism of another major world religion. As the two factions of Islam, the Shiites and Sunnis, battle against each other for the supremacy of their particular beliefs, the brutal decapitations, tortures, and mass murder of innocent people run rampant in a world in chaos. Even traditionally peaceful religions such as Buddhism have resorted to despicable acts of violence, as it is the case in Myanmar where religious intolerance has become endemic.[3] In spite of Prince Siddhartha Gautama (c. 563/480 B.C.E.–c. 483 /400 B.C.E.) non-violent teachings and principles, Buddhist monks in Myanmar are no strangers to violence and conflict. Incidentally, neither Jesus of Nazareth (c. 4 B.C.E.–c. 30/33 C.E.) nor the Prophet Muhammad (c. 570 C.E.–632 C.E.) preached, condoned, or carried out acts of violence against non believers. As it's been said, "It's not God I have a problem with; it's His fan club."⁴

What's the underlying common denominator among different religious manifestations of intolerance and brutality throughout the centuries? Why are there so many factions and contentions within religious groups? Either is Christianity's Catholics against Protestants, or Islam's Shiites against Sunnis, or Buddhism's Mahayana against the Theravada tradition, they all seem to find a common ground in the inherent madness of the human condition; that state of being that is exacerbated by perennial anxiety triggered by fear of the unknown. Indeed, blind religious devotion is, as Freud diagnosed, an expression of collective neurosis. Although he acknowledged that religion has performed a valuable service to civilization by taming asocial instincts and creating a sense of community around a shared set of beliefs, it has also exacted an enormous psychological cost to the individual making him perpetually subordinate to the primal father figure embodied by God.⁵ In the same token, abiding by strict outdated codes of pseudo-morality can only be detrimental to the mental health of both the individual and the society he belongs.

Unlike the Renaissance that emerged from the shadows of the Dark Ages when Christianity flourished, our fortune today may not prove to be so redeeming. In fact, irrational allegiance to the two dominant organized religions has already heralded a new dark age from which we may not recover any time soon, unless their specious dogmas are exorcised by the power of human discernment and compassion.

As it is, organized religion has become but the institutionalized expression of archaic doctrines based on ambiguous writings open to a slew of different interpretations. It has not only lost the way to genuine spirituality, which reigns in the realm of the heart, but turned into a serious collective mental illness with the dangerous symptomatic reactions of fundamentalism. And while each religion sect claims ownerships of righteousness, they have wronged everyone else who doesn't subscribe to their extremism. They have severed the only sacred tie that connects us all into one spiritual group: our humanity.

Nobel Prize laureate Bertrand Russell suggests the way back to sanity this way:

"To find the right road out of this despair, civilized man must enlarge his heart as he has enlarged his mind. He must learn to transcend self, and in so doing to acquire the freedom of the Universe."[6]

In a culture infused with the values of competition, greed, and self-ishness, Russell's proposition might prove to be a nearly impossible task to accomplish.

❀

Attempting to finding out what madness means, two alternative word choices for the same questions may offer a starting point to the investigation; not because of the answers they elicit, but the choice of the questions themselves: is it love or money that makes the world go round? If you choose the former, you're an idealistic humanitarian who believes that love is a powerful transformative energy in the world. You want to promote the development of the enlarged heart that Russell suggests. But if you espouse the expression "money is what makes the world go around," then you stand in a supposedly advantageous position because this is the prevailing attitude; and historically, it has always been this way. However, this is also the way of madness.

As faith is directed by religious zealotry, money is governed by market forces. Operating like the most sophisticated casino in the history of gambling, the capital market is the heartbeat of an utterly insane economic system that must grow incessantly just to maintain its ever-unstable existence. Within this complex gaming apparatus, people's livelihoods become the red chips on the green velvet table of profit where the house (those who control capital) always wins. Whenever profits dwindle, massive unemployment ensues and millions of people lose their only means of survival in a world where capital is the ruthless sovereign. And the unexpected turn of unfortunate economic events, like clockwork, always happens in anticipated cyclical fashion. At the same time, limited natural resources are devoured with voracious abandon to feed the economic beast, while the world population grows at astonishingly fast pace. Indeed, the model of the economic system of capitalism is the quintessential manifestation of institutionalized madness. And even though capitalism is touted to generate great wealth for individuals and nations, it leaves an immeasurable trail of misery and destruction behind the path it blazes through—and the evidences of its wretchedness are as abundant as the riches the system produces.

In addition to its widespread economic dominance in a collapsing world, capitalism has turned economics into a powerful weapon with which to influence, control, and subjugate nations and citizens. By dint of its supremacy in international commerce, capitalism wields an inordinate amount of power with which to exert pressures on countries that refuse to defer to its demands. As nations have become bona fide business entities with income (GNP), debt, and even credit ratings, they must often give in to arbitrary financial demands by organizations such as the World Trade Organization, the World Bank Group and the International Monetary Fund, all of which are administered by the honchos of the system. But this economic pistol is not only brandished for financial gains; it is also utilized as a weapon of diplomatic war through sanctions, embargoes, and trade agreements. Besides, with its destructive cycles of boom and bust, the very nature of the system engenders a great deal of continuous anxiety for workers who own neither the means of production nor the control of their own labor. The constant apprehension about losing one's livelihood—particularly after middle age—is a potent source of stress that can push the red button of madness at any time.

Then, there is the financial madness ignited by greed, which can be initiated by either large corporations or one single wealthy person. As it happens often, once regulations are loosened by business-friendly government administrations, the potential for economic disaster is aggrandized by the temptation to take more risks for increased profits—the ultimate gambling thrill. In one of the largest meltdowns in the history of the U.S. economy, the collapse of the Savings and Loans crisis of the 1980s and 90s threw the financial markets topsy-turvy. Then it came the fall of the dominant Enron Corporation, one of the most innovative and supposedly stable companies in the country. Lastly—but not the least and by no means the last—the economic meltdown that became known as the Great Recession of 2008 brought the world economy to the fringe of collapse. One man who annihilated the financial lives of thousands of people illustrates the zeitgeist of our economic culture. With an insatiable appetite for unrestrained accumulation of wealth, the case of fraudster Bernie Madoff (1938–   ), a multi-billionaire who got carried away with his out of control excessive indulgences, raises the question of greed as a warning sign of madness prompted by an economic system that incites a perpetual pursuit of profit sparked off by selfishness. How much is enough for a madman to live a comfortable life? Apparently there is never enough, for the idea of happiness based on the concept of perpetual accumulation of wealth will never be fulfilled.

As for me, a different kind of madman, I say that happy is the man who is content with his lot, for he'll always have everything he needs to be happy.

In order to make sure that the socioeconomic system runs smoothly, it is imperative to establish a solid governmental foundation. This is common knowledge that has been observed throughout the course of human history. Although political power has always been held by those who wield control of wealth and resources (monarchies, empires, papacy, etc.), since the early twentieth century two dominant forms of government have predominated: communism and democracy. Perhaps it may come as a shock that, though seemingly antagonistic to each other, they are very much alike—and both have been corrupted.

After voicing such a heretic political statement, I must expedite a reasonable argument, lest I may be perceived as a legitimate madman. But it is not as irrational as it seems. Actually, when juxtaposing communism and democracy, it becomes immediately evident that they both share a common madness: they're both afflicted with the illusion of equality; and both embrace the fallacious notion that people are equal. In traditional Soviet-style communism, the politburo governed by proxy on behalf of the people it oppressed. The citizens were supposed to have equal rights, even though the political class had interests of its own. Similarly, in modern democracy there is the illusion of equality by one person-one-vote system, which is an affront to the obvious dissimilarities in individual intelligence, education, and perspicacity that distinguish culturally unique individuals from the hoi polloi. This is not to be interpreted as a pejorative remark on our less gifted fellow-citizens, but a valid observation of the masses and their individual interests. If anything, this argument calls for the realization that the ultimate duty and responsibility of those who are better off—be it intellectually, emotionally, or financially—is to assist those at a lower stage of development to move up the ladder. Unfortunately, people in both political systems have done exactly the opposite: they have taken advantage of their alleged superiority while blowing the trumps of equality. After all, the most effective way to enslave people is to make them believe they are free.

Nowadays, both the principles of communism and democracy have been corrupted. Today's China, for instance, resembles nothing of a traditional communist state (the number of millionaires in the country would make Chairman Mao Zedong (1893–1976) roll in his grave, had his body not been embalmed.) Democracy, on the other hand, exposes not only its corrupted nature across the globe, but also its dangerous manipulative powers that liken it to its opposite counterpart. Under the banner of freedom, which is democracy's ideological flagship, the economic concept of free market sneaked in the system and took it over for good. Powerful economic interests represented as corporations have legitimized their takeover of democracy with the politicized Supreme Court ruling that granted citizenship status to inanimate agglomerates.[7] With an unfair competitive financial superiority to influence the electoral process, the utopian free society has been replaced by the realistic free market economics. Thus, by taking complete control of the manipulative tactics over the intellectually disadvantaged masses, powerful economic interests—ranging from the military industrial complex to fossil fuel extraction—embrace the democratic value of one-person, one-vote system as the ideal way to exert and maintain its oppressive economic domination—and with the seal of approval that the freedom of democracy authenticates.

Once validated as a legal financial contributor to the democratic process, corporations and their lackeys exercise their power with the highest level of efficiency. Their public relations strategies are so persuasive that the voting public support policies that are in direct detriment to their own interests. And after wrenching out the legal right to meddle in public affairs and tilt the balance of power in their favor, now there is no limit to where the free market can control the free society, as the quote below exposes:

"Protected by the free speech provision of the First Amendment, corporations marshal huge public relation efforts on behalf of their agendas. In the United States the 170,000 public relations employees whose job it is to manipulate news, public opinion, and public policy in the interests of their clients outnumber news reporters by 40,000...it is the corporation rather than the state that is oppressing us: 'We are ruled by an oppressive market, not an oppressive state.'"[8]

Like the utopian principles of communism were debunked by the former Soviet Union repressive regime—particularly under the brutal dictatorship of Joseph Stalin (1878–1953)—the noble democratic ideals of the Western World long have lost their authenticity as well. What may have worked fine in the small Greek city-states, democracy (*demos* meaning citizenry, and *kratos* referring to the power of rule) has proven to be equally fallacious in practice, especially at a time when technology allows for omnipresent propaganda and marketing. The noble Greek concept that was poetically elevated by Abraham Lincoln's (1809–1865) statement of "government of the people, for the people, and by the people," has been mercilessly obliterated by the cronies of capital. They have transformed democracy into an authentic kleptocracy (*klep* meaning to steal, and *kratos* referring to the power of rule); in essence, a government of thieves;[9] a "government by those who seek chiefly status and personal gain at the expense of the governed."[10] This is what democracy has become: a farce disguised as political nobility.[11]

In the meantime, they play the game just the same: two dominant political parties—the two sides of the same coin of deception—bickering for political supremacy on behalf of the special interests that placed them in office with their monies in detriment to the welfare of the people who placed them in power with their votes. And from the United States, the erstwhile paragon of democracy in the world, the so-called democratic process almost everywhere is proving to be an ingenious way to corrupt politics, swindle national treasures, and deceive public trust. From Brazil to South Korea, a slew of vexing political scandals of corruption have headlined the news media in recent years. Meanwhile, the two dominant political parties in the United States government, the conservatives and the progressives, both march to the tune of the same dictating drum (capital) that maintains the balance between the seemingly opposing agendas. But perhaps the main difference lies on the etymology of the words themselves: conservatives and progressives. The former, as the word indicates, is traditionalist, stationary, and committed to archaic conventions, fabled beliefs, disciplinary behaviors, among other backward peculiar characteristics. But the latter, as the word indicates, moves forward with time that changes everything, including conventions, beliefs, behaviors, and methods. This basic distinction makes it easier to pick out the better side of the rusty political coin.

However, the problem is not with conservatives, progressives, communists, or democracy itself—and not even with any other form of socioeconomic political organization of a society. The real problem is deeply rooted in the inherent madness of the human condition; the delusion of supremacy over our fellow human beings, the natural environment that sustains life on Earth, and the irrepressible desire to subdue both for egoistic self-interests. The madness is the problem.

Alas, the myopic vision of the modern madman can only see so far. And seeing the forest for the trees seems too lofty an undertaking for poor eyesight in a deranged mind to envision the future.

Nothing dominates the airwaves and the headlines more than the news about the state of the economy. The S&P 500 index, the NASDAQ composite, the unemployment rate, among the other barometers that determine the health of the economy, all seem to overshadow the major challenge of modern time: the unprecedented ecological crises assailing our planet. In fact, the good news about economic growth runs in opposite direction of environmental care needs. Lying behind the optimistic economic prognostics hides the reality that expansion means that the ecological and demographic problem is worsening at a frightening speed. This is perhaps one of the most conflicting dilemmas of our industrial-technological civilization, for the economy must not stop growing to meet the increasing demands of a rapidly multiplying population. One problem feeds on the other while both devour our limited and dwindling natural resources. Unlike positive economic forecasts, the statistics cannot hide the facts.

America is growing by an average of one person every 16 seconds. In the post-World War II era of the great American economic boom, the U.S. population registered 150,000,000 in 1950. It is projected to reach 400,000,000 in 2050. In order to accommodate this multitude of consumers, the United States loses—every hour--50 acres of farm and ranch land to urban sprawl and development, and the nation's water use has nearly doubled since 1950.[12] But if the consumption of energy, food, water, and space were not grave enough, there is the exacerbating problem of disposal of waste—including nuclear waste—of human consumption, mainly garbage and sewage. In comparative perspective, the United States garbage creation has nearly tripled since 1960. In 2013 Americans generated 254 million tons of trash, which represents 4.4 pounds per person per day.[13] Although the U.S. accounts for a large share of the world's consumption, there are billions of people in hundreds of countries desperate to improve their economic status, which under free market economic rules is determined by consumption, and therefore plenty of trash.

In the wake of the United States, one of the top polluters in the world, exiting the important 2015 United Nations Paris Agreement under the argument that it hinders national economic development, the evidences of environmental crises remain asleep in the consciousness of the nation's pseudo-leaders. In addition to the increasing emission of poisonous chemicals in the atmosphere, the trash that's been strewn around the world has reached catastrophic levels. One of the most notorious examples of this ecological travesty lies in the stretch of the Pacific Ocean between Chile and New Zealand; with the emphasis placed on Henderson Island, which was designated a World Heritage Site in part because of its bird life. In this tiny uninhabited island in the South Pacific, researchers have found almost 38 million pieces of trash. The study concluded that 3,750 new pieces of plastic wash up each day on one beach alone; an event that left a researcher appalled:

"Far from being the pristine 'deserted island' that people might imagine of such a remote place, Henderson Island is a shocking but typical example of how plastic debris is affecting the environment on a global scale...Research has shown that more than 200 species are known to be at risk from eating plastic, and 55 percent of the world's seabirds, including two species found on Henderson Island, are at risk from marine debris."[14]

However, the magnitude of the aberrations caused by irresponsible economic expansion is not limited to uninhabited remote islands. What was once one of the most beautiful bays in the world, Guanabara Bay in Rio de Janeiro, has been turned into a filthy cesspool of raw sewage and industrial waste. In less than half a century, a bay that abounded with all sorts of sea life has become the symbolic graveyard of marine wasteland. But Guanabara Bay is just one example among a growing list of large bodies of water becoming contaminated with the dangerous cost of a maddening concept of progress.

In addition to governmental negligence and corporate apathy to ecological threats, there is always the risk of accidents. In the Silverton area of Colorado, a serious spill from the Gold King mine wastewater gushed out heavy metals and toxic waste in rivers and creeks that turned the entire Animas River yellow. Threatening downstream water supplies in at least three states while posing a long-term public health risk, the strong dose of arsenic, cadmium, lead and other heavy metals that settled down to river bottoms will surely pose risks for years to come. But long before the accident, mines in the Silverton area that were first developed in the 1800s had been releasing steady stream of contaminated wastewater into area creeks, leaving some of them lifeless. Researchers have concluded that the negative environmental impact can linger for decades.[15] And as dreadful as these kinds of accidents can be, they dwarf compared to the most hazardous of all contaminants in the waste stockpile of modern industrial civilization.

An old relic of the early days of nuclear engineering, the Hanford Nuclear Reservation was established in 1943 as part of the Manhattan Project that developed the first atomic bomb. Located on south-central Washington State along the Columbia River, the Hanford Site was home of the B reactor, the first full-scale plutonium production reactor in the world.[16] Today, however, it has become a major threat to the local communities of the Pacific Northwest, particularly in the Tri-Cities area. After producing plutonium for nuclear weapons for decades, the 177 underground tanks storing millions of gallons of the most dangerous nuclear waste have been leaking. In a recent incident, the roof of a tunnel partially collapsed triggering the evacuation of workers and one worker tested positive for radioactive contamination on his clothing. Although Hanford officials were quick to announce that no airborne release of radiation occurred, when it comes to contamination of the environment, the truth is always veiled in deception (the 2014 high levels of lead in the drinking water in Flint, Michigan comes to mind). Pressure to expedite the cleanup of the sprawling Hanford Site has been mounting, though the forecast is that will take until 2060 at a cost of $100 billion.[17] The unveiled truth, however, is that until then the potential for other leaks are high, especially considering the deteriorating state of the underground nuclear waste storage.

But all things considered, the risk of leaks in deteriorating nuclear waste containers in underground sites around the country should not be the worst of our concerns. Although critical accidents like the Fukushima Daiichi nuclear disaster remain as probable future occurrences, the most frightening of all cases scenarios is the one that seems to be more likely with every passing day: an all out nuclear war and the ensuing holocaust—the apotheosis of madness.

On July 16, 1945 at 5:29:45 am in Alamogordo, New Mexico, the first atomic bomb was successfully tested. The scientists involved in the project, along with a few dignitaries, had removed themselves 10,000 yards away to observe as the first mushroom cloud of searing light stretched 40,000 feet in the air and generated the destructive power of 15,000 to 20,000 tons of TNT. The tower on which the bomb sat when detonated was vaporized.[18] Afterwards, the only question remaining was on whom was the bomb to be dropped? Germany was the original target, but at the time it was a defeated nation and it'd already surrendered to allied forces. The only belligerent nation still standing was feisty Japan. Thus, on August 6 and 9, 1945 the first atomic bombs ever dropped on a human population was unleashed in Hiroshima and Nagasaki leaving an apocalyptic aftermath. It not only put an end to World War II, but also changed forever the nature and dangers of future wars. As one of the principal physicists on the Manhattan Project, J. Robert Oppenheimer (1904–1967) said after witnessing the earth-shattering force of a nuclear weapon in the New Mexico desert, "We knew the world would not be the same."[19]

Today some 9 countries—more likely 10, including the State of Israel—brandish known nuclear arsenals, and approximately 20 other possess the technology and materials to develop this most potent weapon of mass destruction. In addition, since the breakup of the Soviet Union, nuclear weapons, materials, and technology fell at risk of theft or clandestine sale to rogue states, terrorist organizations, and criminal networks. Expertise is also a dangerous intellectual commodity in high demand. It's been reported that the mastermind of the Pakistani nuclear bomb, Abdul Qadeer Khan (1936–   ), passed nuclear secrets, weapons production technology, and bomb designs to Libya, North Korea, and Iran.[20] Osama bin Laden (1957–2011), too, was eager to acquire nuclear devices to mete out some serious punishments on the infidels in the United States. The truth, however, is that since that turning point day on July 16, 1945 nuclear weapons have become the plague of human civilization; like a technological disease; a pandemic of utterly irresponsible madness. Alas, Oppenheimer was correct when he said that the world would never be the same.

With some experts claiming that an act of nuclear terrorism is inevitable, which the most likely case scenario would be through the release of a "dirty bomb" (a dirty bomb is a conventional explosive packed with radioactive material), the nightmare of the nuclear age makes it difficult to dream about the future. Meanwhile, the Bulletin of the Atomic Scientists says that Earth is now closer to human-caused doomsday than it has been in more than 30 years because of global warming and nuclear weaponry. This advocacy group founded by the creators of the atomic bomb recently moved their infamous Doomsday Clock ahead two minutes; that is, the world is now three minutes from a catastrophic midnight. The bulletin's executive director did not mince words to express the gravity of the issue:

> "This is about doomsday; this is about the end of civilization as we know it...The probability of global catastrophe is very high, and the actions needed to reduce the risks of disaster must be taken very soon."[21]

Nevertheless, we remain in a deep slumber of delusion while immersed in a nightmare from which we seem unable to wake up. We carry on our daily business with mundane concerns about the yield return in our 401-k retirement plan account, but never seem to take into consideration that the future itself has been losing interest to the point of bankruptcy. The mirage about a future that will go on as usual in spite of the overwhelming odds against it is the quintessential madness of illusion. Something has shifted in human nature as we lost ourselves in the alluring power of scientific and technological knowledge. Perhaps, an even more powerful and destructive split than the atom has taken place: the severance of our human nature.

Between 1500 and 1700 there was a dramatic shift in the way people pictured the world and in their whole way of thinking. Before the sixteenth century, people lived in small cohesive communities and experienced nature in terms of organic relationships characterized by the independence of spiritual and material phenomena and the subordination of individuals' needs to those of the community.[22] Despite the monopolistic privileged rules of monarchies, people lived a community-oriented lifestyle. But after the Age of the Scientific Revolution that began when Nicholas Copernicus (1473–1543) debunked the belief that the Earth was the center of the Universe, man did not squander any time to fill in the role himself. As science and technology evolved through the next five centuries, the biped intelligent mammal became the centerpiece of life; "the paragon of animals," as Shakespeare said through the words of Hamlet. But by the time René Descartes (1596–1650) uttered his celebrated statement *"Cogito ergo sum"* (I think therefore I exist), a fatal split in the essence of human nature took place and we haven't recovered from this rupture ever since. As the mind became the sovereign of what it means to be human, it dissociated from equally important components of the holistic essence of humanity, therefore corrupting human nature. Thus, we transformed into selfish intellectual creatures uninterested in the welfare of our citizens, communities, environmental responsibilities, or anything else that does not pertain to an egotistical approach that became the center of the only universe man cares about: himself.

Perhaps the greatest misfortune of the Cartesian division is that it acknowledged the material Universe as a machine and nothing but a machine.[23] And with humanity sitting at the center of the material Universe, it transgressed the individual to a similarly mechanical level of being while disconnecting the mind from the emotions. Thus, like the split of the nucleus of uranium atom that activates the atomic bomb, the infinitesimally small human-atom of the Universe has been split and the explosion of the human tragedy ensued. And to make matters worse, the insatiable economic system aggravates the problem by turning man against man in a savage winner-take-all competitive rage. Meanwhile, the sanctified values of individualism, greed, selfishness, and the unbridled pursuit of happiness (profit) divide communities as the divided man loses the meaning of solidarity and empathy in a world cracking asunder.

Apparently, now we believe that only religion can spare us from a total civilization collapse; not religion in the traditional sense of the word, but the latest one we concocted. Spellbound by our scientific and technological advancements, we've pioneered a novel concept of religious dogma in which our own evolving intellectual knowledge has become the new god. And as our troubles increase, challenges intensify, and anxiety conquers our common sense, we've deluded ourselves, again, that our latest version of god will save us from the chaos we spawned out of the marriage of ignorance and madness. Now that we've created artificial intelligence and sophisticated technological tools, we have become gods in our own right. Today, there is but one God, and His name is mankind, and science is His prophet.[24]

From about 900 to 200 B.C.E., an unprecedented transformational process unfolded in the civilized world. After a long period of widespread violence and tribulations, the consensus for the need to abandon old ways that had proven to be painfully destructive demanded to be actualized. Widespread suffering exacerbated by excessive selfishness engendered intolerable living conditions. A new way to see, interpret, and live in the world became paramount, as it did the realization that nurturing compassion while subduing violence and hatred was imperative to survival. This was an era that brought about the ideas of Confucianism and Taoism in China, Hinduism and Buddhism in India, monotheism in Israel, and philosophical rationalism in Greece. This was the period of the Buddha, Socrates, Confucius, Jeremiah, the mystics of the Upanishads, Mencius, Euripides, among other luminaries of human knowledge. During this period of intense creativity, spiritual and philosophical geniuses pioneered and entirely new kind of human experience. This was the era that German philosopher Karl Jaspers (1883–1969) called the Axial Age, one of the most seminal periods of intellectual, psychological, and religious change in recorded history.[25]

The Axial Age draws an intimate parallel to our troubled historical time. In the last 300 years, human civilization has been going through unprecedented transformations that have brought us to the edge of the abyss of self-annihilation; and now, we must take similar actions as the

Axial sages suggested for correcting the imbalance. Although they lived in different regions of the world—and at a time when communication was slow and limited—they shared a common vision that was often perceived as radical by their contemporaries: what mattered was not what you believed but how you behave. The only way you could encounter what they called God, Nirvana, Brahman, or the Way was to live a compassionate life. Their objective was to create an entirely different kind of human being. They believed that if people behaved with kindness and generosity to their fellows, they could save the world. We need to rediscover this Axial ethos.[26]

Almost 3,000 years after the beginning of the Axial Age, a new age emerged from the terror of the nuclear mushroom. After World War II, the awareness of the urgency for radical transformation of our destructive way of life became evident. Thus, some fifteen years after the introduction of the atomic bomb to an anxious world, an unprecedented social revolution spread like wild fire around the globe. Albeit short-lived, it was a legitimate social revolution led by middle-class youngsters of the wealthiest nation on Earth. It was a time that embraced new ways of thinking in philosophy, religion, socioeconomic, and political organization, while at the same time dispensing with the chaotic and unsustainable status quo. What became known as the Counterculture Revolution of the 1960s ended by the early 1970s, disappearing as mysteriously as it had arrived.[27] But even though many of the participants in the movement for social, political, and economical transformations ended up corrupted by the very system they opposed (many became the infamous yuppies; the opposite of the hippies), a potently charged seed was planted in the parched soil of our withered culture.

It is not like the youth movement of the 1960s gave way to anything remotely similar to what the Axial Age represents. After all, the Counterculture Revolution last barely a decade, whereas the Axial Age took seven centuries to achieve full bloom. It is not even a fair comparison. And even the New Age that came on the footprints of the hippies' sandals, never generated enough power to influence society in meaningful fashion. In fact, to conservative segments of society new age is a quasi-pejorative term, while to progressives it became another amusing fad with a large profitable market to capitalize on. But far beyond the misguided perceptions of conservatives or progressives, the empirical knowledge acquired during the Counterculture Revolution begot a new belief that socioeconomic and political transformations are, indeed, possible.

Unlike revolutions that have been historically carried out by unified waves of passion, the transformations brought about by what becomes classified as an age or era, those take centuries to come into being. It requires the continuous development of individual citizens until they amalgamate into a robust social body based on the principles of human dignity. What must be done, however, is to initiate the transformational process regardless of how long it may take to reach full maturity. As the Axial Age sage Lao Tzu (604 B.C.E.–531 B.C.E.) said, "A journey of a thousand miles begins with the first step."

❀

At the apex of the Counterculture Revolution, the summer of 1967 became known as "the summer of love." Fifty years later, the summer has become scorching hot with hatred, prejudice, social and political upheaval, among other signs of illnesses of the mind and soul. In fact, a whole culture—and market—has been built on the platform of hate. Violence and hatred have become so prevalent and widespread that they are now socially accepted as a norm of daily living. Criminal acts of all sorts—some of which are utterly gruesome and despicable—unjust economic practices, and merciless political decisions have all become expected occurrences. The vicious combination of hatred and violence is now ubiquitously present in politics, economics, entertainment, and numerous other manifestations of its nefarious effects. Indeed, it has become a deadly disease of madness that can only be diagnosed through a sociological examination that, hopefully, will lead to a cure. And sometimes healing takes place unexpectedly. Although the intensity of collective pathological madness seems to be reaching a plateau, it could be brought down by one of the most efficient means of unification: catastrophe. Unfortunately, it's a pity that it takes a calamity for people to come together in mutual aid. But if that is what we need to be cured from the madness of indifference to the sustainability of life and the dignity of our humanity, then disasters might well be the only effective medicine for the treatment of human apathetic madness.

As we begin a new and decisive century facing unprecedented challenges in the history of human civilization, it seems that the only way out of the countless crises we've created is by adopting a different kind of madness; a radically different way of thinking, living, and being. The venerated economic doctrines of capitalism, the worshiping dogmas of religions, the unrestrained pursuit of selfish happiness, the nurturing of insatiable greed and all the other syndromes of what I perceive to be downright madness, all of them can and must be overcome, if humanity is going to make to the twenty-second century. For this to take place, it is important to bear in mind that many things that you probably think are wrong today have been accepted as morally correct in the past; e.g. slavery, serfdom, racial segregation, among many other travesties. Conversely, many other values that you may think are right today; e.g. private property, religious beliefs, free market economics, etc. may likely be deemed to be wrong by future societies. Everything always changes, and right and wrong are relative to a particular time and place.[28]

Today, denying long-standing values upon which modern civilization is buttressed on would be considered a symptom of irreverent madness. If anyone were to decry just one of the sacrosanct principles of economics (private property), politics (democracy), or religion (the belief in God), that person would be ostracized and perhaps even confined to either a mental or penal institution. After all, only a madman would dare to debunk the morality that took centuries to build. But for the madman, it might as well take centuries to topple obsolete pseudo-values, as long as it begins right away. Madness is always willing to wait for timely healing.

Perhaps if more people would come together as though a veritable tragedy were already happening, we might be able to find a way out of this labyrinth of chaos. The reality, however, is that life-threatening adversities are already at hand, and unless we pull together as we would under an emergency—and that is exactly the case—we are but sure of self-annihilation. And if self-destruction is the standard of normality, then I now understand the hidden meaning in the words of American poet Charles Bukowski (1920–1994): "Some people never go crazy. What truly horrible lives they must lead."

NOTES

[1] Jean Jacques Rousseau, *The Social Contract and Discourse on the Origin of Inequality* (New York: Washington Square Press, 1967), xiii.

[2] C. Loring Brace, *The Stages of Human Evolution* (New Jersey: Prentice Hall, Inc., 1991), 9.

[3] Sufyan bin Uzayr, "Buddhism in Myanmar: Extremism and Crimes Against Humanity," *Global Research, Center for Research and Globalization*, August 18, 2014. http://www.globalresearch.ca/buddhism-in-myanmar-extremism-galore/5396471

[4] This anonymous quote shows on the inside front cover dust jacket of Michael Parenti, *God and His Demons* (New York: Prometheus Books, 2010).

[5] Sigmund Freud, *The Future of an Illusion* (New York: W.W. Norton & Company, 1961).

[6] Bertrand Russell, *The Conquest of Happiness* (New York: Liveright Publishing Corporation, 1971), 94.

[7] McConnell v. FEC 2003 (in part). Citizens United vs. Federal Election Commission 558 U.S. 310 (2010) is a game changing constitutional law regarding regulation of political campaign spending by organizations and corporations.

[8] Richard H. Robbins, *Global Problems and the Culture of Capitalism* (Needham Heights, MA: Allyn & Bacon, 1999), 138.

[9] Kleptocracy (from Ancient Greek κλέπτης (kléptēs, "thief"), κλέπτω (kléptō, "steal"), from Proto-Indo-European *klep- ("to steal"); and from the Ancient Greek suffix -κρατία (-kratía), from κράτος (krátos, "power, rule"; *klépto-thieves + -kratos* rule, literally "rule by thieves") is a government with corrupt leaders (kleptocrats) that use their power to exploit the people and natural resources of their own territory in order to extend their personal wealth and political power. Typically this system involves embezzlement of funds at the expense of the wider population. https://en.wikipedia.org/wiki/Kleptocracy.

[10] *Merriam-Webster's Collegiate Dictionary*, Eleventh Edition (Springfield, MA: Merriam-Webster, Incorporated, 2007), 689.

[11] For an interesting overview of the demise of democracy in the modern world see Noreena Hertz, *The Silent Takeover: Global Capitalism and the Death of Democracy* (New York: HarperCollins Publishers, 2003).

[12] Negative Population Growth, *Mother Jones*, May-June 2017, 65.

[13] Ibid.

[14] Mary Bowerman, "Remote island a dump after 38M pieces of trash wash ashore," *USA Today*, May 20, 2017, 1B.

[15] "Experts: Spill leaves long-term risks," *Corvallis Gazette-Times*, August 13, 2015, B5.

[16] "Hanford Site," *Wikipedia*. https://en.wikipedia.org/wiki/Hanford_Site

[17] "Contamination may signal radioactive leak," *Statesman Journal*, May 20, 2017, 6A.

[18] History. http://www.history.com/this-day-in-history/the-first-atomic-bomb-test-is-successfully-exploded

[19] Richard Rhodes, "Living with the Bomb," *National Geographic*, August 2005, 100.

[20] Ibid., 102.

[21] Seth Borenstein, AP science writer, "Atomic Scientists: We're closer to doomsday," *Corvallis Gazette-Times*, January 23, 2015, A6.
[22] Fritjof Capra, *The Turning Point* (New York: Bantam Books, 1983), 53.
[23] Ibid., 60.
[24] Taylor Caldwell, *Dialogues with the Devil* (Mattituck, NY: Aeonian Press, Inc., 1976), 15.
[25] Karen Armstrong, *The Great Transformation* (New York: Alfred A. Knopf, Inc., 2006), xii.
[26] Ibid., xiv.
[27] Todd Gitlin, *The Sixties: Years of Hope, Days of Rage* (New York: Bantam Books, Inc., 1987), 3.
[28] Thomas Nagel, *What Does It All Mean?* (New York: Oxford University Press, 1987), 71-72.

SELECTED REFERENCES

Achbar, Mark; Abbot, Jennifer; Bakan, Joel. *The Corporation*. DVD. New York: Zeitgeist Films, Ltd., 2005.

Andersen/Taylor. *Sociology: Understanding a Diverse Society*, Second Edition. Mason, OH: Cengage Learning, 2008.

Anderson, Kennie. *Land of Hypocrisy*. Black Hawk, SD: Progressive Productions, 2003.

Aristotle. *On Man In The Universe*. Roslyn, New York: Walter J. Black, Inc., 1943.

Armstrong, Karen. *The Great Transformation*. New York: Alfred A. Knopf, Inc., 2006.

Athanasiou, Tom. *Divided Planet: The Ecology of Rich and Poor*. New York: Little, Brown and Company, 1996.

Bates, Theunis, Managing Editor, "Editor's Letter," *The Week*, February 10, 2017.

BBC. "Corruption across EU 'breathtaking'- EU Commission." http://www.bbc.com. 3 February 2014.

Berezin, Robert, M.D. *"Psychiatric Drugs Are False Prophets With Big Profits."* http://www.psychologytoday.com. July 5, 2015.

Blake, William. *The Essential Blake*, Selected by Stanley Kunitz. New York: MJF Books, 1987.

Boal, Mark. "The Agony & Ecstasy of Alexander Shulgin." *Playboy Magazine*, March 2004.

Borenstein, Seth. AP science writer. "Atomic Scientists: We're closer to doomsday."*Corvallis Gazette-Times*, January 23, 2015, A6.

Bowerman, Mary. "Remote island a dump after 38M pieces of trash wash ashore," *USA Today*, May 20, 2017, 1B.

Bowker, John, Editor. *The Oxford Dictionary of World Religions*. New York: Oxford University Press, 1997.

Brace, C. Loring. *The Stages of Human Evolution*. New Jersey: Prentice Hall, Inc., 1991.

Brandt, William. *Arms and Hunger*. New York: Pantheon Books, 1986.

Brookings T. Emerson and P.W. Singer, "War Goes Viral: How Social Media is Being Weaponized," *The Atlantic*, November 2016.

Brookes, Julian. "Why Water is the New Oil?" *Rolling Stone Magazine,* July 7, 2011.

Broussalis, Martin. *Castaneda for Beginners*. New York: Writers and Readers Publishers, Inc., 1999.

Brown, Dee. *Bury My Heart at Wounded Knee*. New York: Holt, Rinehart & Winston, 1970.

Burns, Steve, Executive in Charge of Production. *Collapse: Based on the Book by Jared Diamond* (DVD), National Geographic Society, 2010.

Burton, Neel, M.D., "The Meaning of Madness: Thinking of "mental illness" as more than just illness." *Psychology Today.* https://www.psychologytoday.com. September 24, 2012.

Buscaglia, Leo. *Love.* New York: Ballantine Books, 1972.

Byron, Lord. *The Works of Lord Byron.* Denmark: Wordsworth Edition, Ltd., 1994.

Caldwell, Taylor. *Dialogues with the Devil.* Mattituck, NY: Aeonian Press, Inc., 1976.

Capra, Fritjof. *The Turning Point.* New York: Bantam Books Edition, Simon & Schuster, Inc., 1983.

Carle, David. "A Level of Concern," *The American Legion,* July 2015, 33.

Cartographic Division of the National Geographic Society. *Dawn of Humans.* Washington, D.C., 1997.

Castaneda, Carlos. *The Teachings of Don Juan.* Berkeley, CA: University of California Press, 1998.

Chai, Ch'u with Winberb Chai. *The Story of Chinese Philosophy.* New York: Washington Square Press, Inc., 1961.

Citizens Commission on Human Rights. *The Marketing of Madness: Are We All Insane?* Documentary DVD ISBN 978-1-4031-8759-8.

Collapse, based on the book by Jared Diamond. DVD. National Geographic Channel, 2010.

Corvallis Gazette-Times. "Don't write off Big Pharma," Money & Markets. March 29, 2011, A2.

Corvallis Gazette-Times, "Today in History," January 24, 2017, A2.

Crowley, Michael. "How Wall Street, creator of the financial meltdown, profits at the expense of the middle class." *Reader's Digest,* September, 2010.

Curley, Fia, Associated Press, "Video game addicts can go to 'detox'," *Statesman Journal,* June 12, 2006, 1D, 6D.

Dawood, N. J., translator and notes. *The Koran.* Baltimore, MD: Penguin Books, Ltd., 1974.

Daws, Gavan. *Shoal of Time.* Honolulu, HI: University of Hawaii Press, 1974.

de Assis, Sebastian. *rEvolution in Education.* Lanham, Maryland: The Rowman & Littlefield Publishing Group, 2003.

_____. *Teachers of the World, Unite!* Corvallis, Oregon: The Educational Center Press, 2000.

de Hennezel, Marie. *The Art of Growing Old.* New York: Viking

Penguin Group, 2010.

Della Cava, R. Marco. "Social Networking: Too much of a good thing?" *USA Today, Statesman Journal*, February 15, 2010.

Denenberg, Barry. *Nelson Mandela: No Easy Walk to Freedom.* New York: Scholastic, Inc., 1991.

DeVito, A. Joseph. *The Interpersonal Communication Book*, Fifth Edition. New York: Harper & Row Publishers, 1989.

Doray, Bernard. *From Taylorism to Fordism: A Rational Madness* London: Free Association Books, 1988.

Dunn, Marcia. "7 Earth-size worlds could sustain life." *Corvallis Gazette-Times*, February 23, 2017, A1.

Durning, T. Alan. *How Much is Enough?* New York: W.W. Norton & Company, Inc., 1992.

Editors of Time-Life Books. *The Wild West*. New York: Warner Books, Inc., 1993.

El Essa, Erin. *2016 American Household Credit Card Debt Study,* Nerd Wallet, Inc. Comprehensive details of the study is available at https://www.nerdwallet.com/blog/average-credit-card-debt-household/

Feuerbach, Ludwig. *The Essence of Christianity*. New York: Prometheus Books, 1989.

Fitzgibbon, Will "Files point to $182 mn Halliburton bribery scandal in Nigeria." http://www.indianexpress.com. February 9, 2015.

Foroohar, Rana. "Saving Capitalism," *TIME*, May 23, 2016.

Freeman, David and Timothy Gower, "Big Gulp." *Reader's Digest,* August 2011.

Freire, Paulo. *Pedagogy of the Oppressed*. New York: The Continuum Publishing Company, 1996.

_____. *Education for Critical Consciousness*. New York: The Continuum Publishing Company, 1997.

_____. *The Politics of Education*. New York: Bergin & Garvey Publishers, Inc. 1985.

Freud, Sigmund. *Civilization and Its Discontents*. New York: W.W. Norton & Company, 1961.

_____. *The Future of an Illusion* (New York: W.W. Norton & Company, Inc., 1989.

Fromm, Erich. *The Art of Loving*. New York: Harper & Row Publishers, Inc., 1989.

_____. *The Sane Society*. New York: Henry Holt and Company, Inc., 1990.

_____. *The Revolution of Hope: Toward a Humanized Technology*. New York: Harper & Row Publishers, Inc., 1968.

Ganeri, Anita et al. *Encyclopedia of World History*. United Kingdom: Paragon Books, Ltd., 2009.

Gasset y Ortega, José. *The Revolt of the Masses*. New York: W.W. Norton & Company, Inc., 1957.

Gitlin, Todd. *The Sixties: Years of Hope, Days of Rage*. New York: Bantam Books, Inc., 1987.

Gore, Al. *An Inconvenient Truth*. New York: Rodale, 2006.

Gustavson, Carl G. *A Preface to History*. New York: McGraw-Hill Book Company, Inc., 1983.

Haddock, Doris with Dennis Burke. *You're Never Too Old to Raise a Little Hell*. New York: Villard Books, a division of Random House, Inc., 2003.

Hales, Diane, "Smart Ways To Get Yourself What Out Of Debt," *Parade Magazine*, February 13, 1994.

Hamilton, Edith. *Mythology*. New York: Back Bay Books/Little Brown & Company, Inc., 1998.

Henslin, James M. *Sociology: A Down to Earth Approach*. Needham Heights, MA: Allyn and Bacon, 1999.

Hertz, Noreena. *The Silent Takeover: Global Capitalism and the Death of Democracy*. New York: HarperCollins Publishers, 2003.

Hirsch E.D., Jr., Joseph F. Kett, James Trefil. *The Dictionary of Cultural Literacy*. New York: Houghton Mifflin Company, 1993.

Hoffer, Eric. *The True Believer*. New York: Perennial Classics, an imprint of Harper-Collins Publishers, Inc., 2002.

Hofmann, Albert. *LSD My Problem Child*. Los Angeles, CA: J.P. Tarcher, Inc., 1983.

Holmes, Jack. "A Trump Surrogate Drops the Mic: 'There's No Such Thing as Facts,'" *Esquire Magazine*, December 1, 2016.

Hunt, Cynthia A. and Garrels, Robert M. Water: *The Web of Life*. New York: W.W. Norton & Company, Inc., 1972.

Huxley, Aldous. *Brave New World Revisited*. New York: Harper & Row Publishers, Inc., 2000.

_____. *The Doors of Perception, Heaven and Hell*. New York: Harper & Row Publishers, Inc., 1956.

Jahn, George and David Rising, "Munich shooter called a loner," *Corvallis Gazette-Times*, July 25, 2016, B6.

Kaczynski, Theodore. *Industrial Society and its Future*. PDF document, 1995.

Kaplan, I. Harold, Sadock J. Benjamin. *Comprehensive Glossary of Psychiatry and Psychology*. Baltimore, Maryland: Williams & Wilkins, 1991.

Kauffman, Walter, editor and translator. *The Portable Nietzsche*.

New York: Viking Penguin, Inc., 1982.

Keller, Helen. *The Story of My Life*. Mineola, NY: Dover Publications, Inc., 1996.

Kesey, Ken. *One Flew Over the Cuckoo's Nest*. New York: Penguin Books, 2003.

Khan, Inayat Hazrat. *Mastery Through Accomplishment*. New Lebanon, New York: Omega Publications, Inc., 1993.

Kotler, Steven. "The New Psychedelic Renaissance," *Playboy Magazine,* April 2010.

Krantz, Matt. "11 Drugmakers Wield Pricing Power." *USA Today,* August 26, 2016.

Labier, Douglas. *Modern Madness*. New York: Simon & Schuster, Inc., 1989.

Lasch, Christopher. *The Revolt of the Elites and the Betrayal of Democracy*. New York: W.W. Norton & Company, Inc., 1995.

Loewen. W, James. *Lies My Teacher Told Me*. New York: The New Press, 1995.

Loomis, Ropes Louise, Editor. *On Man in the Universe*. New York: Walter J. Black, Inc., 1943.

Lovelock, James. *The Ages of Gaia: A Biography of Our Living Earth*. New York: Bantam Books, 1990.

Macdougall, J.D. *A Short History of Planet Earth* .New York: John Wiley & Sons, Inc., 1996.

Malthus, Robert Thomas. *An Essay on the Principle of Population*. New York: Penguin Books, 1985.

Martin, James. *The Meaning of the 21st Century*. New York: Riverhead Books, 2006.

May, Rollo. *The Courage to Create*. New York: W. W. Norton & Company, 1994.

McKay, Adam. *The Big Short*. (DVD) Los Angeles: Paramount Picture, 2015.

McLoughlin, Beth. "Brazil's Trump?" *www.usnews.com*, January 19, 2017.

McNall Burns, Edward et al. *World Civilization,* Volume 1, Seventh Edition. New York: W.W. Norton & Company, Inc., 1986.

____. *World Civilization*, Volume 2, Seventh Edition. New York: W.W. Norton & Company, Inc., 1986.

McWilliams, Peter, Editor. *LIFE 101Quote Books*. Los Angeles: Prelude Press, 1996.

Merriam-Webster's Collegiate Dictionary, Eleventh Edition. Springfield, MA: Merriam-Webster, Incorporated, 2007.

Moore, Michael. *Capitalism: A Love Story*. DVD. California: Overture Films, 2009.

_____. *Where to Invade Next?* DVD. North End Productions, Inc., 2015.

Morais, Fernando. *Paulo Coelho, A Warrior's Life*. New York: HarperCollins Publishers, 2009.

Moss, Ralph W. *The Cancer Industry*. Sheffield, U.K: Equinox Press, 1996.

Moulson, Geir, Associated Press, "European nationalists buoyed by Trump," *Corvallis Gazette-Times*, January 22, 2017, A2.

Nagel, Thomas. *What Does It All Mean?* New York: Oxford University Press, 1987.

Neill, A.S. *Summerhill: A Radical Approach to Child Rearing*. New York: Hart Publishing Company, 1960.

Nerburn, Kent, Editor. The Wisdom of the Native Americans. New York: MJF Books, 1999.

News Hour. *Public Broadcast System*. January 5, 2017.

Nies, Judith. *Native American History*. New York: Ballantine Books, a division of Random House, Inc., 1996.

Nietzsche, Friedrich, *Thus Spoke Zarathustra*. New York: Viking Penguin, Inc., 1976.

_____. *Human All Too Human*. Lincoln, NE: University of Nebraska Press, 1986.

O'Hara, Shelley. *Nietzsche within your grasp*. Hoboken, NJ: Wiley Publishing, Inc., 2004.

Orwell, George. *1984*. New York: Penguin Publishing Group, 1977.

Ouspensky, P.D. *The Psychology of Man's Possible Evolution*. New York: Vintage Books, 1973.

Palast, Greg. *The Best Democracy Money Can Buy*. New York: Penguin Putnam, Inc., 2003.

Parenti, Michael. *God and His Demons*. New York: Prometheus Books, 2010.

Parfit, Michael. "Troubled Waters Run Deep." *National Geographic Special Edition*, November 1993.

Parker-Pope, Tara, "Is It Love or Mental Illness? They're Closer Than You Think," *The Wall Street Journal*, February 13, 2007.

Pascal, Blaise. *Pensées*. London: J. M. Dent & Sons, Ltd., 1960.

Pestalozzi, Johann. *Pestalozzi's Educational Writings*. New York: Longmans Green & Company, 1912.

Petersen, Melody. *Our Daily Meds*. New York: Sarah Crichton Books, an imprint of Farrar, Straus and Giroux, 2008.

Poras, Marlo. *Run Granny Run*. DVD. New York: Arts Alliance America, LLC, 2007.

Porter, Roy. *Madness: A Brief History*. New York: Oxford University Press, Inc., 2002.

Postman, Neil. *Amusing Ourselves to Death*. New York: Penguin Books, 2005.

____. *Technopoly: The Surrender of Culture to Technology*. New York: Vintage Books, 1993.

____. *How to Watch TV News*. New York: Penguin Books, 2008.

Potts, Rick. *Humanity Descent: The Consequences of Ecological Instability*. New York: William Morrow and Company, Inc., 1996.

Poundstone, William. "The Dunning-Kruger President: How did a psychology term become a partisan trending topic?," *Psychology Today*, January 21, 2017.

Pressfield, Steven. *The War of Art*. New York: Warner Books, Inc., 2002.

Purcell, Lisa, Editor. *Trees, A Photographic Celebration*. New York: Metro Books, 2007.

Putnam, Robert D. *Bowling Alone*. New York: Simon & Schuster, Inc., 2000.

Quigley, Ann, Book Editor. *Mental Health*. Farmington Hills, MI: Greenhaven Press, 2007.

Reich, Wilhelm. *Listen, Little Man*. New York: The Noonday Press, 1974.

____. *People in Trouble*. New York: Farrar, Straus and Giroux, 1976.

____. *The Murder of Christ*. New York: Farrar, Straus and Giroux, 1971.

Renard, John. *The Handy Religion Answer Book*. Canton, MI: Visible Ink Press, 2002.

Rhodes, Richard. "Living with the Bomb," *National Geographic*, August 2005, 100.

Robbins, Richard H. *Global Problems and the Culture of Capitalism*. Needham Heights, MA: Allyn & Bacon, 1999.

Robertson, Pat. *Right on the Money: Financial Advice for Tough Times*. New York: Hachette Books Group, Inc., 2009.

Rooney, Anne. *The Story of Psychology*. United Kingdom: Arcturus Holdings Limited, 2015.

Roose, Kevin. "The Last Temptation of Ted," *GQ*, January 26, 2011.

Roston, Aram. "Vulture Capitalism." *Playboy Magazine*, December 2010.

Rousseau, Jean Jacques. *The Social Contract and Discourse on the Origin of Inequality*. New York: Washington Square Press Publications, 1967.

____ *Émile*. London: The Guernsey Press Co. Ltd., 1992.

Roy, Mathieu and Crooks, Harold. *Surviving Progress*. DVD. Québec, Canada: Alliance Films, 2012.

Russell, Bertrand. *The Conquest of Happiness*. New York: Liverlight Publishing Corporation, 1971.

Sadiq, Sheraz, Associate Producer for Frontline World. "Timeline: Cochabamba's Water Revolt," Public Broadcast System. http://www.pbs.org/frontlineworld/stories/bolivia/timeline.html

Sartre, Jean Paul. *No Exit and Three Other Plays*. New York: Vintage International Edition, Alfred A. Knopf, Inc., 1976.

Sawyer, Roger. *Slavery in the Twentieth Century*. London: Routledge & Kegan Paul, Inc., 1986.

Schumacher, E. F. *Small is Beautiful*. New York: Harper & Row Publishers, Inc., 1973.

Scull, Andrew. *Madness in Civilization*. New Jersey: Princeton University Press, 2015.

Seigler, Mario. "Artificial Intelligence: The Coming Threat, *Beyond Today*, May-June 2017, 27.

Shakespeare, William. *The Complete Works of William Shakespeare*. New York: Outlet Book Company, Inc., 1975.

Singer, Peter. *MARX*. Great Britain: Oxford University Press, 1980.

Smith, Adam. *The Wealth of Nations*. New York: Bantam Dell, 2003.

Solomon, Robert C. and Higgins, Kathleen M. *What Nietzsche Really Said*. New York: Schocken Books, 2000.

Southern Poverty Law Center, "The Year in Hate and Extremism," *Intelligence Report*, Spring 2016/Issue 160.

Speeth, Riordan Kathleen. *The Gurdjieff Work*. New York: Pocket Books, 1976.

Spence, Gerry. *Give Me Liberty!* New York: St. Martin's Press, 1998.

____. *From Freedom to Slavery: The Rebirth of Tyranny in America*. New York: St. Martin's Press, Inc., 1993.

Stein, Joel, "Tyranny of the Mob," *Time*, August 29, 2016.

Steiner, Rudolf. *The Renewal of the Social Organism*. Spring Valley, New York: Anthroposophic Press, 1985.

____. *Education as a Force for Social Change*. New York: Anthroposophic Press, 1997.

Stott, Carole and Twist, Clint. *Space Facts*. New York: DK Publishing, Inc., 1995.

Street, John. *Politics & Technology*. New York: The Guilford Press, 1992.

Suzuki, David. *The David Suzuki Reader*. British Columbia, Canada: Greystone Books, 2003.

____. *Suzuki Speaks*. DVD. British Columbia, Canada: Avanti

Pictures, 2004.

Szalavitz, Maia and Bruce D. Perry, M.D, Ph.D. *Born for Love: Why Empathy is Essential—and Endangered*. New York: Harper Collins Publishers, Inc., 2010.

Szep, Jason. "Dr. Ecstasy laments the rave drug's notoriety." *Yahoo! News*, December 2, 2005.

Tannen, Deborah. *You just Don't Understand*. New York: Ballantine Books, 1991.

The Huffington Post. "U.S. Oil Industry Giant Paid Millions To A Company At The Center Of A Huge Corruption Scandal." http://www.huffingtonpost.com. March 30, 2016.

The Marketing of Madness. DVD. Los Angeles, CA: Citizens Commission on Human Rights, 2009.

Thomas, Keith, Editor. *The Oxford Book of Work*. Oxford, UK: Oxford University Press, 1999.

Tillich, Paul. *The Courage to Be*. New Haven, Connecticut: Yale University Press, 2000.

Tracy, Erin. "She survived her first distracted driving accident—but not her second," *Merced Sun-Star*, April 10, 2016.

Van Doren, Charles. *A History of Knowledge*. New York: Ballantine Books, 1991.

Vidal, John. "Privatization Has Failed to Address the Water Problems in Developing Nations," *Will the World Run Out of Fresh Water?* Farmington Hills, MI: Greenhaven Press, 2007.

Watch Tower Bible and Tract Society of New York, Inc., 1984.

Waters, Roger. *The Dark Side of the Moon Documentary,* DVD. London, UK: Eagle Rock Entertainment, Ltd., 2003.

Watts, Jonathan. "Rio de Janeiro governor declares state of financial emergency ahead of the Olympics." *The Guardian*. https://www.theguardian.com. 17 June 2016.

Whitehead, North Alfred. *The Aims of Education*. New York: The Free Press, 1967.

Wright, Ronald. *A Short History of Progress*. Cambridge, MA: Da Cappo Press, 2004.

Young, Angelo. "And The Winner For the Most Iraq War Contracts Is…KBR, With $39.5 Billion In A Decade." http://www.ibtimes.com. 3/19/13.

Zielinski, Sarah. "The Colorado River Runs Dry," *Smithsonian Magazine*, October 2010. http://www.smithsonianmag.com/science-nature/the-colorado-river-runs-dry-61427169/

INDEX

About the Author

Sebastian de Assis is a writer, teacher, philosopher, and independent scholar with a profound interest in the daunting sociological challenges of his time.

A graduate of the University of Hawaii at Manoa and California State University at Dominguez Hills, he has lived in several countries and traveled extensively through Europe, South and North America, Africa, and the United States.

He lives in Oregon where he writes in his personal library while listening to Johann Sebastian Bach, Miles Davis, and other inspiring music that nurtures his spirit.

For more information about Sebastian and his work visit www.sebastiandeassis.com.

www.ingramcontent.com/pod-product-compliance
Lightning Source LLC
Chambersburg PA
CBHW021854020426
42334CB00013B/323